Playing
for Time

Playing for Time

Jeremy Lewis

A COMMON READER EDITION
The Akadine Press

Playing for Time

A COMMON READER EDITION published 2000
by The Akadine Press, Inc., by arrangement with the author.

Copyright © 1987 by Jeremy Lewis.

A COMMON READER EDITION and fountain colophon are trademarks
of The Akadine Press, Inc.

ISBN 1-58579-013-3

10 9 8 7 6 5 4 3 2 1

CONTENTS

To Petra

ACKNOWLEDGEMENTS

Since my life has been short on incident and ordinary to a degree (or so it seems to me), the only possible justification for producing a slice of autobiography must lie in its being entertaining, evocative of place and a particular way of life, and somehow symptomatic of a good many other equally unimportant lives. It is, I imagine, extremely unlikely that lecturers in sociology or social anthropology will read so frivolous a work, but if my account of various aspects of middle-class life in England between the late 1940s and mid-1960s excites a sympathetic start of recognition among readers of a similar age and background, I will feel that I have not banged away in vain; if I fail to entertain, however, I can only plead incompetence, and promise to try harder should there ever be a next time round.

I would like to thank the following for making encouraging or helpful remarks, or for reminding me of incidents that were, perhaps, better left undisturbed: Hugo Brunner, Carmen Callil, Digby Durrant, D. J. Enright, John and Christine Kelly, Jane and Alastair Langlands, Hilary Laurie, Jemima and Hattie Lewis (neither of whom, alas, appear in the book, though they represent its natural and undeserved conclusion), my sister, Julia Lewis, Suzanne Lowry, Derek Mahon (who first encouraged such egotistical ramblings by offering me a column on the *New Statesman*), James Michie, Andrew Motion, John R. Murray, Alan Ross (who published three large chunks from the book in the wonderful *London Magazine*), Deborah Singmaster, Charles and Ann and Sprawson, ffiona Swabey, Anthony Weale, Michael Wharton, Eileen Whitcomb, Ian Whitcomb and Terence de Vere White (who kindly corrected my spelling of Patrick Pearse and Cathal Bruga, and pointed out the correct nomenclature of Miss E. Panton Watkinson). I owe special thanks to Carol O'Brien, Michael Fishwick and Ariane Goodman at Collins, whose enthusiasm and encouragement kept me pounding away; to my parents, Mo and Janet Lewis, who could, I am sure, produce a far more accurate and entertaining account of the events described herein; and, above all, to Petra, the dearest of wives, who – although she has heard it all far too many times before – not only brought me endless cups of tea, but put up with my laughing at my own jokes and typing half the night.

Bits and pieces of the book have appeared – usually in rather different form – in the *London Magazine*, the *Spectator*, the *New Statesman*, *Punch*, the *Field* and the *Illustrated London News*, and I would like to thank their editors for permission to reproduce them here.

JML
London, August 1986

PROLOGUE

In the early summer of 1961, I was – to our mutual satisfaction – given the sack by the advertising agency for whom I had been working for the past nine months, initially (and very enjoyably) as a messenger boy, and more recently as an office worker of quite startling ineptitude; and – not for the last time – I relished the irresponsible, liberating thrill of being forcibly removed from a way of life that had become wretchedly uncongenial and for which I was all too obviously under-equipped. I was then nineteen, and a large, top-heavy youth with long fair hair bleached almost white by the sun, an outsize jaw, hands like freshly dug root vegetables, a fruity bass voice, horn-rimmed specs and a face that wore – or so it seemed to me – an expression of remarkable vacuity. Overjoyed to be shot of the tedium of professional life, I sped home to my parents' cottage on the Sussex coast and spent the summer as summers should be spent – swimming two or three times a day, snoozing in deck chairs in the sun, immersing myself in the works of Dickens, Smollett and Surtees, and going for enormous solitary walks across the Downs, in the course of which I wrote and rewrote my entry in *Who's Who* and ran over in my mind the entirely laudatory reviews of books I would never get round to writing.

I had left school a couple of years earlier, during the blazing summer of 1959. I had disliked my public school a very great deal, and had made no impression whatsoever as a scholar, a character or, most importantly, as a sportsman; I snootily assumed that my fellow-pupils – pallid, sweaty-looking boys who tied their black school ties in Windsor knots and combed their heavily 'groized' hair into Elvis quiffs at the front and carefully sculpted 'ducks' arses' behind – were, as the sons of Wolverhampton scrap-metal merchants and Kidder-minster garage proprietors, quite beyond the pale, and my timid disdain was returned with ample interest. When, in the middle of August, my parents received a rather puzzled-sounding letter from my housemaster asking whether or not I intended returning for my final academic year, it was widely agreed that since the weather was so good, and since I so obviously disliked it there, the answer should be 'no'. A message to that effect was rapidly despatched, the deck chairs were rearranged to take in the evening sun, and the future looked rosy indeed.

Despite the sudden and somewhat heedless termination of my school career, we all assumed that I would, almost automatically, follow my father to Cambridge. I had set my heart on reading history there, and had spent long hours in the school library poring over Edwardian volumes on university life, illustrated with autumnal watercolours of ivy-clad cloisters and mossy arches with stooped, gowned figures strolling sedately in the background; I knew the dates and the crests and the alumni and the histories and even the ties of every Oxford and Cambridge college; amid the shouts and the mud and the steaming jockstraps and the adenoidal Midlands voices of school life I had dreamt of the Backs and buttery bills and exchanging waggish repartee over cocoa before a blazing gas fire in my college rooms or standing about in a pub in a duffel coat with a scarf round my neck and a pile of books clutched to my bosom, like the responsible, square-jawed students in the advertisements who – or so we were told – were about to open their first bank accounts, and would never dream of being overdrawn. My father had won a scholarship to Pembroke, and had been a rowing blue (the first and, no doubt, the last from our landlocked, riverless school); many of his friends had been to Cambridge, and I had grown up surrounded by painted oars and rudders and memorabilia of Cambridge life; for no good reason I regarded Cambridge as part of my birthright, and a private, familiar preserve. I had been there only once, from school, and had felt that I was treading sacred ground; and when, some months after I had rashly elected to stay on the beach instead of returning to school to wrestle with 'S' levels and university entrance exams, I went up for an interview at Pembroke, I fondly assumed that a gaggle of elderly, bibulous dons with purple, carbuncular noses and gowns slipping off their shoulders would greet me with welcoming cries, like a prince coming into his own, in much the same way as, on my first day at school, an ancient, egg-stained science master wearing a wing-collar, a black serge suit and a Lloyd George-like bush of white hair had hurried forward to welcome me, kindly but mistakenly assuming that I would repeat my father's saga of success as well as his interest in test tubes and formaldehyde. Instead I found myself confronted by cool, cold-eyed men in suits who made it quite clear that candidates were chosen strictly on the basis of merit, and that the Old Boy network was of no relevance or interest whatsoever; I had been unwise and ill-advised to leave school when I did; I was almost certainly not Cambridge material, but I was welcome to reapply if and when I ever got round to taking my 'S' levels.

Worse was to come, for over the next few months every college I applied to in Cambridge (including, to my extreme indignation, Selwyn, to which I had written in a sudden spasm of condescension), Oxford and even London turned me down without, it seemed, the slightest qualm and, for the most part, without even asking me to go for an interview. The English provincial universities were, of course, out of the question, being reserved for that alien beast, the grammar school boy, with his black blazer with yellow piping, scuffed shoes and National Health specs – though, to make matters worse, it appeared that Oxford and Cambridge colleges were bending over backwards to allow the wretches in, at the expense of their natural clientèle. As rejection followed rejection, I was filled with terrible feelings of melancholy and loss. I felt inadequate and utterly bemused; I seemed quite incapable of improving my lot, but filled in the long hours working as a packer in Harrods or as a casual labourer on Newhaven docks, unloading boxes of plastic flowers and new potatoes from the Channel Isles; by now many of my friends were in their first year at Oxford or Cambridge, and I winced with envy and mortification as I listened to them chatting about college life, or the books they were reading, or the vacations they had spent picking grapes in France or polishing up their Italian in Perugia.

After a year of failure and messing about I realized, with a terrible sense of impending doom, that since I would obviously never get to university, I would have to find myself a job. In this, I received a good deal of enthusiastic support from my mother. Since neither Oxford nor Cambridge had offered me a place, she reasoned, it was safe to assume that universities were a thing of the past, and that the go-ahead young man of today went straight to work and got a head start on dozy, impractical undergraduates reading about the Peasants'

Revolt or the Second Punic War; she had, she told me, always despised university people, and had learnt from an early age that reading was bad for the eyes. In support of her views she quoted my grandfather, a Gloucestershire farmer of unusual ferocity whose only book – Sassoon's *The Memoirs of a Fox-Hunting Man* – was used to prop up the water-tank in the farmhouse attic; he had no time for intellectuals, she assured me, and would almost certainly set his dogs on a don should one wander into the yard and fire a warning shot with his twelve-bore at suspicious-looking men in glasses and corduroy jackets.

As the summer of 1960 drew to its close, it was somehow decided that my future lay in the world of advertising. At prep school I had spent a good deal of time producing newspapers and cartoons featuring men disguised as boiled eggs, and I had written a long play, set in the Graeco-Roman world, in which characters in togas with names like Constipides and Testiculus made important-sounding speeches at one another; I hadn't written a word since, or shown the dimmest glimmer of literary talent, but it was somehow assumed that, whatever Oxford and Cambridge might think, I was bound to be a dab hand at devising waggish or snappy slogans. Besides, advertising was becoming a rather fashionable business to work in; jobs were much sought after by ambitious young men, and there was a good deal of excited, knowing talk about the perfidy of subliminal advertising as spelt out in Vance Packard's book *The Hidden Persuaders*, while the cognoscenti spoke in reverential tones of David Ogilvy's famous shirt advertisements in the *New Yorker* and elsewhere, which featured, for some inexplicable reason, a man wearing a black patch over one eye, like a pantomime pirate who had forgotten to change into the appropriate nautical gear. I wrote off to all the major agencies, in much the same way as I had written to every known Oxford and Cambridge college, and received once more a rain of rebuffs. Among those who – quite rightly – turned me down was J. Walter Thompson, then famous among school leavers and careers masters for its celebrated IQ test, which involved fitting various triangles and oblongs together to make a lozenge or a cube or some other baffling and improbable item of geometry: having failed 'O' level maths four times, I was as floored by this as I would have been by the eleven plus, had I had the misfortune to attempt it – as it was, it was largely reserved for those menacing grammar school boys in their black blazers and scuffed black shoes – and I almost certainly scored nought for both initiative and lateral thinking.

Things were looking grim indeed – not helped by a visit to a careers advisor, a retired major with bloodshot eyes and ginger whiskers who suggested I try my hand at chicken-farming or the wine trade – when I was asked to go along to Baker Street to be interviewed for a job as a trainee with the British branch of one of the larger American agencies. I was told to ask for the personnel officer, who would explain what the job involved and see if I was the kind of chap they had in mind. Whereas the modern personnel officer is privy to company books, knows about cash flow and profit and loss accounts, and is a walking compendium on trade union practices and the intricacies of employment legislation, his old-fashioned equivalent – like old-fashioned prep school masters, or the careers advisor with the red-rimmed eyes and brightly-coloured nose – tended to be a retired military man with a gammy leg and the homely, comfortable air of a tweeded country doctor entrusted with the keys to the stationery cupboard and the office medicine chest containing the full range of powders and potions that could be called upon should a secretary come over faint in mid-dictation, or an aspiring young executive clock in with poached, unfocused eyes and a curious throbbing about the temples. My interrogator turned out to be a former wing-commander with a bushy grey moustache and the patient, kindly look of a pipe-smoking labrador; he wore a cardigan under his lovat tweed suit, his desk was very clear, and I noticed a set of golf clubs in a corner of the room. We got on well together, and after twenty minutes or so he announced that he would give me a go, and took me along a well-carpeted corridor to meet the managing director, who shook me warmly by the hand and gave me my first taste of the advertising man's ceaseless need to justify himself and his 'profession' in what he evidently feels to be a hostile and highly critical world.

Advertising, he informed me – somewhat to my surprise, for I was grateful enough to have a job at all, and felt in no need for an apology in advance – pepped up the economy (without much success, it seemed), kept prices down, informed the consumer of the choices available to him (or, more importantly, her), and brightened up the streets no end with exciting-looking posters and winking neon lights, which he compared to a great gallery laid on free of charge such as the deprived and unhappy citizens of Eastern Europe could only dream of. I was temporarily stunned by this sudden and uncalled-for act of self-justification from on high, and stood in the middle of the room with my mouth hanging open, looking more vacuous than ever; but as the weeks rolled by I came to realize that such pleadings for approval were endemic to the trade, like some unhappy facial tic or impediment of speech. This anxiety about the advertising man's self-esteem and standing in the world reached its climax some months later, when the boss of the parent company in New York came over on a flying visit: a chunky, grey-haired man in a herringbone suit and tractor-soled shoes, he shook each one of us firmly by the hand, gazing manfully into our eyes and making immediate use of our Christian names, before addressing the assembled staff in the office canteen in almost identical words to those employed by our managing director when greeting the most junior member of his staff.

The denigration of advertising was becoming, as it has remained, a popular sport among the thinking classes, and had any of advertising's innumerable and very vocal critics been invited along, his ringing, missionary words might have had some point; but it may well be that the suspension of disbelief that is so essential an ingredient of office life, and so hard for some of us to attain, is especially elusive for the advertising man, which was why those set in authority above us – likeable and entertaining and intelligent as they always appeared to be – felt it necessary to address one another in this curious way, like beleaguered or recusant priests defiantly saying a daily mass in the face of universal hostility and disdain.

The managing director's words still ringing in my ears, I was escorted downstairs to the packing room, which in turn opened onto a cobbled mews that ran along the back of the building. There I was introduced to two elderly gentlemen in knee-length grey housecoats, named – like working-class characters from an Ealing comedy or a film from the 1930s – Sid and Alf. Sid had a brick-red face, rendered still more striking by a large purple birthmark that ran down one side of his face; he had a wide, saurian mouth with a roll-your-own cigarette permanently attached to the lower lip, the smoke from which curled uncomfortably into his eyes causing him to gaze around through narrowed lids, and prompted loud bouts of coughing and horrid hawking sounds as great gobs of phlegm rattled to and fro. Whereas Sid was a loud, jocular figure, Alf was of a sober, clerical cut; both were, as far as I was concerned, touchingly kind and friendly.

Between them they were responsible for despatching and dealing with the parcels and post that flooded in and out of the building in a ceaseless tide of string and brown paper and grey Post Office bags, and all about them were the tools of their trade – scalpels and guillotines and great balls of twine and sheets of cardboard which they thwacked into place with a sideways chop of the hand and franking machines and pots of glue and greasy drawers crammed with stamps and paper-clips and ballpoint pens and rubber bands. Every few minutes there would be the sound of screeching brakes from the mews outside, and a mysterious, black padded glove would open the glass hatch that separated the packing room from the corridor that led to the world outside. This was followed by a heavily helmeted head which – addressing the room in an angular, uncomfortable way, as though its owner was poised on the executioner's block – enquired in a gruff and lugubrious monotone whether there was anything for Sun Engravers, or the *Daily Mail*, or whoever its employers might be; Sid or Alf would then hand over to the gloved black hand some artwork or a printing block or – most exciting of all – a can of film featuring a red-faced man in a cardigan draining a glass of beer, smacking his lips and simultaneously winking and giving a thumbs-up sign to the camera; the hatch would slam shut, and seconds later the mews outside rang to mighty explosions and revving sounds as the man in the helmet sped away, like a woebegone overweight knight, his precious cargo tucked away in the pillion behind him. Here, I felt, was the urgent heart of our trade, and I gazed upon its mysterious comings and goings with wonder and with awe.

My fellow messenger boy, Robert, was a jolly, rubicund youth with a large, carrot-shaped nose, an interesting crop of blackheads, and a shock of straw-coloured hair that shot from the side of his head like an inverted ice-cream cone. He wore a smart charcoal grey worsted suit with a nipped-in waist and tight, tubular trousers, carried an umbrella at all times, and sported a virulent clubman's tie which, he told me in a confidential undertone so as not to alarm the old retainers, marked him out as an Old Chigwellian. Robert spent a good deal of time practising imaginary cricket strokes, and occasionally brought back dreadful memories of school by executing a swift rugger pass with a newly arrived parcel: as had always been the case, I was invariably caught entirely unawares, letting it crash to the ground with an ominous breaking sound. He had an easy, joshing way with Sid and Alf, punching them lightly on the upper arm and coaxing a smile from the cautious, worried Alf; I admired and envied his friendly, self-confident approach but was far too stiff and shy to attempt it myself, and spent the long hours wishing I had the nerve to read the book in my pocket while Robert burbled cheerfully on about beer and football and the new girl with the Bardot pout and blue and white flared gingham skirt who sat behind the till in the canteen as we filed slowly past with our trays of steak and kidney pie and spotted dick with custard.

As for the work itself, I soon discovered that the life of a messenger boy suited me to perfection: indeed, it still seems to me to have been the most entirely enjoyable type of work I have ever done, involving as it did much travelling of a sedate and therapeutic kind, ample opportunities to daydream or read interminable nineteenth-century novels or inspect art galleries and City churches, and – most important of all – a complete absence of responsibility. Every now and then an important, harassed-looking young man or a highly polished secretary with a beehive hairstyle would descend from the offices above and stand drumming their fingers on the counter of the packing room, where Robert was busily engaged in improving his golf swing with an upside-down umbrella, Sid and Alf were franking the innumerable letters that offices exist to produce, or performing extraordinary feats of dexterity with strips of cardboard and binding twine, and I was sitting on my hands and swinging my legs to and fro, a look of utter vacuity illuminating my features. When the drumming failed – as it always did – to elicit any reaction, the emissary from on high demanded that the item in their other, non-drumming hand should be taken round *prontissimo* to such-and-such a newspaper or studio; after which they turned on their heels, and disappeared aloft as swiftly as they had come.

These peremptory visits excited volcanic grumblings from Sid and Alf and muttered threats of resignation; they then proceeded to wrap up the offending item very slowly indeed, muttering fiercely all the while, before interrupting Robert's display of spin bowling or my musings on Captain Cuttle or Mrs Todger's boarding house to order one of us to be on our way. Every item, I soon discovered, had its particular hazards: a large piece of artwork could be carried away or bent in half by a high wind; a can of film – containing, no doubt, the beer-loving man in the cardigan – once burst open on the top deck of a Number 2 bus, unravelling down the gangway and heading eagerly for the staircase at the back and the open road beyond; a teetering pile of hat boxes bound for Great Marlborough Street could well come toppling to the ground in a flurry of tissue paper, spilling their dainty, lurid contents all about and inducing paroxysms of shame as helpful, kindly passers-by hurried to retrieve the latest models as they bowled along the pavement and came to rest in the gutter or propped up against a lamp-post favoured by the local dogs. Once outside the packing room, though, all London lay before us; and of time, it seemed, there was no end.

By far the most frequent and enjoyable trips were to the newspaper offices in Fleet Street. For all the drumming of fingers and cries of '*Prontissimo*' from the floors above, the delivery of their precious cargoes was a slow and decorous business. Carrying the advertising block and my book in one hand and my umbrella in the other – the product of the lost property office in Victoria, to which it rapidly found its way once more – I would climb aboard a Number 13 bus, inch my way down Baker Street peacefully reading on the upper deck, sit for at least forty minutes in a mammoth traffic jam in Oxford Street while all about us angry motorists raged and hooted and banged the roofs of their cars, the bus accelerating to something approaching walking speed as we flashed down Regent Street, and – if I'd finished my book or felt like stretching my legs – jump off at the Strand and walk the rest of the way from there. Having gone all that way, it seemed only right to spend a few minutes in the Soane Museum or the Temple Church; after which I re-boarded a Number 13 travelling in the opposite direction, and made my way slowly back to the office.

These expeditions to Fleet Street and Holborn were particularly magic and evocative on dank, dark winter afternoons, when the fog came down, the stallholders' paraffin lamps flared the length of the Farringdon Road, and the slimy cobbles and dark, mildewed, untenanted warehouses that loomed like close-packed cliffs on either side of Saffron Hill exuded all the sinister, romantic gloom appropriate to the site of Fagin's lair. My head aswarm with the doings of Mrs Jellyby and Mr Jaggers and Ralph Nickleby and the indolent Eugene Wrayburn, I found the Temple and Lincoln's Inn and Clerkenwell Green and the river and the tiny, crooked courts and alleys that twisted away off Fleet Street and Ludgate Hill a dear, familiar land in which it came as no surprise to wander into dusty, sunless City gardens such as Arthur Clennam knew as a child, or to come across, in the upper reaches of the Farringdon Road, a blackened, greasy chophouse of the kind preferred by Mr Guppy, with hard wooden seats and high, draught-excluding partitions dividing one table from the next, serving meat and two veg followed by marmalade pud for all of 3/6.

My love for this part of London was made all the greater by the fact that this was still – but not for much longer – a blackened, coal-burning city in which the public buildings were mercifully uncleaned, the grass in the parks was (less pleasingly) coated with a fine black grit, the cuffs and collars of a shirt were begrimed after half a day, and a finger thrust up the nose came down again ringed with soot. Long before I had ever heard of Dickens I loved nothing better than the famous pea-soupers that suddenly blotted everything out, bringing the traffic grinding to a halt, deadening all sounds, and giving the streets over to pedestrians who loomed out of the murk like sluggish yellow underwater beasts, and vanished again as quietly as they had come. Brutally unaware of pensioners and asthmatics coughing their last or fighting for air, and utterly indifferent to the plight of the homeward-bound motorist, I lavished on London's last season of smog the kind of enthusiasm that is normally reserved for the first flowers of spring or the countryside in autumn; quite apart from which, a fog with the consistency of brown Windsor soup gave one the perfect excuse to take even longer than usual to find one's way back to the office or even to call it a day, in much the same way as a frozen pitch or a sudden deluge of monsoon-like rain – so earnestly prayed for, and so seldom delivered on time – had sometimes led, in days gone by, to the cancellation of a house match or a game against a muscular rival school, in both of which I would have otherwise almost certainly suffered immediate disgrace.

The office Christmas party was held on a particularly fine foggy night that year. It was, the notice boards informed us, to be a Spanish evening: we were all to dress up as pallid, washed-out looking señors and señoritas, and the office wags spent the days before the great event drumming their heels on the ground and clicking their fingers above their heads. Even Robert – a more improbable Spaniard than most – temporarily abandoned some careful teeing-off with the upside-down umbrella in favour of a preparatory stamping of the foot and narrow-eyed tossing of the head, causing his curious cone of hair to bob to and fro like the windsock at Northolt Aerodrome. The very idea of dressing up as a toreador filled me with a nameless dread, and I had a strong suspicion that I would prove as inept with the castanets as I was with bat and ball or the parcels of breakables which Robert still sent spinning in my direction; moreover, though I was diffident and self-conscious to a ludicrous degree – so much so that, if offered a glass of wine or a cup of tea I found it impossible to control the trembling of my hand, causing the drink to spray about the room and the pieces of crockery to clatter together like the bones in a *danse macabre* – I resolved to defy the notice boards and go as something else. I was living at the time with some friends of my parents in a large house in Ladbroke Square: apart from an embarrassing moment on my first evening in the house when I blocked their lavatory so effectively that despite my best endeavours with pails of water and a broom-handle a team of experts had to be summoned, while I stood wretchedly by wringing my hands and wishing I were elsewhere, we got on extremely well, and when I explained my predicament they hurried to be of help. My host liked nothing better than dressing up, and had once disguised himself so successfully as a cardinal – using his wife's petticoats, a profusion of lace, a cummerbund and a dinner jacket worn the wrong way round – that some visiting South American ladies had knelt to kiss his ring; between them they unearthed some ancient, musty-smelling Chinese garments, gave me a pair of slit eyes with which to peer through my horn-rims, glued a cotton wool beard to my granitic, unChinese-like chin, pinned a paper skullcap and a black woollen pigtail to my even less oriental hair, ordered up a taxi, and sent me stumbling out into the night.

The party was to be held in a large house, since demolished, at the bottom of Park Lane – next door to, or at least very close to, the

famous Londonderry House, which was just about to be swept away
to make room for that dire symbol of London's ruination, the Hilton
Hotel. As I sped towards the office party, I suddenly realized that I
had quite forgotten to bring with me the roneoed note - with
castanets in each corner, a Mexican hat in the middle, and
embellished with many a '*Caramba!*' and '*Olé!*' - ordering all staff to be
present in Spanish dress, and giving the exact address to which I
should be heading. All I knew was that I should look out for a large
house at the bottom of Park Lane, so I ordered the taxi to stop
somewhere behind Apsley House, and set out through the fog
towards the sound of revelry. By now I was beginning to regret
having come as a Chinaman: the ancient clothes were poor protection
against the cold, my appearance seemed to excite little confidence in
those I encountered in the gloom, and my spirit of defiance - never
strong except at a distance - was quickly beginning to wilt.

Eventually I stumbled upon what seemed a large enough house,
wandered in through the open front door and, finding no one about,
strolled up a great flight of stairs, along interminable corridors and
round dark and gloomy wells, expecting at any moment to hear the
clack of the castanet and a mighty drumming sound as a great army
of clerks hurled themselves into the fandango. But not a sound was to
be heard in this empty, echoing house; and at last I came across a bent
and elderly occupant who, politely disguising any surprise he may
have felt at coming across a complete stranger very badly disguised as
a Chinaman, suggested I try further up Park Lane, and kindly
escorted me back to the front door. I like to think - probably quite
wrongly - that I had somehow drifted into Londonderry House only
weeks before the demolition men removed it for ever: but that, I
suppose, is something I shall never know.

As for the office party itself, I felt wretchedly conspicuous and ill-
at-ease in my musty Chinese dressing gown and pigtail: still more so
since most of my fellow-workers had, very sensibly, made the most
perfunctory gesture in the direction of Spain and had turned up in
shirts and jeans, with the odd pair of castanets or papier mâché
sombrero as a way of showing willing. Sid and Alf were sitting with a
clutch of cheerful-looking cleaning ladies and people from Accounts;
their hair was full of streamers, and the table in front of them was stiff
with empty bottles of pale ale. Sid, I noticed, was wearing a large red-

and-white spotted handkerchief tied about his head, which gave him a vaguely piratical look, appropriate to the Spanish Main; Alf, on the other hand, had on a maroon cardigan, a pale green shirt, grey flannel trousers held up with braces and (or so I liked to think) a pair of check Pirelli slippers, and I could only assume that he had cunningly disguised himself as a Spanish office packer enjoying an evening out. My friend the personnel officer seemed to have muddled Germany with Spain, and was striding jovially about in a pork pie hat and a pair of knee-length shorts; while far away, in the middle of the dance floor, Robert – fully togged out as a toreador by courtesy of a firm of theatrical costumiers – twisted and strutted in a wild and sensuous flamenco with the girl from the canteen with the Bardot lips, a three-cornered hat uneasily balanced on his unusual cone of hair. My colleagues were understandably baffled by my unpersuasive stab at Spanish national dress, and I spent much of the evening fending off cross or puzzled enquiries about what I was supposed to *be*; I resolved that, if I were to try to buck the system in future, I should do so in a slightly subtler and more devious way.

The idyllic life of a messenger boy was, alas, far too good to last. Early in the New Year Robert was promoted upstairs to something called the production department to begin the next stage in his training, and a couple of months later I delivered my last load of hats to Great Marlborough Street, and followed on behind. Apart from the peremptory visits from the important-looking young men in shirt sleeves and the equally impressive girls in Jaqmar scarves, my experience of life upstairs had been restricted to watching grave men in suits trooping into the projection room to watch films of bears driving lorries or the red-faced man downing yet another pint of gaseous bitter and giving the thumbs-up sign, and to an occasional, rather bemused visit to the art department on the top floor of the building, which was staffed by jolly men with carefully sculpted beards, clad in mauve shirts, lime-green ties, thick black corduroy trousers and suede desert boots: in an endearingly old-fashioned way, such a uniform suggested artiness and bestowed a certain licence and eccentricity on its occupant, just as the grey herringbone suit, thin squared-off tie and button-down shirt of the aspiring account executive were (it was fondly hoped) redolent of the clean-cut New

Frontier of JFK, of innovation, informality and responsibility rolled into one.

On the day of my elevation the personnel officer – no longer, alas, in his knee-length shorts and pork pie hat – led me along a brightly-lit corridor on the second floor, and into the small cluster of rooms that formed the production department. As he flung open the teak door I was reassured – but not entirely surprised – by the familiar spectacle of Robert's bowling arm in action: only this time, instead of bowling an imaginary ball, he sent a knot of office paper flashing down the room towards a purple-featured man in his forties, with tight, well-oiled curls, a bright red bow tie and the bunched and weaving stance of a boxer, who was standing in front of an olive-coloured wastepaper basket with a ruler in his hand with which he lashed out at the paper ball, sending it spinning over the head of the fielder, a grizzled, elderly man with a tattoo on his right forearm. As I quickly discovered, cricket played an important part in the life of the production department; but at the sight of a newcomer they courteously broke off the game – scribbling the score on a pad of paper for future reference – and the man with the purple face hurried forward to explain what the work involved, and what was expected of me.

As far as I could understand, we were responsible for booking advertising space in newspapers and magazines, and then delivering blocks or artwork to them; my first job would be to cut out the finished ad from the paper in which it had appeared, gum it into an enormous leather-bound scrap-book with a bright white glue that smelt of marzipan, and write in underneath the date on which it had appeared, the size of the advertisement and the amount it had cost the agency. Like cleaning shoes or peeling potatoes, this turned out to be the kind of work I have always enjoyed: it may have lacked the variety and the opportunities of travel associated with being a messenger boy, but it was agreeably undemanding, left the mind free to wander as it would, and reminded me pleasantly of long hours spent as a child sticking postcards and Christmas cards into almost identical albums.

This important work was done in a small annexe separated from the main office by frosted lavatory glass: it overlooked the mews, from which sudden revving sounds and the screech of brakes announced the coming and going of those padded, helmeted knights of the road with whose gloves and visors I had become so familiar. I spun out my labours with the scissors and the glue for as long as I could while realizing that, sooner or later, I would have to pretend to be an ambitious and serious-minded office worker and take my place in the main office along with Robert and the grizzled warhorse. Robert, it seemed, was even more at home with these fellow-sportsmen than he had been with Sid and Alf: indeed, he seemed to be in a fever of excitement, practising drop-kicks with the same olive-coloured wastepaper basket that doubled up as a set of wickets, displaying an encyclopaedic knowledge of beer and sex and cracking jokes of the kind I priggishly associated with commercial travellers wearing pork pie hats – alarmingly similar to that possessed by the personnel officer – while propping up the bar, to the accompaniment of a good deal of winking and leering and nudging of the elbow.

Faced with such competition, how could I hope to prove myself a comparably convivial work-mate, let alone an urbane and sophisti-cated man of the world of the kind that flitted through the French and Italian films I so eagerly devoured, with huge overcoats draped across their shoulders and cigarettes dangling dangerously from their lower lips, as though held in place by a tiny dab of glue? Although I had, at a rather early age, nourished heady dreams of being invited into the bathroom to soap the back of our Austrian au pair girl, and – since baths seem to loom large in such matters – became unreasonably excited by English comedies in which heavily made-up French girls in bubble baths got their toes stuck, for some curious reason, in the cold tap and had to be rescued by embarrassed men in tweeds and college scarves, carefully averting their gaze as they disconnected toe and tap, my knowledge and experience of sex was nil; I liked beer well enough, but had drunk little of it as yet, and found it hard to remember the difference between bitter, mild and stout, let alone the other brews which my fellow-workers ordered up in the pub round the corner with such enviable assurance; I laughed hard and long at Robert's jokes, the milder of which had almost certainly started life on the back of matchboxes or in Christmas crackers, but could no more have unleashed one of my own than lead the singing of 'Auld Lang Syne' or 'For He's a Jolly Good Fellow', or – most agonising of all, occasioning massive feints of inattention or a sudden hacking cough – join in a hearty rendition of 'Happy Birthday to You'. From the beginning, I'm afraid, I must have seemed a killjoy, a prig and something of a snob; and although my colleagues always treated me with a kindly, patient concern, as though I could not quite be trusted to be out on my own, a small contretemps which occurred a week or so after I had joined the department made me realize early on that my face was unlikely to fit.

Although advertising men are eager to be thought of as tireless human dynamos, fizzing with ideas as they pace up and down the office waving their hands in the air, or burning the midnight oil, black coffee to hand and collar buttons undone, while the rest of the world settles down to a TV dinner, life in our department at least was torpid to a degree. Much of the morning in particular was given over to playing office cricket; and although the pitch ran right in front of my desk, so that the ball often landed in my In Tray or flew angrily over my head like a great white wasp, I invariably waived my turn at the wicket and sat instead behind my desk with a stuffed expression on my face, trying to look as though I were enjoying myself while wishing that they would let us have some peace and quiet so that I could concentrate on the book that lay open on my lap.

After a while I abandoned the pretence of being an appreciative spectator, wearing the kind of clip-on smile appropriate to a member of the royal family while watching a display of tribal dancing – and I would have had to be sportsmad to the point of lunacy to find the spectacle of Robert bowling a piece of crumpled memo paper at a middle-aged man with a ruler *that* compelling – and, bringing my book up on to the desk, settled down for a long and total immersion in *Nicholas Nickleby*. As I read greedily on about the doings of Lord Frederick Verisopht and Sir Mulberry Hawk, the thwack of ruler on paper ball and the eager cries of the cricketers faded into an agreeable background drone: this, I felt – swinging one leg over the arm of my chair – is what office life is all about. Hardly had I reached this point before the book was suddenly torn from my hand: my boss with the purple nose, risking life and limb as he strode across the pitch in the face of one of Robert's demon balls, stood glowering angrily down at me. This was not, he informed me – his voice atremble with indignation – a public library; if he found me reading again in office hours he would have no alternative but to— Overcome with emotion, he turned sharply about, seized the ruler from the warhorse, and subjected Robert's bowling to the most terrible punishment. How on earth was I to fill in the long hours? Should I carve my name on the desk instead, or write out the plots of Dickens's novels on the clean white sheet of blotting paper with which each desk was so thoughtfully provided?

Not all our time was given over to indolence, however. Every now and then I was, to my horror, asked to ring up the *Daily Mail* or the *Sunday Express* and book space for one of the advertisements that had been cunningly concocted by the artists in the mauve shirts and carefully sculpted beards and the jocular, disillusioned copywriters with their red-rimmed eyes and extended lunch hours and corduroy suits and half-completed novels tucked untidily away in the drawers of their desks along with a rich collection of rubber bands, paperclips and discarded toffee papers.

For as long as I could remember I had hated the telephone above all else, so that the mere sound of its voice left me paralyzed upon the spot, as though some venomous serpent lay coiled upon my desk, or sent me rushing from the room with pounding heart, my eyes wide with terror like some unhappy Pompeian fleeing in vain the advancing lava flow. If I found myself alone in the office with a ringing telephone I stepped sharply out into the corridor and headed off in the direction of the lavatories with a brisk and purposeful air; were my colleagues present, I found myself unexpectedly overcome by a protracted fit of coughing very similar to that provoked by the prospect of community singing, or urgently involved in important talk with a puzzled passer-by, who found himself buttonholed and engaged in inconsequential conversation for as long as the bell continued to ring, before being gratefully released and allowed to go on his way. Such dodges were of no avail, however, when I was asked to make rather than receive a call; in this case, having postponed the awful moment for as long as I possibly could by pretending that the line was engaged or the advertising department unobtainable, I would wait until the office was as empty as it was ever likely to be, bend low over my desk, my shoulders hunched over the receiver like an American footballer with the ball in his possession, and, with trembling fingers, dial the hateful number.

Once through, I would ask in a quavering voice for the display advertising department – speaking in little more than a whisper lest I be overheard by my colleagues who, I was certain, were waiting on my every word. More often than not the words came out in such a torrent that the operator was unable to understand anything I had said, so that I had to start all over again; or they fell foul of a frog in my throat, which I expelled with a volcanic rasp, deafening the operator and at once engaging the attention of my fellows who, until then, had been quite unaware of these titanic goings-on. By the time my request had been deciphered and I had been put through to the right department I was so unnerved that I either forgot what I was supposed to say, or placed quite the wrong order, which caused a good deal of sighing and raising of eyebrows on the part of the warhorse and the man with the purple features.

To avoid such scenes in the future, I decided to take drastic action. Whenever I was asked to ring up a newspaper I walked sharply out of the office, taking with me some forbidden book, climbed aboard a Number 13 bus, just as I had in the days gone by, trundled peacefully down to Fleet Street, delivered my message in person to a slightly surprised member of the advertising department, and trundled slowly back again. My fellow-workers were still absorbed in the same game of cricket as when I had left them an hour before, or busy with the darts board which Robert had recently introduced; no one seemed to have remarked on my absence, and within a few weeks I was combining such expeditions with a short stroll round the Wallace Collection on the way home. The nightmare of the office telephone had, for the time being at least, been vanquished and put to flight.

Even so, I felt increasingly bored and restless and unhappy, and I must have radiated gloom, like a trainee curmudgeon or a portly spectre at the feast. Far from trying to make the most of it, or to learn something of this curious and entertaining trade, I splashed about in glutinous pools of self-pity. Surely, I felt, life had more to offer than this? How I longed to be at university, and how I winced when I met friends on vacation and listened to their indolent, luxuriant talk of pubs and punts and proctors. My friend Tom tried to cheer me up by telling me that, after Eton, Cambridge seemed dull and anti-climactic, full of ink-stained swots in spectacles held together with strips of Elastoplast, like embryonic scoutmasters; to me however it seemed like a lost land of which I knew every detail, but would never visit or call my own.

I read simply in order to escape: into the lurid, tangible world of Dickens, so much more vivid and enjoyable than that of everyday; and into dreams of benevolent rural bliss, of a world of rose-bowered cottages and smiling peasantry of the kind that appeared in the paintings of George Moreland, or in my hero's sicklier passages, in which the dutifully good – more often than not overweight and interminably smiling City men or retired chandlers in indecently tight trousers – lived out their blameless lives in a shimmering pastoral idyll. I had lived all my life in London or on the rusty, storm-lashed South Coast, and my experience of rustic life was restricted to occasional, daunting visits to my ferocious Gloucestershire grand-father and his Surteesian world of flint-eyed, bottle-nosed hunting men and shouting and guns and dogs; yet as I waited for the tube at Notting Hill Gate on my way to work, or ate my sandwiches in a tiny blackened cemetery off Baker Street, the pigeons eagerly hoovering up the crumbs about my feet, I read my way through Kilvert and Parson Woodforde and 'The Winter Walk at Noon' and, best of all, E. V. Lucas's once-celebrated country anthology, *The Open Road* – a small format volume printed on India paper, which I liked to imagine browbeaten Wellsian clerks tucking into their knapsacks or the pockets of their Norfolk jackets as they set out for a bicycling bank holiday along the dusty white roads of the North Downs.

By now it must have been apparent to my boss with the empurpled features and the warhorse that I was not the stuff of which aspiring advertising agents are made. No one could deny that I had made a first-rate job of pasting advertisements into scrap-books, but beyond that, it seemed, I had alarmingly little to offer. I showed no interest whatsoever in the work upon which I was bent; my mind was obviously elsewhere; not only did I spurn the cricket pitch and make heavy weather of incoming telephone calls, but I jumped whenever spoken to, spoke in an incomprehensible rumble, and moved with strange, convulsive jerks, like a puppet whose master had taken to the bottle or had trouble in working out which string was which. One sunny morning the purple-faced one called me into his office and asked me to close the door behind me. Placing his elbows on his G-plan desk, and interlacing his fingers like a housemaster preparing to admonish in a firm but kindly way, he asked me what I was reading and how I spent my evenings. Had I been a bright or ambitious youth I would have told him that I had just finished a work by Marshall McLuhan or *The Affluent Society*, and that after work I hurried away to learn about typography and block-making at the London College of Printing, or browse through the literature at the Institute of Practitioners in Advertising; instead, I thought hard and long before revealing that I had just finished *Barnaby Rudge* and was wondering whether to move on to *Little Dorrit* or *Our Mutual Friend* – perhaps he had views on the matter? – and that I had spent the last three evenings in a tiny cinema in Westbourne Grove seeing what must in fact have been one of the last ever showings of Marcel Pagnol's masterly trilogy about the adventures of César and Marius in Marseilles between the wars.

At this my boss sighed heavily and gazed at the ceiling with the pensive look of one who was about to embark on an unpleasant but unavoidable course of action, and was anxious to choose exactly the right words before setting forth; and after half a minute or so he asked me, in the most considerate and helpful way, whether I felt I was altogether suited to the cut and thrust of advertising life, and whether I shouldn't perhaps give some serious thought to the future ... So touched was I by his air of concern, and by the delicate, roundabout route he was taking to the moment of dismissal that I hastened to cut him short, and set his mind at rest. I was sure he was right, I said; I had been coming to much the same conclusion myself; he *must* not worry himself on my behalf; only the other day I had, in fact, decided to take advantage of the £10 assisted passage, and make a new life for myself in Australia (I sometimes filled in the long hours after delivering a 'telephone' message to Fleet Street by reading the papers in Australia House, and some unusually quick thinking enabled me to come up with this implausible version of my future). A look of intense relief suffused my boss's benevolent, bloodshot features; it was hard to know which of us was the more delighted by the outcome; without going so far as to forgive me for reading at my desk, he shook me warmly by the hand, assured me that I had made the right decision, and told me that of course I could stay on to the end of the month; and with that my career in advertising was over.

A week or so later I waved goodbye to the boss and the warhorse and Sid and Alf, and went to the pub round the corner for a final drink with Robert. Coming back to the bar after a visit to the lavatory, I found him practising his golf strokes with a rolled-up copy of the *Evening Standard*. In a messy, impermanent world, some things, at least, remained endearingly the same.

CHAPTER ONE

Unholy Trinity

In the weeks – and even months – that followed my dismissal from the world of advertising I don't remember giving a moment's thought to my future prospects: we lived in a tiny, perpendicular cottage within a wave's break of the front, and I happily reverted to my familiar and vastly preferable habits of reading in the sun, swimming enormous distances and striding about the Downs while the golf balls whizzed about my head like a barrage of enemy fire. I did, however, stir myself to the extent of writing a rather vague letter to Trinity College, Dublin, asking them if they would like to offer me a place to read history.

According to an authoritative-looking book I discovered in the Seaford Public Library, the college of the Holy and Undivided Trinity had been founded towards the end of the sixteenth century by Queen Elizabeth, was loosely modelled on its Cambridge namesake and closely associated with the Protestant Ascendancy in Ireland, whatever that might be, and numbered among its old boys a gaggle of playwrights including Congreve, Goldsmith, Synge, Wilde and Samuel Beckett and assorted literary men like Swift, Burke, Bishop Berkeley and – for some curious reason – both Sheridan le Fanu and Bram Stoker, the originator of *Dracula*. I knew, too, that it was considered very 'wild' by those in the know, that it was inhabited by the tweedier type of English public schoolboy, much given to blowing hunting horns and being sick out of windows from a great height, and that it was possible to gain admission on the strength of 'O', let alone 'A', levels. It sounded like perfection; but I received no acknowledgement from this ancient seat of learning, and after a week or two I gave it no more thought.

As summer turned to autumn, and the sea began to get too chilly for more than the occasional dip, I began – in a torpid, gloomy manner

– to bend my mind once more to the horrid business of earning a living. Perhaps the *Brighton Argus* would take me on as a cub reporter? What could I offer the British Council? (Nothing, it seemed.) Should I have followed the advice of the retired major doubling up as a careers advisor and sought employment in the wine trade, or as a chicken farmer? With every day that passed I lowered my sights still further, and I was scanning the small ads for possible employment as a trainee clerk when, in early October, a letter arrived bearing an Irish stamp. Inside was a letter from someone who signed himself off as the Senior Tutor of Trinity College, Dublin; he informed me that he would be delighted to offer me a place, that term began next day, and that I should report for duty at once if I wanted to take advantage of his kindly offer. Redemption was suddenly at hand; I need worry no more for at least four years; I hurried away to have a bath and wash my hair, for it was well known that the Irish were an insalubrious people, and it might be my last opportunity for many weeks to come.

That afternoon I set off for London in the train, heavily encumbered with luggage and feeling not unlike a Victorian traveller en route for darkest Africa. I took a taxi from Victoria round to my aged Auntie Annie in Onslow Gardens, where I refreshed myself with a cup of tea and took note once more of the carefully pasted-up instructions to unwary occupants of her diminutive bathroom ('Pull Chain down STRAIGHT') before setting out to find a travel agent who might be able to shed light on the mysterious regions to which I was bound, and advise me on how best to get there in order to meet the Senior Tutor's deadline. Despite my Geography 'A' level and the Irish stamp, I wasn't altogether sure whether Dublin was in the North or in the Republic. Which part of the island was I heading for? Would I be needing the passport my mother had so carefully packed beneath my underpants?

A couple of hours later I clambered aboard the London to Holyhead train at Euston. I settled into a dimly lit compartment and opened *Mr Sponge's Sporting Tour*. The spirit of adventure, never strong at the best of times, ebbed unhappily away in the half-light, and I was engulfed in the same feelings of homesickness that, only a couple of years earlier, had marked me out as the Wettest Boy in the School, sobbing into my *New Statesman* as the train drew out of Paddington, while all about me manly, rugger-loving boys lit up enormous cigars and hurled inflated contraceptives out of the window with cries of virile glee. My only companion was a cheerful, red-faced Irishman in a knobbly white jersey. 'Trinity, eh,' he exclaimed, after examining the labels my mother had glued so carefully to my impressive range of trunks and suitcases. 'By God,' he said, 'they'll have your guts for garters,' and disappeared in the direction of the bar, chuckling to himself in a highly gratified manner. He returned shortly after, clutching several bottles of stout and a scotch egg; and as the train hurled through the Midlands on its way to Anglesey he described with a hideous relish the misdeeds of Trinity students, till my head reeled with tales of mass intoxication and the smashing of windows and undergraduates being chased across Dublin by infuriated beetle-browed Gardai wielding clubs the size of baseball bats.

At one o'clock we arrived in Holyhead, and I humped my luggage aboard the Dun Laoghaire steamer. The Celtic world lay all about me in the darkness: swarthy, diminutive North Walians in blue jerseys and wellington boots; beefy, red-faced labourers from Roscommon or Mayo, the mud of Coventry or Camden Town still adhering to their boots, tossing down pint after pint of Guinness at the bar and singing songs of a kind I had never heard before; censorious young seminarians in black macs and homburg hats, with pursed lips and sunken eyes, thankful to be leaving behind them the tainted soil of heathen England; waxen-featured nuns looking queasy and cross-eyed, but unwisely refusing to exchange the smoky, sweaty squalor of the second-class lounge for a breath of fresh air (some years later one of these unhappy ladies was sick all over my typewriter, and I mopped it up with the weary unconcern of a veteran). I felt, as I was often to feel in the future, very large, very blond, very conspicuous and irredeemably Anglo-Saxon.

Of the four-hour crossing I now remember little. Greatly daring, I joined the red-faced labourers at the bar and ordered – in as low a tone as could possibly be mustered – the first of the several thousand pints of Dublin stout that were to pour down my throat over the next four years; I treated myself to a pork pie and a cold sausage roll, and washed this unpleasing mixture down with another pint of the same; like a true Englishman, I disdained the steamed-up lounge with its background chorus of retching and groaning, and strode round and round the deck – noticing as I did so a handsome, strong-featured girl in a corduroy coat, with auburn hair, an exciting-looking bosom and in one hand a copy of *The Tin Drum*, which she was quite incapable of reading in the darkness and the Force Eight gale. With her wide mouth and good cheekbones and hair lashing about her face, she looked like a duplicate Brigitte Bardot who had been unexpectedly parachuted onto the wildly bobbing deck; I fell instantly in love with this radiant apparition, and remained so for the next eighteen months at least. And at about six o'clock on a rainswept, silver-grey morning I caught my first sight of a view that would, in days to come, move me more than once to tears of joy and regret: the delicate, elegant cones of the Dublin Hills and the Wicklow Mountains to the south and, to the north, Howth Head and the great sweep of Dublin Bay.

An hour or so later I had trundled into Dublin aboard a foreign-feeling black and orange train, examined a notice in Westland Row Station warning Irish girls about the perils of London life and giving the addresses of various priests in Hammersmith and Kentish Town, and deposited my faithful cases in the left-luggage office. By now I felt hungover, underslept and ruinously indigested: the long night, the Guinness and the pork pie were taking their toll; it was still raining; and for all its seedy elegance, Dublin seemed to exude a sour smell of stale stout and old socks. I wandered into Trinity, and the graceful Georgian squares looked sombre and granitic in the chilly morning light, with here and there a broken window, and the odd unshaven figure groping its way in a dressing gown, towel over the arm and sponge-bag in hand, towards the College Baths, where enormous enamel tubs awaited it, like private swimming pools, with a claw at each corner and vast brass taps belching steam and boiling water. I spotted someone I'd known at school coming towards me and, feeling too reduced to explain what I was doing there, I dodged behind a pillar until he had disappeared in the direction of his room; I bought a postcard of the Front Square – the sky a cobalt blue, the grass a fluorescent lime – and sent home a gloomy message to the effect that Dublin seemed quite dreadful and that they should expect me home within the next day or two.

Quite how I filled in the rest of that terrible day mercifully escapes me, but some time towards the end of the afternoon I was allocated digs in a distant suburb by a brisk lady with something of the school matron about her – to my disappointment she failed to offer me a spoonful of radio malt – and bundled into a taxi of the kind I was later to spot breaking down in Guatemala City or the Jordanian desert. During my time in Dublin I never found a taxi-driver who had the faintest idea of where he should be going or even the dimmest acquaintance with the geography of the city. Talkative, kindly men, they invariably justified their ignorance by explaining in apologetic tones that they were 'up from the country' or 'standing in' for a brother or a cousin. To make matters worse, the clutches of Dublin taxis, once pressed in, failed to spring back of their own accord, but had to be hooked out with a nimble motion of the toe – which may well have explained the winkle-pickers worn by these rustic men. After a good deal of revving and reading of maps and hooking out of the clutch and backing wildly out of cul-de-sacs into the flow of oncoming traffic we eventually reached our destination, a pebble-dashed semi in a small street overlooking Dublin Bay, with the hills looming up behind and the odd fuchsia bush lending a dash of colour to the greyness all around. I unloaded my cases from the boot, watched the taxi-driver shoot unsteadily off in the wrong direction, and – dreading what further horrors lay in store – rang the front-door bell, wincing in a well-brought-up way at the dainty resonance of the two-tone chimes.

The mere sight of my landlady as she flung open the door in greeting redeemed the day; and from then on I knew that all would be well. Mrs Todd was a grey, garrulous lady, kindliness made flesh; in return for a very modest rent she not only gave us the best sitting-room in the house, but expressed a positively maternal fondness for washing out underpants and hanging socks to dry in the family kitchen. The Todds were Protestants, and evidently regarded the establishment of the Republic as a temporary aberration, at the end of which the pillar boxes could be painted red once more, and life resume a more familiar shape. Mr Todd, a silent genial man who spent his days watching BBC television – coming in on the train that morning I had been impressed by the outsize television aerials on top of all the houses, bending in the direction of Wales like arms stretched out in supplication – told me proudly that, far from being kings of Ireland, his ancestors came from Teddington. Their daughter Sylvia – her beauty marred only by the mauve legs so common in those days among Irish girls, and attributed by us dietary experts to the national aversion to fresh veg of any kind – had recently landed a job with the local branch of the Swastika Laundry. Every evening Mrs Todd cooked us a high tea of fried eggs, black pudding, bacon and fried potato bread, followed by soda bread and bright pink strawberry jam and washed down by several mugs of mahogany-coloured tea; at ten o'clock, worried that we might be worn out by our researches into early Irish society or the contents of the King's Wardrobe, she insisted on giving us a little 'supper' of cakes or sandwiches or the occasional fried egg. On one occasion, unwilling to hurt the good lady's feelings but unable to look the egg in the eye, I went for a brisk walk after this late-night snack, taking the unwanted egg with me in the palm of my hand. As soon as we were out of sight I hurled it over a high wall, and went on my way rejoicing and dusting my hands together. Five minutes later, as I retraced my steps, I found the egg once more, looking like a bedraggled jellyfish on the pavement before me: I assume it had landed on a late-night gardener who had tossed it back over the wall with a grunt of irritation.

I found myself sharing these fine digs with two other freshmen. The first of these was a lugubrious Bristolian named Holmes. Holmes was a pleasant enough fellow, but lacking in the social graces. He used to block the lavatory with tiresome regularity, striding away from the scene of the crime without a backwards glance; the fact that we had to share a bathroom with our hosts made this all the more offensive. He was also a smoker of the squalid school: though still in his teens, his fingers were already stained a horrid hue of orange; he affected a 'National Service' style of dragging, with the fag end held between the thumb and the first two fingers, and the lighted end smouldering in the palm of the hand, safely out of sight from an enquiring sergeant major; and he was much given to smoking in bed, singeing the sheets in the process. Still worse, he used to stub out his fag ends on the nearest piece of furniture, and instead of depositing the extinguished remains in an ashtray or a wastepaper basket he would put them in his jacket pocket, which was soon bulging over with the remains of ancient cigarettes. This disagreeable habit led him into trouble one evening, after he had been out drinking in the middle of Dublin with some depressing fellow-Cliftonians. Holmes used to ride a motor-bike, and would set off for Trinity every morning in a virulent yellow crash helmet, which we thought rather ungentlemanly; he also wore a paper-thin mock suede jacket, into the pockets of which he fed his collection of stubs. As he was speeding home from the pub on the night in question he pocketed an insufficiently extinguished cigarette end; his jacket began to smoulder, exciting interest among the passers-by; within minutes he was ablaze, like a demon rider, and had to be hosed down by a suburban gardener out tending his roses in the Ballsbridge area of the city. After that, he was more careful about his cigarette ends; nor was I sorry to lose the company of the mock suede jacket, which was the colour my mother referred to as 'dog's mess'.

Although I shared a room with Holmes, I became far more friendly with the third inhabitant of the digs, Michael Shore. Shore was a small, swarthy youth with glasses and a motheaten black beard, and he bore an astonishing resemblance to Yasser Arafat of the PLO; indeed, I have long suspected that he may well have become Yasser Arafat shortly after graduating from Trinity, for he was beginning to show revolutionary tendencies towards the end of his time in Ireland, and I have neither seen nor heard from him during the years in which Arafat has been a household name. Shore's father was a prosperous knife-grinder in Sheffield; I soon put it about that, far from being plain 'Mr Shore', he was in fact Lord Shore, in the hope that this would lead my friend to attract the kind of deferential treatment due to a prospective peer of the realm, for Trinity was heavily staffed with minor or bogus nobility, and ambitious landladies vied with one another for the number of Etonians they could squeeze on board. Sadly, my ruse was unsuccessful: although I had a very great deal of time for Shore, finding him a congenial drinking companion, a good joker and an enterprising traveller, and losing patience only when he was, as sometimes happened, overcome by a sudden burst of ineffective pyromania, he had no great public presence, and was sadly under-valued by the less discerning undergraduates.

Next morning, Shore, Holmes and I took another black and orange train into the middle of Dublin, and strolled with a nonchalant proprietorial air through the back gate of Trinity, past the games fields, and into the main body of the college. How different it all seemed from the day before! The sun was shining; the broken windows seemed to have been miraculously repaired; the whiff of stout drifting down Dame Street from the Guinness factory seemed pregnant with raffish promise; the undergraduates looked and sounded delightfully urbane and well turned-out, with tweed jackets, corduroy trousers and a Woosterish absence of chins much in evidence, and loud, self-confident, reassuringly familiar Home Counties voices cutting imperiously across the hideous and alto- gether alien accents of the Ulstermen and the melodious burr of the men from the South. The Ulstermen in particular I found baffling, never having encountered their kind before, and I assumed at first I must have come across a nest of exiled Glaswegians. Many of them wore green blazers with a boar's head emblazoned on the bosom in silver filigree; most of them had a decidedly post-war look, with much Brylcreem in evidence and the gnarled, rather shiny features I remembered from my childhood in London in the late 1940s. Beside them – and beside the equally knobbly, equally diffident Southern Irish – the English looked well-fed, dashing, opulent and (to the native eye, no doubt) intolerably arrogant, overbearing and loud as they revved up their MGs in the middle of the night and bayed at one another across the Dublin streets. They also, as I soon discovered, behaved very much worse than the Irish, reversing the national stereotypes of the fierce, drunken Irishman and the quiet, diffident Anglo-Saxon, and causing much pursing of the lips and twitching of lace curtains in what was, for all its flamboyant reputation, an eminently respectable city.

Shore and I had both enrolled to read history, and after a good deal of examining notice boards and cross-examining bottle-nosed college porters (curiously togged out in tailcoats and black jockeys' caps) we eventually found ourselves squeezing onto benches in a lecture room in the Museum Building, a draughty mid-Victorian monstrosity much admired by Ruskin. My fellow-scholars, I was glad to note, included the auburn-haired girl with the exciting-looking bosom who had made so strong an impression on the Holyhead boat, and a stout, disreputable figure with prehensile fingers, a very loud brown and white tweed jacket and a rolling, nautical gait, who became, and remains, one of my closest friends.

After five minutes or so the door of the lecture hall was flung open with a theatrical bang, and a figure bearing a striking resemblance to Ludwig van Beethoven strode on stage. This, we learned, was the Professor of History, and he had come to initiate us into the mysteries of his calling. Clutching the lapels of his gown in either hand, and fixing his noble gaze on a clutch of acanthus leaves on the ceiling above us, he began to intone in a fine, resonant brogue. 'History,' he informed us, very much to our surprise, 'is the past'; and he continued in this inspiriting vein for the next three-quarters of an hour before disappearing with equal abruptness through the door by which he had entered. As we were soon to learn, the work expected of dons and undergraduates, and relations between the two parties, were altogether more reminiscent of eighteenth-century Oxford than of contemporary Oxbridge: terms were six weeks long; although we expected to snooze our way through a certain number of lectures, we were seldom required to write more than two essays a year, and these were often returned (if at all) a term later than that in which they had been written; visits to one's tutor were – for English students at least – restricted to a termly call asking for his signature to a form entitling the bearer to large discounts on flights between London and Dublin.

In the square outside, we gathered – automatically, it seemed – into little groups, each of us instinctively recognizing that to which he or she belonged: the English public schoolboys, the green-blazered Ulstermen, and the Catholic Irish – a third of the total – who had received special dispensations from the Archbishop of Dublin to attend this hotbed of West Britons, Orangemen and undesirable aliens from over the water. Additional interest was supplied by several Nigerians, looking ill-at-ease in brand new blazers and cavalry twill trousers with creases so rigid that the garments would almost certainly have stood up by themselves had their owners been mysteriously hoisted out of them; a middle-aged Copt in his ninth year reading agriculture, who made a beeline for the girl with the auburn hair and the exciting-looking bosom; and the occasional American from the mid-West – clad invariably in a beret, a black mac, jeans and gym shoes, clutching a copy of *Le Nouvel Observateur* and wearing a smile of goofy benevolence – who had read deeply in J. P. Donleavy's *The Ginger Man*, and had hurried over to Dublin in the hope of re-enacting its hero's fabulous misdeeds.

Shore and I found ourselves drawn into conversation with an eager, pinch-faced youth in a black leather jacket, grey shirt and utilitarian tie, who rather threw us off balance by asking us for our views on existentialism within seconds of our being introduced. His politics were fiercely to the left, which must have been frustrating in a university which was - at least as far as the English contingent were concerned - frivolous and apolitical to a degree that would have seemed both incredible and reprehensible some seven or eight years later. He had occasion more than once to chide me for not taking life in general, and politics in particular, as seriously as I should, and took me to task with especial vehemence at the time of the Cuban Missile Crisis; he seemed maddened by my apparent indifference to the fate of mankind, thrusting his cadaverous face close to mine and angrily ramming his message home with a wagging motion of the right-hand index finger, while I gazed anxiously over his head hoping relief was at hand. He had all the humourless credulity of the born believer, and this provided us with a source of harmless amusement in the weeks ahead. I remember telling him that the Provost of Trinity - a blameless mathematician from Ballymena - was, in fact, a dentist from Mullingar who had been struck off the register for professional misconduct, and was gratified to hear him repeating this tale elsewhere in a conspiratorial whisper; some time after that I informed him that a bovine, elderly-looking undergraduate whom I had nicknamed 'the bank manager' had indeed managed the Stowmarket branch of Barclays, at which the eager believer hurried off to reprimand the manager for his bank's investment policy in South Africa just as he was setting off for a round of golf, drawing a puzzled rebuff in response.

★ ★ ★

After London, Dublin seemed surprisingly small and rural: I felt as though I had been suddenly thrust into the company of garrulous, weatherbeaten farmers in forceful tweeds after consorting with dignified and ashen-featured City gentlemen in black jackets and bowler hats and old-fashioned striped trousers of the kind associated with T. S. Eliot, wedding guests and hen-pecked clerks in English comedies of the 1930s. Whereas London buildings were blackened with grime and grit, their Dublin equivalents - though tending to decrepitude - retained their ruddy, youthful glow; the air was sweet with the rustic whiff of burning peat; while London seemed to spread out for ever, the Dublin Hills loomed up at the end of Fitzwilliam Street - that mighty and, as yet, unviolated sweep of Georgian terraced houses – like some gigantic stage prop that had been wheeled out to keep Dubliners' urban aspirations firmly in their place.

After the sobriety of London, Dublin seemed wonderfully seedy and raffish: for all its eighteenth-century elegance – and the great town houses of the Anglo-Irish in Merrion and Fitzwilliam Squares, with their enormous intricate fanlights and Italian plasterwork and huge sash windows and well-worn flags, seemed infinitely grander and more elegant than anything one might come across in Blooms-bury or Belgravia – the city had something rotten and rancid about it, as though it were built upon a shifting, unstable compost of straw and horses' messes and dead rats and old tweed jackets and unmentionable alcoholic drinks. Every now and then – or so we read in the vigorous local papers – the front would fall out of some decrepit Georgian terrace on the north side of the city, crashing into the street and unkindly exposing the inmates to public view as they went about their business, eating meals or climbing into bed or out of the bath or straining eagerly forward to pick up *This is Your Life* on a flickering black and white television set; the houses all around would then be propped up with great triangles made of wood, and life would continue as before.

Everywhere was within walking distance, even our digs in distant Blackrock; I liked nothing better than poking about this beautiful, battered city, strolling down the quays that ran on either side of the Liffey – a diminutive, strong-smelling stream, like a miniature Thames or Seine, lined with plain-featured merchants' houses and porticoed and pedimented public buildings – or venturing into dainty, immaculate suburbs inhabited by retired colonial officials or the dentists with which Dublin seemed so richly endowed, or picking one's way through crowds of barefooted, puce-faced tinkers' children, many of them clad in outsize brown overcoats that flapped about their ankles and quite covered their hands, to inspect some decaying church or terrace we'd seen from the top of a bus.

As for Trinity itself, it had the look of a very large and agreeably coarse-grained Oxford or Cambridge college which had comman-deered an unreasonably large area right in the middle of Dublin, opposite the curving classical front of the Bank of Ireland – or, in pre-Union days, the Irish Houses of Parliament – and within hailing distance of the river in one direction, and Grafton Street in the other. Designed, we were told, by Sir William Chambers, the main frontage of Trinity, which looked away up Dame Street towards the Guinness brewery and Christ Church Cathedral, was massive, benign and grey, with a kindly and somewhat faded blue clock placed bang in the middle of the central pediment; beneath the clock was the Front Gate, manned at all hours of the day and night by the red-faced porters in jockey caps, where enquiring undergraduates could read notices about Gaelic clubs, hurling matches, a cricketing tour of southern England, a meeting of Fianna Fail students or a debate in which Reginald Maudling would bend his mind to some vexed and vexing issue of British domestic politics. It was at Front Gate that the loud and hectoring English minority gathered before lunch to watch the world go by and look each other up and down and group together before setting off for the pub: among the regulars I noticed the middle-aged Copt, hurrying helpfully forward to relieve the better-looking girls of their heavy loads of books, and so strike up a fruitful and pleasurable friendship.

Beyond Front Gate was a large cobbled eighteenth-century square – or crude approximation to a square, containing as it did all manner of indentations and intrusions – which contained, in addition to dons' and undergraduates' rooms leading off staircases, a Chapel (Church of Ireland), a very elegant Examination Hall, a Hogarthian Dining Hall, and Trinity's answer to King's College Chapel, the great blackened Library, reeking of ancient leather-bound volumes, with its huge barrel-vaulted ceiling and bright white busts of Irish bishops and Greek philosophers and the famous Book of Kells, on one page of which Queen Victoria had thoughtfully signed her name. Towards the back of this enormous square stood a free-standing Victorian campanile, with allegorical women in helmets at every corner; as far as I know, its bells were never rung, but it came into its own in the summer term, when enterprising but ticketless undergraduates, suitably disguised in dinner jackets, concealed themselves in its intricate heights on the afternoon of the Trinity Ball, letting themselves down on a rope as soon as it was safe to do so and sauntering off to join in the merriment. Behind the campanile were the Rubrics, red-brick late seventeenth-century buildings with a line of Dutch gables running along the top: they were the oldest buildings in Trinity, and the sets of rooms – which were lighter and brighter than most – were much sought after by influential sportsmen and bachelor dons. In those days – things have changed greatly since – two or sometimes three undergraduates would share a set of rooms, which were made up of two bedrooms, a sitting-room and a midget kitchen consisting of a gas ring and a sink; as in an Oxford or Cambridge college or the Inns of Court, the sets led off a staircase at the bottom of which was a lavatory and a painted black noticeboard giving the names and floors of the various occupants. Although at least a third of the undergraduates were women, none of them were then allowed to live in college, and visitors were supposedly expelled to their digs – or to an old-fashioned 'hall of residence' – by eleven o'clock in the evening.

On the other side of Front Square to the Library stood an Edwardian monstrosity called the Graduates' Memorial Building, containing solitary rooms for the lonely or the misanthropic, a good many snooker tables, an ancient telephone box, and the reading rooms of the two rival debating societies, the Hist and the Phil. Most undergraduates joined one or other of these self-important bodies in their first term, attending the odd debate – in which elderly-looking students wore white bow-ties and ribbons with medals on round their necks, clutched their lapels in an important way, and spent a lot of time banging gavels – and using the reading rooms to shelter from the rain or to retreat to when uncertain of what to do next or overcome by a sudden fit of nerves. Freshmen apart, these soporific, sombre rooms, with their begrimed plate glass windows and ancient leather armchairs and copies of *Punch* and the *Field* and the *Irish Tatler* in maroon beribboned leather folders and portraits of Burke and Mr Gladstone, were haunted by aspiring Irish politicians and trainee clubmen snoozing the afternoon away with their hands crossed over their trainee paunches and copies of the *Irish Times* spread open across their faces; the silence was broken only by the steady drone of the sleepers, the sudden snort of one who was rudely awoken, the buzzing of flies against the glass, the gentle tick of the clock on the mantlepiece, and an occasional rumble of conversation as two elderly undergraduates – both wearing mud-coloured suits with leather patches on the elbows, and both inclining to corpulence – discussed in measured tones the issues of the day.

Behind the GMB stood the grimmest of Trinity's three squares, Botany Bay. The grass in the middle had been asphalted over and turned into a sombre tennis court; and since the buildings all about were austere and barrack-like, and built of Wicklow stone the colour of grey worsted, the overall tone of the place was on the glum side, and made more so by the fact that undergraduates like Holmes were allowed to park their Vespas and motorbikes on one side of the Bay, and spent a good deal of time revving their engines and screeching their brakes. The only good thing about Botany Bay – apart from the jollity of its inmates – was its proximity to the mighty College Baths. Altogether different was New Square, which lay behind the Rubrics, had been built in the dashing, genial 1820s, and exuded levity and light. Between the two squares stood a tiny Greek temple which housed the University Press; unlike its more ambitious equivalents on the other side of the Irish Sea, it had no aspirations beyond printing the university calendar and exam papers, and it was occasionally burst into – or so we were led to believe – by enterprising undergraduates anxious to learn what lay in store for them.

Opposite the heavily guarded temple stood Woodward's famous Museum, in which the Professor of History had unravelled the mysteries of the Past, with its stone acanthus leaves and Byzantine vaults and columns. Beyond this lay the games fields, echoing to hearty cries and the dreadful thwack of boot on ball; the Fellows' Garden, in which so few fellows were seen to spend their time that towards the end of the 1960s it was covered over by a library extension and new lecture halls made of the dripping grey concrete and dirty plate glass so admired by fashionable architects and go-ahead dons; and – moving back to where we started out – the imposing Provost's House and Garden in which, or so my friend in the black leather jacket and utility shirt believed, the disgraced dentist from Mullingar went about his mysterious ways.

Sealed off from the rest of Dublin by a high stone wall surmounted by sharply pointed iron rails, the symbol and a relic of a lost Ascendancy, Trinity was tolerant, benign, indolent and indifferent, a place in which the idle and the industrious, the bright and the astonishingly dim, ex-National Servicemen and Catholic boys and girls from the wilds of Mayo or County Cork were left to sink or swim together. I came to love it more than any institution or set of buildings I have ever known; and the genial ambivalence and absence of gravitas that were so strong a feature of Trinity life left me, like so many of its graduates, hopelessly adrift once the gates of Paradise had clanged to behind us and the key had been firmly turned.

★   ★   ★

Very swiftly we settled into an agreeable if rather dull routine in which Shore and I – like a couple of mildly jovial clerks – commuted in from the outer suburbs, snoozed through lectures on Basil the Bulgar-Slayer and the True Nature of St Patrick, enjoyed a quiet lunch in one of the innumerable pubs that clustered round the gates of Trinity (in the course of which I once discovered, to my great delight, the snapped-off head of a toothbrush in my steak and kidney pie), and spent the evenings dozing over a gas fire reading poems by Yeats and Robert Graves, our stomachs squealing and groaning as they sought to digest the inevitable intake of fried black pudding and potato bread. From time to time we would visit the Gas Company Theatre to watch Miss E. Panton Watkinson take the leading part in one of Ibsen's gloomier masterpieces, or take a bus to Glendalough (signing our names in the visitors' book of some evidently underfrequented hotel beneath those of W. E. Gladstone and the Secretary of State for Ireland), or even – perhaps the high point of our university life to date – enjoy a Pickwickian evening with the bank manager and his equally stolid flatmate and golfing companion.

Pickwick had long been one of my favourite books, and I had rapidly persuaded Shore – though not Ian Whitcomb, my friend with the prehensile fingers – to share my enthusiasm; in a whimsical way we saw ourselves, for a day or two at least, as reincarnations of Tupman, Winkle and Snodgrass, with the rotund and benevolent figure of the bank manager unwittingly doubling up as Pickwick. Strenuously eager to enjoy ourselves, we arranged with the manager and his colleague to see *The Mikado* at the Bus Station Theatre. During the interval Shore – who was later to make a speciality of passing out in the lavatories of Dublin theatres, from which he was flushed out in the early hours by puzzled cleaning-women – dashed his spectacles to the ground in emulation of our elderly hero, at which the bank manager, who had no spectacles to dash and cheerfully confessed that, as far as *Pickwick* was concerned, he had 'never got round to reading it, old boy', looked understandably nonplussed.

The climax of this brief, uneasy friendship was occasioned by the manager asking us round to his digs for an evening of minced pies and mulled wine. With what relish we sat in the sombre, dingy gloom of the manager's bed-sitter in Rathmines, lit only by a sweet-smelling peat fire, making old-mannish conversation and taking mature, reflective sips of hot red wine made palatable with cloves and sugar and slices of lemon! How solid and comfortable and reassuring was the manager himself, with his friendly double chin and the roll of fat hanging over the back of his collar like a raw sausage that had been taped to the nape of his neck and his unremarkable tweeds and his comfortable slippers that lacked only a faithful, prune-eyed labrador to bring them at his master's beck and call! In a new and alarming world, in which so many of our fellows seemed to me at least to be alarmingly smooth or blasé, strutting about in modish suede or leather jackets and tasteful tweeds and fashionable French corduroy trousers so heavily corrugated that their owners looked like freshly ploughed fields sprung suddenly to life, how consoling it was, and how good for one's fatuous self-esteem, to watch the manager slowly filling his pipe, or to glimpse his golf bag in the corner, or to await his commonsensical verdict on the Arian Heresy or the Great Divide between the Celtic and the Roman Churches ('There's really nothing to it, old boy. Now let me explain ...')! Heady excitements such as these, however, were few and far between: more often than not of an evening Shore and I would sit in companionable silence in some suburban lounge bar, admiring the Spanish wrought iron and the purple wall-to-wall carpeting, and wondering whether this indeed was the life of wild debauch of which we had heard so much.

Rather different from these genteel hostelries was a very antique, rather English-looking pub in the maze of little streets between St Patrick's Cathedral and the Liffey. It doubled up as a residential hotel, peopled almost entirely by elderly gentlemen who appeared to have come down in the world. The poet Derek Mahon – who was a year or so ahead of us at Trinity – had, we were told, spent an entire term there, and we decided to try it out for a night or two. It was, like most adventures, more enjoyable in retrospect than at the time. The mattresses appeared to be stuffed with straw; since none of the floors were straight, the beds tilted at disconcerting angles; the lavatories had no locks, and more than once I surprised an elderly resident with his trousers round his ankles.

Most disconcerting of all was a disagreeable item discovered in the butter dish at breakfast on our first morning. One of the elderly inmates had evidently sneezed while tucking into his bacon and eggs; the offending item had shot out of his nose and embedded itself in the butter. Gingerly we chiselled our way round it until at last it was left standing on a slender stem of butter, like Nelson on his pillar. When we reassembled for breakfast the next morning, we were surprised to find it still there, but hemmed in by fresh supplies of butter. Again we carefully cut our way round it; still it managed to survive, remaining in place until our stay had ended and (no doubt) for many days thereafter.

Deep inside this delapidated hostelry was a small and gloomy bar, kippered with smoke and lit only by a skylight, in which ancient Irishmen in cloth caps and ankle-length tweed overcoats spent their evenings drinking Jameson's and bottled stout (no draught was available, and the bottles were plugged with corks rather than crown tops) and singing those infinitely sad, infinitely moving songs of which the Irish – unlike the English – have enviably retained such a number. I found – and still find – that many of these songs were guaranteed to bring out the goose-pimples, and wished, as a very obvious Englishman, that I could either fade into the furniture, decrepit as it was, or suddenly stumble on a cache of unexpected Irish ancestors, thus enabling me to look my companions in the eye as they sang steadily on about the villainies of England and the sufferings of Ireland.

And, of course, Ireland and its history were beginning to prove wonderfully seductive. How easily we sympathized with those waves upon waves of Normans, Flemings, Welshmen, English and Scots who, within minutes of their arrival, had become (or so our tutors assured us) *hiberniores ipsis hibernicis* or – having the best of both worlds, like the angular, weatherbeaten Anglo-Irish one spotted striding down Grafton Street in Old Etonian ties and riding macs, or Trinity's own crop of gaitered Church of Ireland clergymen – Irish to the English and English to the Irish! Who could fail to be moved by Ireland's melancholy, haunted history, by the hieratic chanting of

Synge, by the plangent music of Seán Ó Riada (Ireland's Bartok, and surely a far greater composer than most of those celebrated in this discordant century), or even the mighty tub-full of mediaeval Irish butter – an aged antecedent of Kerrygold – that had been dug out of the Bog of Allen and was to be seen, along with Celtic crosses and buckles and elaborate gold shields, in the National Museum of Ireland? Who could doubt that Yeats was the greatest of poets, or that the 'foremost of those that I would hear praised' bore an unmistakeable resemblance to the girl with the auburn hair and the exciting-looking bosom?

As we began to discover the country about us, our academic aspirations withered in the undemanding Irish air. Stubbs's *Charters* lay unopened and unmourned, 'Was Early Irish Society Tribal? Discuss' remained a matter of permanent indifference. The garrulous, genial charms of Dublin pub life began to lure us from the paths of virtue; rowdier clerks than before, we began to return home reeking of stout and excess. Mrs Todd took all this in good part, clapping her hands together and summoning Mr Todd from the televison set as Shore, overcome by alcoholic fumes, slid under the table just as she placed the evening's quota of black pudding and potato bread before him, repeating the performance as her husband came hurrying to the scene. We were beginning to find, and lose, our feet; all Ireland, and the future, lay before us.

CHAPTER TWO

The Prep School Special

Back in England in early December, I did my first – and, as it turned out, my last – vacation job. My friend Ian – he of the prehensile fingers and rolling nautical gait – lived in a large and homely block of flats in the middle of Putney Heath, replete with wrought-iron gates, clip-on Tudor beams, neatly trimmed hedges and enormous pale green bathrooms in which the tiles on the walls rose like Aztec pyramids or the setting for an Esther Williams film. Ian found us both jobs as assistant draymen in a local brewery, and within a day or two of our arrival back home we were reporting for duty. Once again, I stayed with our family friends in Notting Hill Gate; but whereas I had left them a glum and down-trodden clerk, I returned in an altogether more bumptious vein. And far from leaving the house in the rush hour clad in a shiny grey suit from Burton's, umbrella in one hand and potent reading matter in the other, I now stole away at five in the morning in jeans and gym shoes and a thick winter woolly. How great a change, it seemed, had been wrought in how little time!

As for the drayman's life, it seemed to me, in my euphoria, to be vastly preferable to office work – if inferior to that of the messenger – despite the uncongenial hours, the muscular strain of flicking crates on and off the back of a lorry or rolling barrels into position for them to be pushed or hoisted through the trap door in front of the pubs into the vaults beneath, and the somewhat tedious conversation of my full-time colleagues, between whom I sat squeezed in the cab of the lorry, uneasily athwart the gearstick. Like many working-class southern Englishmen, they communicated in a series of grunts and four-letter words, and their reading matter was restricted to the pages of the *Mirror* and the *Sketch*: after the Irish they seemed sadly inarticulate and short on both native culture and a sense of history – an impression that was reinforced by an Irishman in the brewery, who spoke to us about the buildings of Dublin and the great burial chamber at New Grange and the unhappy fate of Lord Edward FitzGerald with an eloquence and an enthusiasm I found it hard to imagine my more stolid compatriots, likeable and jocular as they were, bringing to the work of Inigo Jones or the Battle of Flodden Field.

Not surprisingly, the draymen found hurrying round London delivering large quantities of beer to be thirsty work, and every now and then the lorry would pull into a quiet side street so that we could refresh ourselves from one of the crates on the back. The drained bottles were carefully cracked across the neck and replaced in the crate, to be explained away as 'breakage'. According to the regulars, prodigious quantities of the beer produced by the brewery were consumed in this way: we were often told – in awestruck tones – about one of the old hands who had drunk so much of his employers' beer that his insides had rotted away and been replaced by a system of metal and rubber pipes and plungers which clanked and hissed as he strode about, and a stout, red-faced man in brown overalls was pointed out as the phenomenon in person.

With the money I'd made at the brewery I decided to spend a few days after Christmas in Normandy with my sister Julia and Tom Pomeroy, the kindly Old Etonian who had tried to console me with tales of the tedium of Cambridge life. We took a cargo boat from Newhaven, and spent the first night in a draughty hotel in Dieppe. It was so cold that I went to bed in all my clothes, including an American army jeep coat, as heavy as a suit of armour, which my father had worn in the war: somewhere near Beauvais he had stumbled on a dead sheep which he had promptly skinned and cured, so providing his coat with a home-made sheepskin collar. During the night the temperature dropped to unheard-of depths, and after a good deal of wrestling with top-heavy wardrobes and recalcitrant dressing tables I managed to lift the carpet from the floor and lay it on top of the threadbare blankets provided by our hosts.

France in those days had a magic and a sense of style that seemed – and, no doubt, still seems – entirely lacking in England outside the somewhat rarified worlds of London clubs and ancient schools and universities and draughty country houses. I admired and envied the French for the way they smoked their cigarettes, dangling from the lower lip or held low down between the first and second finger (so much so that I unwisely bought a packet of Gitanes but was immediately overcome by terrible waves of dizziness and nausea, as though of hemlock I had drunk); for the ingenuity of their neon lights and the way in which the neon was pinned to the building itself instead of being backed, as in Britain, by hideous sheets of lurid plastic; for their washed-out sky-blue overalls; for the way in which they managed to plunge their hands far deeper into their pockets than we could, while simultaneously shrugging their shoulders; for their clean white table cloths and their long zinc bars; for the precarious dash of their cars and metros and buses; for the *chic* of their shop fronts which, even in a provincial town like Dieppe, seemed brighter and grander and altogether more elegant than even the smartest shops in Bond or Jermyn Streets. I tried to console myself by remembering Churchill and the war and re-reading André Maurois's Colonel Bramble and (even better) Pierre Daninos's Major Thompson, but none of it quite rang true any more, and hard as I tried to persuade myself to the contrary, England seemed sadly small and scruffy whenever one returned.

All this was very confusing. At prep school in particular we had been led to believe that the English were – apart from their other, self-evident virtues – a clean and tidy race; rather like the Dutch or the Scandinavians, but more dashingly so, and with none of the regimented, rather antiseptic neatness of our Nordic cousins across the sea. Travellers from the Latin countries in particular brought back distressing accounts of clogged and groaning lavatories in France (made worse by the absence of *seats*) and flea-ridden Italian *pensioni* and corpulent, loudly buzzing bluebottles hovering hungrily over grime-encrusted vats of paella and moussaka. The Continent, it seemed, was a realm of seedy chaos, in which diarrhoea and even dysentery were a recreational hazard for those rash enough to sample the food (greasy), the water was best avoided, telephones and public transport were subjects of jocular disdain, and the unwholesome French, instead of wrapping their bread in dainty paper squares, strode brazenly about with baguettes tucked under their armpits, scattering ash as they went. Only the Swiss matched up to, or even surpassed, our exalted standards of hygiene; but no one could really take them seriously, and their compulsive cleanliness was thought to be going too far, and sadly symptomatic of a dull devotion to chocolates, cuckoo clocks and numbered bank accounts.

I began going to Europe at about the time that my housemaster was informed in a somewhat peremptory way that I would not, after all, be returning for the next academic year, and every time I went there I was struck by the great gulf set between patronizing post-war stereotypes and what I saw all about me. Whereas the average Englishman – supposedly a natty dresser – shambled to and fro in creased and shapeless trousers, a nylon shirt with string vest all too plainly visible beneath and a terrible maroon jersey, while his wife was before long to bring shame upon the nation by striding purposefully about in lime-green polyester trouser suits with flared trousers and white high-heeled shoes while clutching giant white handbags that looked as though they had been stuffed with rocks, the French in particular managed to look maddeningly stylish and neatly put together; whereas the Continentals were – not unreasonably – accustomed to eating in a sensible, civilized way with proper knives and forks and highly polished crockery and efficient, supercilious waiters in black trousers and long white aprons, we seemed glumly reconciled to a world of chipped mugs and tea slopping about the saucer and plastic spoons and paper cups and pub tables covered with pools of beer and ash trays brimming over with fag ends and screwed-up packets of crisps; and whereas in Europe the old, much-derided world of the *haute bourgeoisie* lingered benevolently on, England seemed poised on the edge of becoming, in the very worst sense of the term, an essentially working-class culture, brought low by a pernicious combination of crude commercialism and soggy, guilt-ridden notions about 'class' and 'rights' and 'equality'.

★   ★   ★

Back home, such gloomy thoughts were quickly blown away by a breath of sea air and a brisk walk on the Downs – two of the ingredients essential, my mother believed, to 'transforming' even the most 'washed-out' and pasty office-worker into the picture of health, the others being early nights, plenty of swimming and extensive exposure to sunlight. Insofar as the climate allowed, all were readily available in the small town in which we lived. As generation upon

generation of prep school boys will remember, Seaford is a windswept
seaside resort halfway between Eastbourne and Brighton. Despite its
setting in the Downs, even its keenest admirers (of whom I am one)
would be hard-pressed to describe it as a place of beauty: bungalows
abound, and the prevailing impression is one of rust-streaked
concrete, peeling stucco and giant pneumatic hammers constantly
repairing the storm-lashed promenade, on which hunched, heroic
figures battle against the wind, one hand holding a hat in place while
the other fights to control an enormous dog on the end of a string. In
the early 1960s Seaford was still largely populated by cane-swishing
prep school masters in egg-stained tweeds, retired tea-planters with
a taste for golf and stern-looking elderly ladies in demob suits and
pork pie hats who moved about the town with giant strides and – or
so I liked to think – smoked huge cigars in the privacy of their heavily
hydrangaed gardens. The lower orders were represented, in part, by
a great army of retired tobacconists who, as is well known, head in
droves for the south coast from all parts of the United Kingdom
within minutes of ringing the till one final time and drawing down the
blind forever. Seafordians of all varieties tended to be hardy, ruddy-
featured folk: large-boned ladies of a pensionable age could be spotted
stumping down to the sea in blue and white striped bathrobes at all
seasons of the year, casting contemptuous glances at those unwilling
to take the plunge in late November or early March ('Do you men
ever swim to Newhaven?' a muscular septuagenarian once asked my
father and me, before setting out for a distant lighthouse at a slow but
determined breaststroke).

We had first lived in Seaford towards the end of the war, while my
father was doing his stuff as a medic with the Guards Armoured
Division on the other side of the Channel; he had, it seemed, been
sent on in advance, equipped with a spade and a large collection of
Everyman Classics, which he read in some discomfort while lying in
his slit trench. The town – like most of the south coast – was a
restricted area, sealed off from the rest of England in preparation for
D-Day; the prep schools had been evacuated, the beaches were
peppered with pill-boxes and angry black spikes pointing out to sea
like gigantic rusty nails, and the streets were full of drunken Canadian
soldiers who peered unsteadily into prams through bloodshot eyes in
the hope that an appreciative word about the monster within might

lead to further acquaintance with the lady at the helm. Even then, my sister and I seem to have spent most of our time on the beach, if the family photograph albums are to be believed: we sit or squat on the shingle, great swathes of barbed wire behind us, our skins the colour of caramel and our hair almost silver in the dazzling summer light; straight-featured and well-built, we look uncomfortably akin to Hitler's ideal Aryan family, diminutive versions of those under-dressed, bone-headed Germanic heroes who skipped about the sand dunes in the opening shots of Leni Riefenstahl's film of the 1936 Olympics, or indulged in mass eurythmics aboard a hideously regimented 'Strength through Joy' liner on some pre-war mission of badwill.

Since then I have often wondered, as most of us must, how I would have behaved had I been born in Germany twenty years earlier. Despite my liking for the music of Nazi marching songs, and a certain sympathy for those anti-urban early ecologists, descendants of the earnest, idealistic *Wandervogel*, who formed so important an ingre-dient in that unwholesome stew, I like to think – though who can tell? – that I would have taken the side of virtue. Be that as it may, I suspect my disapproval would, at best, have taken the form of disdainful grumblings from behind the scenes: my admiration for those brave enough to actively oppose Nazi bestiality is matched only by my irritation at those smug, pharasaical souls who take it for granted that they would not only have sided with the forces of light but, unlike the cowed majority, would have proved instant and active members of the opposition.

In my private version of the war – which, despite all the evidence, I continue to half-believe – we watched Spitfires and Messerschmitts dog-fighting in the cloudless sky above us and bombers droning overhead like malignant wasps en route for London and points north, and picked our way home to tea through a litter of unexploded bombs; in fact my experience of aerial combat was restricted to falling off the swings on the Salts Recreation Ground and cracking my head open on the tarmac underneath, and to gazing glumly out of the yellow perspex eye pieces of a gas mask in the attic.

To celebrate VE Day we went to eat cakes and wave miniature Union Jacks with two great-aunts who lived in Blatchington, a genteel and relatively sheltered part of Seaford with a golf course to hand and a large number of rhododendron bushes concealing spacious Edwardian houses inhabited by solicitors in lovat green tweeds and rival teams of maiden aunts. Auntie Mary, the forceful character, was a short, stout woman, with bristly grey hair and pendulous jowls of the kind unflatteringly referred to as dewlaps. She was, I suspect, a kind old thing, but her gruff voice, ferocious gaze and more than a touch of the regimental sergeant major made her a force to be reckoned with. She looked, at first sight, as though she might have been a member of the pork pie hat and demob suit sorority, but in fact she cherished a melancholy, unrequited and life-long passion for a major over the road. As a motorist she was a public menace: this was hardly surprising, since once she had lowered her massive frame into the bucket seat of her navy-blue Vauxhall, little could be seen above the windscreen but the top of her head and her hands, firmly gripping the wheel in the approved ten-to-two position. She died while I was at Trinity: on the day of her funeral, as we were walking away from the church, my Aunt Annie turned to her surviving sister, tapped her watch and said in a sepulchral tone 'Ada, I think she must be nearly there by now.' If Mary's motoring was anything to go by, she must have spent a good deal of time mounting the kerb and driving very slowly down the middle of the road and knocking down innocent pedestrians on the way to the Pearly Gates: but, like most of my family, she was a stickler for punctuality, so Annie's prognosis may not have been too far out after all.

Auntie Ada was the only remotely rich relation we had, and certainly one of the saddest. Even as a young and – judging by the photographs – very fine-looking girl in the early 1920s she had a wistful, dark-eyed, haunted look about her. She had spent a good deal of time in China, and her house was crammed with pop-eyed turquoise china pekes, lacquered gold and black wardrobes with impenetrable oriental locks, jade Buddhas on circular black stands, and glass cabinets in which tiny, scarlet-clad figures enacted forever the forgotten rituals of Imperial China; and over them all there hung a curious musty smell that remains for me – quite wrongly, no doubt – the quintessential whiff of the Orient. While out East the sad Ada met and married an elderly, well-heeled Yorkshire mill-owner; within a few months of their marriage he was dead.

Ada returned home to England, where she moved into a large, red-brick, tile-hung, white-painted Edwardian house in Blatchington with her spinster sister Mary. With its hydrangea bushes, tennis court, clipped hedges, tradesman's entrance, polished brass, vegetable gardens, crunching gravel drive and bell-push discreetly positioned under the dining-room table within reach of the proprietorial toe, it was exactly the kind of house Richmal Crompton's William Brown must have lived in; unlike William, Ginger and Henry, those great-nephews and great-nieces who occasionally paid a visit were very much on their best behaviour, speaking only when spoken to, politely picking at neatly trimmed cucumber sandwiches and sipping lemonade from a jug of frosted glass, over which was draped a muslin net held down by a ring of small glass beads, and exhaling sighs of relief as polite farewells were said, and the benign but somewhat daunting elderly aunts disappeared from view, still waving, in the back window of the car.

★   ★   ★

In the summer of 1950 I returned once more to Seaford along with sixty other boys between the ages of eight and thirteen, all of whom were fellow-pupils at one of the innumerable prep schools for which the town was celebrated on account of the health-giving properties associated with bright sun and strong south-westerly winds. From our flat in Prince of Wales Drive my parents drove me to Victoria Station in their converted Macfisheries van; no doubt they parked without any difficulty in the forecourt of the station, and no doubt it never occurred to them to lock the doors, or slot into place the removable perspex windows, before striding purposefully off in the direction of the Seaford Prep School Special. I puffed along behind, carrying a small maroon canvas bag containing a sponge bag, two wooden hairbrushes on the back of which my father, a masterly carpenter, had carefully incised my initials and filled them up with bees' wax (to my everlasting regret, I left both brushes in a seedy hotel in County Tipperary some thirteen years later), a spare pair of pants and a second set of school socks, knee-length woollen grey affairs with two maroon bands about the top, held in place by black elastic garters.

My main luggage – consisting of a large blue trunk with wooden bars, and a black tin tuck-box containing the regulation allowance of boiled sweets, a balsa wood aeroplane kit, a brand new pair of football boots and, carefully concealed at the bottom, a stuffed animal of some kind or other – had, as luggage did in those days, gone on in advance and was even now being unpacked by white-coated school matrons with thermometers in their bosom pockets and upside-down watches dangling from their lapels.

My mother had, I knew, taken a disrespectful and cavalier approach to the school's formal clothes list: she refused – quite rightly, I felt – to equip me with a pair of black elastic-sided pumps on the grounds that such shoes were ugly, common and of no possible use in civilian life, and sent me instead with some brown idlers from America, which looked oddly out of place and excited a certain envy; the stipulated quantity of vests was utterly ignored, for vests were thought to be ludicrous, undashing garments which no reasonable person would deign to wear (I hope to meet my Maker without having ever worn such a garment); when the summer term came round, I found myself the only boy in the school not to come equipped with a floppy grey hat of the kind preferred by elderly bowls-players and chinless curates in Ealing comedies, for – as a child of the 1930s – my mother had, as we have seen, a strong belief in the curative powers of the sun, and considered such headgear absurdly effete and old-mannish. To my surprise and relief, none of these minor omissions drew the fire of the head matron, a stout, heavily bewhiskered lady of alarming aspect but kindly disposition, as broad as she was high, who had rented my mother a cottage in Seaford shortly after the VE Day celebrations, and no doubt realized that any protests would be in vain.

As I boarded the Prep School Special I noticed with some surprise that many of the smaller boys appeared to be smoking heavily, despite the fierce No Smoking notices pasted to the windows of the compartments; no doubt their parents had dumped them at the station with a gasp of relief and hurried away to the station bar without a backwards glance, and from behind the glass of the carriage windows these sardonic, puffing orphans watched fur-clad, behatted mothers make fussy, tearful adjustments to their loved ones' hair and clothing, while the loved ones squirmed with shame and their fathers tapped their umbrellas and took discreet, embarrassed glances at the clock. I was greatly impressed by this display of heavy smoking, though puzzled by the absence of stubs and by the fact that a good deal of loud and heavy inhalation was unaccompanied by the customary clouds of smoke: much later I realized that these heroic eight-year-olds were in fact smoking thin sugar cigarettes, the glowing tips of which had been daubed a virulent pink. All this mercifully distracted my attention from the sudden, dreadful departure of the Prep School Special, crammed to overflowing with boys and girls from the prep schools in which Seaford abounded – including one for backward or especially wicked boys who were, to judge by the quantity of sheets hung out to dry, even more given to mass bed-wetting than the rest of us.

Twenty years ago, Seaford's prep schools began to disappear, like mighty dinosaurs creeping off to die: parents in Esher and Tunbridge Wells tended instead to send their children to local schools as weekly boarders or day boys or girls; headmasters and governing bodies were made gratifyingly aware of the property value of the many acres of land they were sitting on; blackboards and canes and rolls of honour were committed to the flames, and the games fields that had been so distinctive a feature of the town were covered with desirable residences suitable for retired tobacconists. Particularly melancholy was the disappearance of the buildings themselves: Edwardian prep schools, like golf clubs, embody English institutional architecture at its best, and Seaford in its heyday was chock-a-block with white mullioned windows, overhung balconies with curious box-like fire escapes attached, dormer windows with mattresses propped out to dry, belfries, weather-vaned clock towers and well-raked gravel drives. Our particular school was a low-slung, rambling building: like many south coast houses of the 'cocktail shaker' vintage it had a green roof, and was covered with white painted pebbledash. Like all the Seaford schools, it stood amidst cosy suburban streets; it was, however, insulated by tree-lined playing fields; and in the small garden in front stood the school flagpole and a small slatted white box on legs that housed the all-important Meteorological Instruments.

I quickly discovered that all the masters except the French master – who was a bear-like Belgian, and one of the most entirely benign men I have ever met – had a strange, missionary obsession with the English climate. The geography master in particular – a musclebound veteran of the Battle of Jutland, with tattoos on his forearms, much given to lashing out clips to left and right, and famous for his demonstration of how to climb a rope without the use of the legs, during the course of which his enormous biceps bulged and creaked as he hauled himself aloft – keenly impressed upon us the superiority of our climate to all others. At least once a week he showed us the correct method of ventilating a room by flinging open the bottom of a sash window to let in the cool, fresh air, and dragging down its upper part to let out our tepid exhalations, at which the large grey clouds that had been amassing over Seaford Head suddenly turned to rain and the Force Eight gale that howled through the bottom of the window picked up our careful tracings of the coalfields of Great Britain and sent them spinning about the room. Those unlucky enough not to share the blessings of our climate, he informed us as the rain spattered against his horn-rimmed specs, were unlikely to understand or benefit from so healthy a system of ventilation, which was why Frenchmen in particular tended to look wizened and anaemic; and since appreciation could be heightened by understanding, small teams of boys were deputed every day to read the rain gauge, measure the strength of the wind, and take accurate readings of the maximum and minimum temperatures recorded over the past twenty-four hours, taking care to reset the thermometers with a small magnet which was kept in the slatted white temple on the front lawn.

This close attention to the weather was matched by an equally ferocious interest – shared, it seems, by parents and staff alike – in sanitation, drainage and the regular movement of the bowels. 'The Water Supply is excellent and the Sanitation perfect,' the school prospectus assured anxious parents, adding that 'the latter system, of iron piping, is annually inspected by one of the leading sanitary engineers of London'. A couple of pages later, in the 'Timetable for a Full School Day in Winter', the prospectus touched lightly on a central ritual of prep school life in its fleeting reference to 'lavatory assembly' from 8.40 to 9.15 every morning. Each of the school's ten lavatories had a shiny brass number attached to its door, and the master whose turn it was to supervise 'lavatory assembly' was equipped with a scoreboard and ten well-made wooden tickets, each with a corresponding brass number carefully screwed to it. After breakfast we assembled in our classrooms for some well-ordered homework and metronomic opening of the bowels. Ten boys were issued with a ticket each, and sent off to do their best; as each returned to base – like a Battle of Britain pilot limping back to Biggin Hill after a fearful combat in the skies – he would hand his ticket in to the duty master, who ticked him off on the scoreboard before passing the ticket on to another eager lavatory-goer. Only when this essential ritual had been completed, and every boy had done his best, could the business of the day begin. Occasionally a boy would faint on the job or malinger beyond the bounds of credibility: a junior master would then be despatched to hammer on the door of his cubicle and, if need be, climb over the partition from the lavatory next door to rescue the ailing youth. On one occasion a thrill of excitement ran through the school when it was learnt that a lavatory had collapsed under the fattest boy in the school, leaving him asprawl among shards of intricate Edwardian porcelain.

Nor was the prep school master's involvement in such horrid matters merely administrative or theoretical. Helping to deal with mass bed-wetting was an occupational hazard similar to that presented to coal-miners by lethal pockets of gas or deficient pit props, since on more nights than I care to remember one of us weak-bladdered types would enjoy those delicious but deceptive prep-school dreams in which the narrator, caught short in a park or surburban garden, finds the bush or secluded tree of his dreams, and awakes to find himself almost afloat in the shallow V of his horsehair mattress. With luck such flooding took place fairly early in the night, in which case the extent of the damage could be concealed and the sheets made dry once more by rubbing them briskly together, like a washerwoman tackling a particularly stubborn stain, or simply through the warmth of one's body. Every morning we were supposed to pull back our sheets and blankets to air the bed, which was then re-made after we had washed and dressed in the approved military manner: the bed-wetter could usually be spotted by his anxious, furtive demeanour and by the unconvincingly casual way in which he left his pyjamas over the offending stain. More often than not the crime went undetected, but occasionally the master on duty would help the matron to manhandle a mattress onto the balcony beyond, where it was propped in the sun to dry.

Equally unnerving – and then I will drop such unwholesome matters, large as they loomed in our lives at the time – were the bugs that ran through prep schools, like miniature versions of the plague. They were usually announced by a hideous retching and splashing from the back of the class, interrupting a discussion of King Alfred and the Cakes or the Theory of Pythagoras, and causing all heads to swivel sharply away from the blackboard to the source of the disturbance. At times like these the prep school master displayed those nerves of steel that had, no doubt, served him so well in Bomber Command or on the Western Front, standing impassively by the blackboard, chalk in hand, and commanding our full attention once again as Matron escorted the waxen-featured sufferer to the San, the school maid wiped from the highly polished boards the sorry remains of school sausage and spotted dick, and the rest of us fought to keep nausea at bay as the horrid whiff of Jeyes Fluid drifted across the room towards us.

Bugs like these were especially prevalent in the autumn and winter terms. The sickness and diarrhoea were dreadful, but recuperation was a delightful and enviable business, and one which the wise schoolboy spun out for as long as he possibly could. Nothing could be more enjoyable than to lie in the sick room in the attic, with the rain drumming against the dormer windows, alternately dozing and reading about the Saint or Bulldog Drummond, listening to the familiar sounds of school life and knowing that one was utterly immune from them all: to bells being rung to announce the beginning or the end of a lesson, to the roar of one's fellows streaming out into the yard at break, and – best of all – to the shrill, peremptory blast of a referee's whistle, the thwack of boot against leather, the cries of the players and the dreadful baying roar of the supporters on the touchline.

At lunchtime the junior matron would suddenly appear – at the sound of her approach the wise sufferer would feign lassitude or a restless, feverish sleep – and take one's temperature, placing one cool, efficient hand on one's forehead and with the other consulting the watch that hung upside-down from the lapel of her well-ironed white housecoat; after which the school maid would appear with a tray containing a mug of Bovril and two slices of dry toast. The late afternoon was the most magical time of all, as the room and the sky outside grew ever darker in the dusk, so much so that I dreaded the moment when the curtains were drawn and the bedside light switched on. Such treats came my way less frequently than I might have wished, despite my valetudinarian tastes: I was a distressingly healthy youth, and since I was already manifesting a startling ineptitude at, and hatred for, organized games, opportunities to lie in bed listening to the referee's whistle from a safe distance did not occur very often.

More will be said later about my prowess on the games field: although I disliked both forms of football in particular, and offered up unheeded prayers for flooded pitches and immobilizing Cold Snaps, I suffered more – since my prep school was a genial, kindly place – from frozen fingers than from the opprobrium reserved for those who combine incompetence with an almost complete absence of the Team Spirit. My mother had suffered a good deal from chilblains, and often begged us to rub her throbbing, swollen toes: after a short session on the footer pitch my hands turned beetroot mauve and my fingers seemed locked in the claw-like posture favoured by werewolves or by the normally imperturbable Carl Petersen when Bulldog Drummond had pushed his luck a bit too far. Once back in the changing rooms, I found it quite impossible to undo the clinging rubber buttons on my games shirt, let alone reknot my maroon school tie or rebutton my regulation grey flannel shirt, and as my hands thawed out – unwisely hurried on their way by placing them on the hot water pipes that ran along one wall of the changing room – they were shot through with a terrible tingling ache that made me leap up and down on the spot like someone who had inadvertently plugged himself into the mains.

The two headmasters were themselves keen sportsmen, and the leaner of the two had been a cricketing blue: kindly overlooking my failures in that department, they asked me every spring to join them and the Head Boy in watching the Boat Race on their flickering black and white television set, the screen of which – encased in a vast frame of highly polished wood – must have been all of four inches across. My father had rowed for the victorious Cambridge team in 1936 and had borne off all kinds of trophies at Henley, so much so that he had been picked to row in the Berlin Olympics and, though set on a medical career, had been offered the opportunity of stardom by Columbia Pictures on the condition that he had all his teeth removed and replaced by a set of glistening, unnaturally regular gnashers: the Boat Race and those who rowed in it loomed larger even in the 1950s than they do today, and the opportunity to join the two heads in their chintz-embowered sitting-room while my fellows were lying on their beds and enjoying their compulsory after-lunch 'rest' filled me with a vicarious sense of pride. Despite John Snagge's enthusiastic commentary, it was hard to make out what was happening on the tiny, flickering screen. The two boats were almost entirely obscured by sheets of impenetrable electronic snow: every now and then one of the two headmasters would lean forward and strike the set severely on its side, and the picture would briefly right itself in time to show one of the two boats – it was always Cambridge in the lead – flashing under Hammersmith Bridge; more scientific efforts to right the picture by twiddling the large brown knobs led to a complete blackout or a sudden, disconcerting glimpse of the two crews awash in a turbulent, foam-flecked sea.

For the cricketing head in particular, the high point of the school year was the annual match between the Old Boys on one side, and a mixed bag of masters and boys on the other. Obsessive Old Boys were an important ingredient in the life of the school, donating money, providing tiny, timid-seeming sons to carry on the grand tradition, making long-winded speeches on Prize Days (their jokes exciting convulsions of merriment and much slapping of the thighs from the assembled staff, and looks of bafflement from the boys), and donating cups and shields for important sporting occasions. The annual cricket match was a red letter day in the Old Boys' calendar, and from early in the morning the school was suddenly aswarm with elderly men in white flannels and blazers of virulent hue, lugging outsize cricket bags about the changing rooms, eagerly bowling to one another in the nets, and addressing one another by their surnames in the school slang of thirty years before. Many wore a motheaten First XI cap from before the First World War, perched on a bald or grizzled head like a tiny bird balanced on the back of an elephant; others tottered onto the field in the colours of I Zingari or the MCC.

After a suitable salad lunch in the dining-room – the Old Boys joining the heads on the top table, while the junior masters were banished to sit with the boys – the entire school gathered about the cricket pitch to pay homage to their seniors, many of whom had drunk deep from the contents of the headmaster's cellar. For some reason the Old Boys usually opened the batting: the younger masters stalked importantly onto the field, a select handful of senior boys trailing in their wake, like gulls behind a tractor, while the lean headmaster, wearing his Oxford cap and now entirely in his element, arranged the fielders as the Old Boys' opening pair – a retired colonel and a senior partner in a distinguished firm of stockbrokers – took up their positions at the crease.

It was thought good form for one of the boys to open the bowling, and it was tacitly understood that the Old Boys would make suitable allowances for the youth of some of their opponents: after a good deal of ferocious banging of the crease and consultation with the umpire and gazing sternly about the field, the retired colonel was bowled out first ball by a tactless thirteen-year-old and stumped back to the pavilion looking vexed and out-of-sorts; and the match was under way. The headmaster – allowing valour the better part of discretion – ensured that the public humiliation of the Old Boys continued in a similar vein, and worse was to follow when the junior masters came into bat. Ignoring signals from the more diplomatic members of staff – including the Bursar, who saw his funds disappearing by the minute – they treated the Old Boys' bowling with scant respect, lashing the ball for sixes about the ground, smashing the glass in the school greenhouse and more than once disturbing Matron as she snoozed in a deck chair behind the fives courts before distributing orangeade and meat paste sandwiches to the whole school during the tea break.

The heartier masters – including the muscle-bound veteran of the Battle of Jutland who, apart from climbing ropes without the use of his legs was a nimble performer on the horse, reserving an especial scorn for those of us who failed to clear it in a single spring, bruising our tenderest parts on its further edge in our downwards flight – liked nothing better than to appear after 'rest' in a pair of knee-length shorts and a blazer with a whistle in one pocket, and to hurry us on to the games field with much eager rubbing of the hands and bending of the knees and jumping up and down on the spot. This same boisterous spirit was much in evidence on Guy Fawkes Night: the boys were assembled in dutiful lines around the edge of the school yard, while the masters – clad in duffel coats and fiery tweeds – rushed excitedly about letting off rockets and putting matches to catherine wheels, and laughing merrily as some giant firework, belching flames and emitting the most horrific explosions, shot off at a tangent, ploughing through the assembled boys or zigzagging wildly among their legs like a ferret struggling to escape from a sack. Much as I liked the great sprays and jets of colour, I dreaded the bangs, surreptitiously holding my hands over my ears whenever I saw one of the more jocular masters preparing to apply his cigarette lighter to a particularly bad-tempered variety of squib.

Much milder entertainment was provided by various peripatetic lecturers who addressed the school in the gym on Saturday evenings in winter, alternating with showings on the ancient school projector of *The Ghost Train* and English comedies featuring Will Hay, George Formby and Sidney Howard. Such lecturers tended to be retired colonial officers or elderly clergymen, much given to describing the wildlife of the Downs and to imitating the cries of various wild animals with curious sucking and squeaking motions of the hands and lips. Such talks were helped on their way with slides; a reliable senior boy was deputed to change the slide upon the banging of the lecturer's staff, and a good deal of mirth was occasioned when the slide came on upside-down or inside-out, or the projector caught fire and had to be hurriedly unplugged and taken outside to cool down. A particular favourite among those lecturers was – or claimed to be – a retired deep sea diver, who appeared at least once a year, clanking dramatically on to the stage in a diver's helmet and mud-coloured uniform and lead-lined boots and carrying with him various barnacle-encrusted items of equipment and mementoes of the long hours he had spent moving sluggishly about the sea bed. He told us of encounters with sharks and giant man-eating squids, many of which he had despatched with the rusty-looking dagger he wore about his waist, and he illustrated his talk with slides of weed-encrusted wrecks and bad-tempered electric eels. His lectures were altogether more successful than those of the vole-loving clergyman or the unexciting colonial officer, and when, at the end, the stouter of the two headmasters rose to thank him for coming so far to address us on a wild November evening, and the head boy called for three cheers, we joined in with a wild abandon. Years later, at Trinity, I learned from Ian Whitcomb – whose own prep school was a couple of hundred yards up the road – that our heroic diver was a fraud, a retired clerk from Three Bridges whose knowledge of the deep had been gleaned from *The Wonder Book of the Sea* and boys' magazines, and who made a modest living travelling round the prep schools of the south coast in a diving uniform hired from a theatrical costumier.

Every Sunday we exchanged our grey v-necked jerseys and corduroy shorts for smarter grey flannel suits, and walked a couple of miles into the middle of Seaford for the weekly schools' service. We travelled in crocodile, with a couple of masters bringing up the rear; similar crocodiles of boys and girls converged on the parish church from every direction, each instantly recognizable by the colour of the cap – ours were maroon – the stripe of the tie and the crest on the pocket of the grey flannel jacket. The service itself seemed a long and tedious business, in the course of which the Vicar of Seaford would from time to time interrupt his sermon to transfix an inattentive nose-picker with a beetle-browed stare, or call for silence in a voice of thunder. As we plodded wearily back to school one Sunday early in 1952, kept going only by the prospect of Yorkshire pudding and fluorescent jelly, we spotted the bulky figure of Matron pedalling unsteadily towards us: she informed us in sepulchral tones that the King was dead, before wobbling slowly down the road to spread these unhappy tidings to the crocodile of more senior boys that was bringing up the rear. Over lunch that day the masters looked grave and responsible, and the school flag was hung at half-mast; the year before, when Mr Attlee's Labour Government finally fell, they had seemed suddenly purposeful and jocular, as though the Anti-Christ had suffered a well-deserved rebuff, and now public events were intruding once again on our pleasantly well-ordered lives.

A year or so after Matron had broken to us the grave news about the death of King George VI, we were given the day off to celebrate the Coronation. We watched the proceedings on another flickering postcard-sized television set of the kind associated with the Boat Race, only this time belonging to a jovial and excitable Irish family whom we had lived next to during the war. In the afternoon my parents took me into Brighton and went on board HMS *Eagle*, the famous aircraft carrier, which was conveniently anchored off the pier and was, we had learned, open for the day to prep school boys and members of the general public. Once on board, my mother swiftly broke away from the official tour, and instead of inspecting flight decks and rows of stacked-up aeroplanes we found ourselves in a mess room eating thick slices of bread and margarine and drinking teak-coloured tea which the sea dogs poured for us from gigantic aluminium pots.

We rejoined the official party in time to climb on the bridge where, like the other prep school boys present, I was allowed to take the wheel and consult various knobs and dials. Although I had never shown the remotest interest in boats or in the minutiae of mizzen masts or starboard watches I had, as a very small boy, set my heart on joining the Navy, and the subsequent discovery that I was as blind as a bat and that bespectacled boys were ineligible for the Services had thrown me into a quandary about careers from which I have yet to recover; visiting the *Eagle* rekindled for a short time these vain aspirations, which were further inflamed by reading C. S. Forester's Hornblower novels and the works of Captain Marryat. Not surprisingly, as a virile symbol of Britain in the 1950s, HMS *Eagle* tended to feature a good deal, usually in detailed cross-section for mechanically-minded boys and Meccano buffs, in Marcus Morris's eponymous comic, along with Tommy Walls, PC 49 – the artist of which, we were proud to note, was an Old Boy of the school – Harris Tweed, Jeff Arnold, Luke, a blue-eyed and flaxen haired St Paul looking surprisingly similar to the head boy, and Sir Wilfred Grenfell, a kindly soul who seemed to have spent a good deal of time driving teams of huskies across the wastes of Labrador and setting an example to us all. Although we were forbidden to read *Dandy* and *Beano* at school – let alone *Hotspur* or *Radio Fun,* which were strictly for the lower orders and featured common-looking boys with unbrushed hair and diamond-patterned socks which, like William's, fell down about their shoes – *Eagle* was thought to be informative and salutory reading, and still more so when fears about imported American Horror Comics rose to fever pitch.

Once or twice a term bevies of parents descended on the school, and mothers would be spotted peering into inky desks with a fixed smile on their faces, while pin-striped fathers gazed moodily about them, their hands clasped behind their backs in the manner perfected by the Duke of Edinburgh. The hotels and boarding houses of Seaford did brisk business at times like these: gongs were polished, cruets laid out, antimacassars straightened and collecting boxes set

out in the hall. My parents occasionally stayed in a wind-swept and
rust-encrusted family hotel on the front; the landlady's husband – or
so we were told – had a drink problem and was given to epileptic fits,
and I lived in dread of finding him foaming noisily and crashing into
the furniture when I went downstairs to play ping-pong in the
basement.

Walking about the town on weekends such as these, one came all
too often across parents and fellow-pupils eating silent, uncommunic-
ative meals in tea-shops – the mother gazing anxiously about, the
father stealing a glance at *The Times* and wishing he could have a drink,
the son living in dread of being spotted, as he always was, by an
unkind fellow-pupil – or inspecting the animals in Drusilla's near
Alfriston, or fighting their way to the end of the pier in Brighton in
the face of a stiff southwesterly gale, or queuing to see *The Dam Busters*
or *The Wooden Horse* at the cinema in Eastbourne. Spotting a friend in
such places was a strained, uneasy affair, with both parties pretending
not to notice that the other was there, and keenly avoiding one
another's gaze. I dreaded my friends' parents, let alone the friends
themselves, being dismissed as 'common' or 'suburban' or 'ordinary-
looking', and no doubt they, as well-brought-up members of the
middle classes, were going through similar convulsions themselves –
improbable as that seemed to me, since both my parents were large,
handsome and extremely youthful looking, and far from conventional
in appearance or demeanour. A rather tiresome friend of mine – a very
good-looking boy who announced at the age of eight that he wanted
to be an eye surgeon, and never veered from his chosen path – had
a dashing, widowed mother from St John's Wood who caused a
certain scandalous excitement by regularly booking into a raffish-
looking pub in the middle of the town rather than one of the 'family'
hotels: she, I knew, would never be labelled 'common' or 'ordinary',
but others were more of a liability.

Such weekends were rendered hideous for both parties by
convulsions of sobbing on my part so cataclysmic that my parents
very sensibly cut their trips to the minimum and stayed put in
London instead. Saturday morning would find me in a boisterous,
cheerful mood, for I knew that all that afternoon and the whole of
Sunday still lay ahead; the afternoon was clouded by the knowledge
that Sunday was hurrying ever closer, and I would return to school

that evening in a gloomy, apprehensive vein; Sunday was a complete washout, in which I fought in vain to stem a tidal wave of tears and racking convulsive sobs so dire that by the time I was dropped back that evening I looked more like a sodden pile of rags than a robust, healthy-looking boy of between eight and twelve – for the passing of the years brought no improvement in my conduct. Since I enjoyed my prep school a great deal, such lachrymose behaviour was hard to explain or forgive; by Monday morning, however, I was trundling happily forward once again, making feeble jokes for the entertainment of my friends and failing to distinguish myself in any way whatsoever.

When I was about eleven my parents decided it would be a good idea to emigrate to Canada, and it was agreed that I should, as a precaution, take my Common Entrance early in case we came back and I wanted to go on to a public school. I was to take the exam privately in one of the master's houses – a cosy 1920s building with a thatched roof, bogus beams, diamond-pane windows, dark stained doors and Welsh tiles on the floor. The exam was to be invigilated by the master's wife, and while we were waiting for the clock to strike nine she asked me in a casual way whether I had been following the Queen's tour of the world aboard HMS *Britannia*. I had no particular interest in the Queen or her doings beyond thinking that she looked engagingly like Minnie Mouse and would look very much at home in a small house on the Kingston Bypass, bustling about the kitchen in a flowered apron with a whisk in one hand; I told her that I hadn't paid that much attention to the tour, at which she became very agitated, told me how fascinating it all was, and, unfolding a copy of the *Daily Telegraph*, proceeded to point out in great detail on a map of the world all the places the Queen planned to visit and the islands on which she would be confronted by row upon row of naked tribal dancers and frenzied drummers, while all about her stood stiff-looking naval officers in white uniforms and cocked hats, bejewelled swords by their sides.

I was grateful to the master's wife for her kindly if misguided belief that I was interested in such things, and dutifully studied the map as she bustled to and fro clearing her dining-room table and setting out pencils and paper. A couple of minutes later she told me to put the *Telegraph* aside, counted off the seconds like a linesman starting a race, handed me the geography paper and told me to fire away. As my eye shot down the list of questions I noticed a blank map of the world on which we were to mark the route to be taken by the Queen, and the principal ports of call; when I looked up, not quite sure whether to register gratitude or bewilderment or both, the master's wife carefully averted her eyes and kept them firmly on her knitting.

Later that term the head boy - a handsome, clean-cut boy, a wizard at games and no slouch as far as the grey matter was concerned - was gazing out of his form window in an abstracted way, over the laurel hedge and the crunching gravel drive and the miniature meteorological station, to where the clouds were scudding angrily over Seaford Head. At that moment two 'oiks' from the town came by carrying an air gun. With his scrubbed pink-and-white features and neatly combed hair and rosebud lips, the head boy must have presented an irresistible target, and they shot him in the eye. Revolution, it seemed, was in the air; it was time to be moving on.

CHAPTER THREE

Spade Beards and Boiler Suits

Long-suffering readers may remember how, some pages back, I described my first term at Trinity College, Dublin, in the autumn of 1961. I'd like now to take matters a stage or two further, with special emphasis on the auburn-haired girl with the exciting-looking bosom with whom I had fallen irrevocably in love after spotting her striding about the deck of the Holyhead–Dun Laoghaire steamer with a copy of *The Tin Drum* clutched firmly in one hand, and who was – to my extreme irritation – being keenly pursued within minutes of her arrival by a middle-aged Copt in his ninth year studying agriculture. As it turned out, the discriminating Copt was soon joined by a rabble of ex-National Servicemen with 'O' levels in Geography and Fretwork, Old Salopians, French barons in unusual-looking cars and well-appointed youths in hacking jackets and corduroy trousers, all of whom were fellow-students of mine in this ancient and undemanding university, and rivals for her hand.

Anxious – I knew not how – to compete with this overpowering opposition, I called in at Harrods before sauntering down to the Aer Lingus terminal opposite the Brompton Oratory to start my journey back to Dublin. I had my hair cut, and then went on to spend a sizeable chunk of my East Sussex County Council grant on what seemed to me to be the ultimate in sophistication, and exactly the kind of garment that was favoured by the smooth-looking under-graduates who edited the college magazines or bustled importantly about the tiny stage of Players, the university theatre, waving their arms in the air and calling one another 'darling': a nut-brown suede jacket with a long row of bone buttons down the front – each of which had, for some unexplained reason, a sheep's skull engraved upon it – a natty collar which could be worn turned up in a Continental mood, and slanting, low-slung pockets into which I could thrust my hands like a French *ouvrier* or an undercover policeman.

It was, I suspect, a rather hideous garment, in that it had no waist and was of the then-fashionable bum-freezer variety; but I loved it as I had loved no garment before, and all that night – to Holmes's irritation – I kept switching on the light to make sure that my new acquisition was still safely suspended on its hanger behind the bedroom door, and to marvel at the smoothness and the fuzzy, bruised-looking shimmer of the suede. It also enabled me to discard, with a terrible ruthlessness, a moss-coloured bogus suede jacket I had bought in Brighton a couple of years earlier, which bore an unmentionable resemblance to the dog's-mess-tinted jacket into which Holmes had, only the term before, so unwisely thrust his smouldering cigarette ends. Its stunning replacement would surely, I felt, prove an invaluable item in my armoury, and could hardly fail to impress the girl with the exciting-looking bosom, if only at a distance; I planned, however, to keep it in reserve for the really big occasion, and for everyday use I sported a checked tweed jacket – of which, twenty-five years later, I remain as fond as ever – a dark blue high-necked jersey, green corduroy trousers and fawn-coloured desert boots. So equipped, I set out once more to pursue a life of quiet study and seclusion.

By the end of our second term, Shore and I had abandoned all pretence to scholarship and devoted ourselves instead to a routine of agreeable indolence punctuated by bursts of rather bovine drunkenness, often lasting from the opening of the pubs at eleven in the morning until they closed again twelve and a half hours later. Although Dublin pubs were swiftly succumbing to the blandishments of piped music, Spanish wrought iron, mauve wall-to-wall carpeting, plastic tulips and uneasy, carbuncular barmen togged out in scarlet bum-freezer jackets and clip-on bow ties, it was still possible to track down pubs of the kind we felt we were entitled to. The best of these tended to be empty, cavernous halls, with marble black-and-white floors, decrepit red leather benches, nicotine-stained walls, a resident cat and elaborate, stained wood dressers behind the bar with a wealth of mirrors and tiny shelves and bevelled glass cunningly inlaid.

Many of these fine establishments were lit from above by way of a grimy, yellowing skylight; the light filtered down at an angle, as if from a transept window, losing what little brightness it had as it fought its way through a cloud of motes and dancing dust before settling on a solemn, pallid 'curate' in a long, white apron engaged in the slow, hypnotic ritual of pouring a pint of stout – knocking off the 'collar' of foam with an ivory palette knife, adding some more stout, knocking once again, adding some more, until the elaborate rites had been completed and a satisfactory pint prepared.

Such pubs tended to be frequented by elderly, bony-featured men in caps, who combined the singing of fiercely Republican songs with affectionate memories of life in the Royal Navy or in Camden Town, and long lists of relations dotted all over England; some years later, on the day that Churchill died, I found myself sitting in just such a pub within viewing distance of the Front Gate of Trinity, and was pleased to note the locals' indignation when, after a good deal of symptomatic dithering and uneasiness, flying the flag at half mast one minute, then hauling it down, then running it up again, the university authorities finally decided to call it a day and fly no flag at all.

During the 'holy hour' – from half-past two to half-past three – we would emerge blinking into the daylight before plunging into a cartoon cinema in Grafton Street, where Donald Duck and an aggressively unamusing American comedy team called The Three Stooges alternated with long and entertaining stretches of the news in Gaelic. These invariably featured President de Valera – looking like a bad-tempered Muscovy duck that had somehow been fitted out with a pair of gold-rimmed spectacles and a stiff collar with rounded ends – watching a display of Irish dancing in County Limerick, or greeting a group of glum-looking seminarians of the kind one frequently encountered bicycling round Dublin, like flocks of disapproving crows. Other favourites were the Archbishop of Dublin sprinkling holy water over the assembled Aer Lingus fleet – the aeroplanes gathering round him like enormous, eager dogs, their noses pointing appreciatively in his direction – and the jovial-looking Prime Minister, Sean Lemass, a toothy, Brylcreemed individual not unlike Stanley Matthews, who seemed to spend a lot of time, trowel in hand, laying the foundation stones for the diminutive skyscrapers that were already beginning to ruin the looks of this graceful, if tumbledown, city.

Going to the cinema in Dublin was an altogether more exciting business than it was in London or on the south coast. To begin with, Dublin neon lights tended to be more inventive than their English counterparts, with a particular favourite at the end of Westmoreland Street making great play with a frying pan and a flying sausage; inspired by the elegance of French neon and the comicality of the Irish, Shore and I hastily founded the Neon Lights Appreciation Society in a bid for popularity, but the membership never exceeded two, and the society was disbanded a year later after an outing to Times Square, which was deemed a grave disappointment. The cinemas of Dublin, like the fish and chip shops, throbbed and glowed with puce and marzipan illuminations. They were guarded by giant commissionaires decked out like Panamanian admirals, with cauliflower-sized epaulettes, great scrolls of gold braid at the end of each sleeve, still more up the outside leg, a twist or two on an outsize sergeant major's peaked cap, and medals of various kinds hanging from a chest that looked as though it had been pumped up in emulation of the Michelin Man or my old hero, Desperate Dan.

Life became still more exciting once one had taken one's seat inside. Unlike their passive English counterparts, Dublin cinema-goers reacted keenly to the goings-on on the screen, shouting advice and encouragement to the actors, helpfully answering the unobservant hero's questions ('Where are you, darling?' 'She's over there, you chump!'), and displaying understandable signs of vexation when the heroine – about to be savaged by a wart-encrusted monster from the deep or propositioned by an unwholesome-looking man in a mackintosh – appeared oblivious to their warning cries.

Although the shouts of the cinema-goers could be irritating at times, I was grateful to the Dublin habit of providing a free running commentary when I went to see an alarming film in which a girl in a wheelchair, left alone in a sinister country house, unwisely and infuriatingly insisted on wheeling herself out in the middle of the night to investigate mysterious lights and hollow tapping sounds – why she couldn't have left well alone, or gone to sleep wearing a pair of ear-plugs, was quite beyond me – only to light upon unhappy corpses in dinner jackets standing rigidly to attention in the deep freeze, or floating about the swimming pool. At several stages in the proceedings both Shore and I were reduced to removing our specs and cowering down behind the seats in front of us, in much the same way as Dublin cinema-goers took cover from a storm of cinematic assegais or when caught in the crossfire between James Stewart or Henry Fonda and assorted varmints in stovepipe hats and over-extended sideburns; luckily the locals, for whom such horrors were an everyday event, continued to provide the full service of advice and exhortation, so enabling us to pick up the threads as soon as the girl in the wheelchair had closed the door of the deep freeze and wheeled herself back to bed, and merciful daylight had flooded the screen once more.

Every now and then the film of the day would jerk violently and inexplicably forward – invariably in mid-scene, and more often than not in mid-sentence. This was a sure sign that the censor had been about his business with a pair of pinking shears. Needless to say, the shears were most busily employed when it looked as though a peck on the cheek might lead on to unmentionable sins. Violence was a different matter, and horrid scenes of torture and mutilation, involving bottle after bottle of tomato sauce, went by without a tremor of the official's hand. Additional excitement was caused by the Dublin habit of getting up and leaving three-quarters of the way through the main film. This proved particularly frustrating when watching the kind of thriller in which the mystery appeared to have been cleared up, and the villain named, whereas in fact another half-an-hour at least would have to pass before matters were finally resolved by the maverick man from the Yard with a hunch that things weren't *quite* as simple as they seemed. The bogus ending inevitably provoked a mass exodus, made all the worse for those of us who were still trying to keep our eyes on the screen by the local habit of bringing with them ankle-length overcoats and the most gigantic items of luggage, some of which had to be manhandled out of the cinema by two or more members of the audience. All this meant that the screen was entirely obliterated for at least five minutes, by which time the vital clue had been lost forever. One afternoon Ian remonstrated with a party of premature leavers, employing an unflattering epithet in the process; at this a particularly ferocious-looking Dubliner, with bloodshot eyes and unsteady gait, rounded on the unhappy Shore, assuming him to be the guilty man, and sent him spinning back in his seat with a mighty crack to the jaw.

Much as I enjoyed laughing at the Irish news and the doings of An Taoiseach, I was moved almost to tears by *Misé Eire* and *Saoirse*, two documentary films that described the events of 1916 and the subsequent civil war. The combination of the ancient, sputtering film of O'Connell Street in ruins, of the dashing, lethal figure of Michael Collins, of self-evidently brutish Black and Tans, of ancient crones clutching shawls about their faces and keening into the camera, with peat-stacks and donkeys and mist-enshrouded mountains in the background and Séan Ó'Riada's plangent, heart-rending music not only made me feel, as an Englishman, an insensitive, wooden-pated brute but heightened the notion – now, I feel, a mistaken and misleading one – of Ireland as a fundamentally foreign country.

Taken in conjunction with the songs we heard in the pubs (melancholy or boisterous, and made more so by an accompanying fiddle or penny whistle), a visit to Parnell's cell in Kilmainham Jail, intoxicating doses of Yeats, Synge and Joyce and rather more reluctant reading of nationalist historians like Eoin MacNeill, they had the schizophrenic effect of giving me a strong if vicarious – and agreeably second-hand – sympathy for Irish Republicanism, while at the same time regretting that so congenial and so familiar a country – which seemed, in some ways, less strange and less alien than Scotland or even the North of England – was no longer 'one of us', at least as far as formal politics were concerned.

Already ensnared by, and temperamentally suited to, the ambivalence of Ireland by its nimble ability to reconcile apparent contradictions and a weakness for pointing in two opposite directions at the same time, I became gripped by the national obsession with race and genealogy, which seemed quite as intense and as pervasive as the more familiar English interest in class, and with the ways in which the definition of 'real' Irishness would be shifted and shifted yet again to suit the whim or the convenience of the speaker. Men whose families had been in Ireland since the Norman invasion or the sixteenth century might find themselves repudiated as alien stock, as being not 'true' Irishmen; property developers anxious to demolish Georgian terraces were helped on their way by round-tower loving nationalists ranting about 'oppressors' architecture', yet those very same nationalists would, in expansive or proprietorial mood, claim for their own not only Jonathan Swift or Bishop Berkeley – who came from the same Protestant Ascendancy that had built the allegedly 'English' terraces – but the entire Brontë family (on the grounds that Patrick Brontë had been born in County Down) or Robert Graves (who grew up in Wimbledon, but whose father had written 'Father Flynn').

Like many before me, I noted that many of the great Irish patriots from Wolfe Tone to Roger Casement came, inconveniently, from the Protestant Ascendancy, while two of the heroes of 1916 – Cathal Brugha (*né* Charles Burgess) and the sinister scoutmaster Patrick Pearse – appeared to have English fathers. I found the ambiguity and the complexity of Irish attitudes to England endlessly fascinating and utterly maddening; and although I remained as fond as ever of England, my sudden immersion in this hitherto unknown and sadly seductive world had the cumulative effect of setting me at a slight tangent to England and English goings-on that was to remain with me for a good many years to come.

Equally ambivalent, though in very different ways, was Ian Whitcomb, my friend with the prehensile fingers and the rolling nautical gait, who found himself wrenched between two apparently incompatible ways of life. A fellow-observer of the clerk in the diving-suit, Ian had also been to prep school in Seaford – to a red tile-hung establishment of a similar vintage to my own which he referred to, like a house from the pages of Rupert Bear, as 'Nutlands'. Nutlands life had left him agreeably obsessed with a cosy, bachelor world of tweed jackets with leather patches on the elbow and carpet slippers and baccy pouches and sherry-drinking, in which half-mad masters strode angrily about swishing their canes and hurling pieces of chalk with terrible accuracy at lazy boys at the back of the class, and the head – a titanic figure in a gown and mortar-board – worked himself into a frenzy of rage and righteous indignation at schoolboy crimes. So vividly did he evoke this lurid world, and so bitterly did he recall ancient slights and feuds with, in particular, a boy with hair that rose to a point like a lavatory brush or a giant Brillo pad, that every now and then he would appear in Seaford – once at least on a bicycle, wearing an orange and black striped blazer – and insist that I accompany him on an expedition to the half-magical, half-dreaded world of Nutlands.

Instead of walking boldly up the drive and asking to be admitted, he preferred instead to creep up on it through the surrounding undergrowth, darting from one rhododendron bush to another when the coast seemed clear, and freezing like a statue when the headmaster suddenly appeared on the terrace or flung open the window of his study. Our activities invariably attracted the attention of the head – a mild-looking man in a cardigan, with neither cane nor mortar-board to hand – who, fearing that a child-molester or a flasher with trouser bottoms cunningly attached to the hem of his ancient mackintosh was at large in the school grounds, came hurrying to the scene only to find one of his more popular Old Boys, accompanied by a complete stranger, standing rigidly to attention, one finger to his lips, behind a rhododendron bush.

It was this side of Ian that delighted, for a few weeks at least, in ruminative, geriatric evenings with the bank manager and his fellow-golfers, and found endless comedy in club bores and half-witted majors and chinless vicars of the Miles Malleson variety, all of whom were far funnier and more vivid in his account of them than they ever turned out to be in the flesh. He saw the world, not as it was, but through a filter of films that featured Will Hay and Frank Randle and the down-trodden clerk of *Darts are Trumps*, of *Film Fun* and *Radio Fun* and *Dandy* and *Beano*, of Jack Buchanan and George Formby and Ealing comedies; like a kindly alchemist, he made magical the mundane and everyday, and it was as an entertainer that he was rapidly, and quite rightly, making his mark at Trinity. He was, and is, prodigiously talented: within weeks of his arrival he was designing posters for the Players Theatre, writing and performing songs, playing in various groups and in the jazz club, inhabiting worlds very different from Shore's and my clerk-like routine, let alone that of the bank manager and his cronies on the links.

One evening he invited back to his digs one of the Nigerians from our history set – a shy, formal figure, looking ill-at-ease in his brand-new cavalry twills, dark blue blazer and flawless silk cravat. It was generally believed that jazz and the blues owed far more to the African than to the European musical tradition and that Negroes were, by definition, superior practitioners since the beat was in their blood: Ian hoped that an evening spent listening to jazz and ragtime records would not only help our timid colleague to relax and feel at home, but provide useful evidence for the direct links between straw-skirted tribal dancers and Little Richard or Fats Domino.

He had bought for the occasion a Fuller's walnut cake which, in time-honoured schoolboy fashion, he cut into segments with a ruler; and after handing his puzzled-looking visitor a slice of cake and a cup of tea, he set to work with the gramophone records. To his dismay, his visitor seemed utterly unmoved by the sudden blast of rhythm and blues: far from flinging off his blazer and hurling himself into some kind of uncontrollable rhythmic frenzy – fingers flicking, eyeballs rolling, knees atremble and pelvis pumping rudely in and out – he looked stiffer and more baffled than ever, politely picking at his slice of cake and discussing Gilbert and Sullivan or the Leges Henrici Primi – a subject dear to the heart of a sardonic, lady chain-smoking professor of whom we stood in awe – while the music pulsed and thundered all about. After this disappointing experience Ian became firmly convinced – rather unreasonably, I suspect – that the African contribution to popular music had been greatly exaggerated.

In the meantime I too was anxious to make an impression on my fellow-undergraduates, and the auburn-haired girl in particular: to this end I supplemented my new suede jacket with a boiler suit and an enormous carrot-coloured beard of the spade shape favoured by Karl Marx, which clipped on over the ears, reached down to the middle of my chest, and had a slot conveniently placed to allow food and drink in, and air and verbiage out. Michael Shore proved a willing accomplice (too willing for Ian, who saw him as little more than a stooge): I had already persuaded him that *Mr Sponge's Sporting Tour* was the finest novel ever written, and now he readily joined me in buying a matching boiler suit and beard, except that his beard was black to match the colour of his hair. For three weeks or so neither of us removed our beards and boiler suits, wearing them during meals, lectures, while cashing cheques in the Bank of Ireland, in pubs and the tea-rooms of Brown Thomas, Dublin's answer to Fortnum & Mason – where all about us genteel Dublin matrons in hats daintily picked at cream-laden pastries – and while drinking warm stout in a tent at Leopardstown race course during those tedious intervals between the races, eyeing from behind my whiskers the oblivious object of my desire who stood hemmed in by a circle of admirers in hacking jackets and brown felt hats.

Sad to say, the beards and the boiler suits amused and impressed us a good deal more than our fellow-undergraduates or the population of Dublin as a whole: I was pleased to note a sudden glint of irritation in the eyes of the Professor of Irish – who sported a very similar beard to my own, albeit a genuine growth rather than the product of a theatrical costumier's at the far end of Dame Street – but the girl with the exciting-looking bosom seemed oddly unimpressed by our exploits. Nor was she moved when – in a desperate bid for sympathy – I affected a wooden leg as well and stumped across Front Square in an ostentatious, piratical manner, my right leg executing a sweeping semi-circle with every step I took. In disgust, I decided to call a halt to the whole abortive business: the beards – which were becoming increasingly itchy and hot and encrusted with the remains of stale stout, fried eggs and potato bread – were abandoned for ever, though I continued to wear my boiler suit when, for a short time, we took up beagling in the Wicklow Mountains. I was glad to note that not a single hare was caught during the course of these proceedings, and since they involved a good deal of falling into ditches and wading through sulphurous bogs, our suits excited a certain envy among our more conventionally clad fellow-sportsmen.

When it came to matters of sex we were absurdly innocent and shy, while suspecting (wrongly, more often than not) that those about us were leading lives of unbridled lust. When I read in novels or autobiographies – written, like this, in middle age – of precocious puffings and fumblings and youthful initiations in bushes by smiling, buxom girls or experienced Older Women, of a world in which pimply youths with barely broken voices unhooked brassières with the insouciance of old-fashioned bedroom bandits and tore open packets of contraceptives with a steely self-assurance while all about them the night air was rendered dreadful with the grunts emanating from purloined parental Morris Minors, I felt that my life had, indeed, been a tepid and unadventurous affair; nor could I understand how such things could be done in the back of the family saloon, since by the time I was fifteen I was far too tall to have fitted sideways into a Morris Minor, let alone the Ford Anglia we drove at home. Nor had I in any way matched practice to theory since those distant days in Battersea when I had dreamt, while still in knee-length shorts, of soaping the Austrian au pair girl's back at her express invitation.

Being large, bespectacled and plain, I was not an object of desire in my first terms at public school, and so missed out – mercifully – on the mass ravishings and sweaty midnight raids to which long-lashed small boys were subjected by muscular brutes of eighteen with 'groized' locks and Windsor knots in their ties; nor, when my turn came round and I became a muscular brute myself, did my contemporaries seem to indulge to quite the same extent in those scuffling forays on the changing-room floor – accompanied by dreadful yelps and the unwholesome elastic snap of underpants being forcibly removed – that had seemed so common a hazard of life in those Stygian, steam-clouded regions some four or five years earlier. Even so, as we sat in well-ordered rows on brown metal and canvas chairs in the Great Hall watching *The Lavender Hill Mob* or listening to a talk – illustrated with the speaker's own slides – on the geology of Antarctica, I knew that all about me over-heated boys were plunging their hands into one another's pockets, the bottoms of which had been cunningly unstitched.

My most important contribution to the sex life of the school – made in conjunction with an indolent, willowy Parsee who disgraced himself by peroxiding his hair and wore, for religious reasons we were told, unusual undergarments made of yard upon yard of muslin, like the wrappings of a mummy – was to buy a bottle of hair-restorer, which we rubbed into our denuded groins in the hope that a great forest of hairs would suddenly sprout between our legs, so enabling us to stride into the shower-room with the same aggressive swagger as the self-confident, booming sportsmen of whom we stood in such resentful awe. To our dismay the restorer – a glutinous amber liquid, the label of which showed a bald and smiling man with sparks leaping from the top of his head – failed to do its stuff. This was disappointing news – almost as disappointing as the failure of All Bran to print a testimonial my sister and I had addressed to them a year or two earlier describing its regularizing powers and enclosing 'before and after' photographs of the kind employed in their advertisements, in which grey and sluggish-looking pensioners from Southend or Clacton-on-Sea were transformed into brisk and smiling senior citizens after a bowl or two of the restoring bran.

Nor was my experience of such matters any more advanced now that I was an undergraduate at the same university as the fabulous Ginger Man, whose adventures were so torrid as to be available only in an edition published in the elegant dark green covers of the

Olympia Press in Paris. Although one of my more depraved and dissolute friends reported an encounter with a 'scrubber' in a Dublin hotel, in the course of which he seemed to have lost heart when confronted by layer upon layer of corsetry and old-fashioned undergarments, like a man with a tin-opener struggling to fight his way into a suit of armour, I felt myself to be the Lothario of my generation when – my heart thumping like a sledge-hammer – I asked an apple-cheeked girl in my history set to join me for a restorative cup of coffee after an especially enervating lecture on the Battle of Clontarf.

As for the girl with the auburn hair and exciting-looking bosom – whose name, I had now learned, was Fenella, only spelt, by her own dispensation, ffenella – I cast calf-like glances of admiration in her direction as we gathered in our gowns for the occasional snooze-inducing address on the Workings of the King's Seal or the Pelagian Heresy, grinning in a complicit manner when one of the dons, despairing of his ability to bring the Middle Ages vividly to life, urged us to go and see Charlton Heston in *El Cid*, then showing at one of the gigantic neon-lit emporia in O'Connell Street, in the hope that this, if nothing else, would lodge something of mediaeval Europe in our obstinate, unreceptive brains.

My cause, such as it was, took a giant step forward in the spring of 1962, when a French Week was held in Dublin. Despite the pleasing parochialism of their newspapers ('NUNS STUCK IN LIFT' was a particular favourite), the Irish were, I soon discovered, very anxious to prove themselves not just more spiritual and more sensitive, but more sophisticated and more 'European' than the Protestant dullards on the other side of the Irish Sea, and spent a good deal of time pretending that, by some miracle of geography as well as of national psychology, they were far more a part of the Continent and of Catholic Europe than the plodding Anglo-Saxons.

A French Week provided the perfect opportunity for Dubliners to prove their innate mastery of clever foreign ways. French flags suddenly sprouted along O'Connell Street, flying side-by-side with the orange, white and green of Ireland; plays by Anouilh and Sartre were staged, and a season of French films – much savaged by the pinking shears – was mounted at one of the artier cinemas; there was much excited talk of Beckett and Joyce and the Franco-Hibernian literary tradition; the odd baguette was to be found looking ill-at-ease among the sweets, tinned carrots, bottles of stout and elderly, limp cabbages that seemed to be the stock-in-trade of even the classiest Dublin grocery shops.

Best of all, some Paris *gendarmes* were invited over to undertake traffic duty in central Dublin. In those days there was no driving test in the Republic: cars could often be spotted racing one another three abreast down a narrow two-lane street; Dublin buses drove at twice the speed of their London equivalents, mounting the kerb in their haste and crushing pedestrians against the granite walls of Trinity as they hurled round the corner of Nassau and Grafton Streets. The presence of a clutch of mustachioed *gendarmes*, swirling white truncheons and emitting cross, censorious blasts on their whistles merely aggravated the customary confusion, since whereas Dublin drivers were quite likely to drive on the wrong side of the road if left to their own devices, the visiting policemen actively encouraged them to do so.

Shore and I decided to do our bit for Franco-Hibernian relations by attending a wine tasting in a Dublin hotel. Most of our fellow-tasters turned out to be highly respectable ladies from the inner suburbs, anxious to point out that the new Catholic meritocracy had not only left far behind them the demeaning image of the drunken Irish, but were more than a match in matters of *savoir faire* for the old Anglo-Irish Ascendancy in their riding macs and Old Etonian ties, let alone the benighted English over the water. Clad in trim two-piece suits in forceful shades of Irish tweed and overpowering hats with Celtic brooches on the side, and occasionally dragging behind them a neatly turned-out husband in a black or grey alpaca suit of the kind then favoured by gangsters, mortuary attendants and upwardly mobile Irish businessmen, these ladies approached the occasion with the same high seriousness and spirit of reverence with which they would, later in the day, attend an improving lecture on Camus or Cezanne at University College or the National Gallery of Ireland.

Among these rather daunting matrons, it was a relief to spot the voluptuous figure of my heroine, clad – as she invariably was – in skin-tight white jeans, boots, a poncho and a broad-brimmed black hat of the kind associated with bullfighters and a certain kind of arty Englishwoman. Like us, she had come along in the expectation of an afternoon's free drinking at the expense of the French Government; like us, she had graduated from draining – rather than merely sipping and then spitting out into a silver salver – her sample of the wine in question to commandeering those of her more restrained and obedient neighbours, and was rapidly approaching that stage of jollity at which the flinging of bread rolls and a certain thickness of speech were imminent. The matrons looked frostily unamused; Shore slid gracefully under the table, disappearing from sight so neatly and so quietly that the organizers understandably assumed that he had hurried off to another appointment, never suspecting that he was lying stretched out among the matrons' thickly stockinged legs and sensible shoes, his head thrown back and a faint droning sound emitting from his throat. I knew, from past experience, that he would remain there until his discovery, many hours later, by a member of the hotel's cleaning staff; seized with a sudden bravado, I moved across to where ffenella sat and, trembling with excitement and emboldened to unimagined heights of bravery by the wine I had consumed, addressed some incoherent words in her direction.

We were now – by my standards at least – on the most intimate terms, and as a grey and rainy spring led, almost imperceptibly, into a grey and rainy summer, I began to see rather more of ffenella. On odd afternoons I went with her to the old, raffishly elegant Bailey, gazing uneasily over my pint at the self-assured Trinity bloodies as they stood with their legs apart in front of the fire and riffled through the racing pages of the *Irish Times*, that finest of newspapers, or discussed in loud, imperious tones the night's losses at poker, or the party at which two members of the Gardai who had come to investigate the sound of broken glass had been put to sleep side-by-side in the bath after partaking of too much undergraduate hospitality, or the controversial burning of a carpet outside a nunnery (the Mother Superior had been moved to protest in the warmest tones), or the celebrated occasion – mythical or not? I never knew – when some boisterous, tweedy marksman had taken a pot shot at the Junior Dean as he was walking rapidly across one of the Trinity squares, sending him scurrying for safety like Bugs Bunny with Elmer Fudd in hot pursuit (according to a variant of this story, the Junior Dean – expecting the worst – had mistaken the removal of a champagne cork for the blast of a twelve-bore, and had taken appropriate evasive action).

Towards these well-heeled, hard-drinking idlers I felt a curious mixture of emotions, of embarrassment and indignation crossed with a certain pride and that cringing desire to be thought of as one of the boys that the stylishly badly behaved brings out in even the mildest and most timid of men. As yet I knew none of my Irish fellow-students, nor was I to do so until, some terms later, I started writing for the Trinity literary magazine (of which Derek Mahon and Michael Longley were the resident luminaries) and, to our mutual surprise, became engaged to a girl from County Down. Watching the Bailey bloodies gathering loudly before its doors shortly before opening time or elbowing the locals off the pavements or wildly revving the engine of a Triumph TR 2 or an old MG with spokes in the wheels, I felt, in a priggish way, that if I were a Dubliner, or one of those rather old-fashioned Ulster undergraduates I had spotted walking decorously about in a buttoned-up blazer with a silver filigree boar's head stitched on the breast pocket, I might well find these particular Englishmen exceptionally hard to take. Left to my own devices I would probably have taken ffenella to meet – and, indeed, shake hands with – the mediaeval mummies in St Michan's Church on the Quays, or to stride about the grounds of Powerscourt House, with the Sugar Loaf looming up in the distance, or to inspect the Japanese prints in the Chester Beatty Museum; but this was the world she knew and liked, and it was, after all, the 'wild' Trinity of which I had heard so much.

Apart from the middle-aged Copt and a sad, good-looking undergraduate who was hopelessly and unhappily drunk throughout his entire career at Trinity, and for many years thereafter, perhaps the most lurid, and certainly the most entertaining, of ffenella's great army of admirers was a curious, short-legged figure straight from the pages of Surtees, who was invariably clad in a mustard-coloured tweed suit overlaid with a huge and ferocious check – very much the kind of garment preferred by Lord Scamperdale and Jack Spraggon in Leech's gloomy engravings or, it would appear, by the cigar-puffing Evelyn Waugh when working in his library. Beneath the suit he sported a canary-coloured waistcoat and a sky-blue bow tie with white polka dots, and he wore a carnation in his buttonhole. His face was brick-red, and his hair, which was the same colour as his waistcoat, shot from his head in irregular cones like a close-up photograph of the sun's rays or, to continue the Surteesian comparisons, like that of the *faux bonhomme* Mr Jawleyford – though he had none of the latter's distressing faults of character, being the soul of benevolence and kindliness.

One of his false teeth had long ago fallen out and had been replaced with a rusty nail, which, he claimed, was useful for spearing certain items of food: he spoke very fast, screwing up his face a great deal as though in agony, fixing his subjects with a demented pale-blue stare, banging his brow with the palm of his hand again and again as he repented of some florid indiscretion ('I tell a lie! I tell a lie!') and running his hands wildly through his custard-coloured hair as he strove, like a huckster at the races, to inject a note of firm sincerity into his speech ('I kid you not'). Ffenella he approached with what seemed to us to be an enviable mastery, fussing over the wine list – his fingers drumming ceaselessly the while – and discussing the vintage with the head waiter in a low, important drone, or manfully seizing the tiller as we churned through choppy seas to visit a small and inhospitable island off Howth Head, inhabited solely it seemed by cross-looking seagulls with cold grey eyes.

Mr Jawleyford treated Shore and me with the kindly condescension appropriate to an ex-National Serviceman in his last year at Trinity when addressing a couple of peculiarly callow twenty-year-olds. When Shore revealed that he wanted to buy an old crock so that we could fill in the long hours touring the West of Ireland – a highly congenial activity that was to occupy a good deal of our time over the next three years – Mr Jawleyford was all eager attention. He was, he assured us, an expert judge of a car, with years of motoring experience behind him; second-hand car dealers were notoriously bad eggs; without his assistance, Shore and I would be utterly led astray.

We answered an advertisement for a black district nurse's car, for sale in a Sandymount garage, and gratefully accepted Mr Jawleyford's insistence that he come along with us to supervise the transaction. No sooner had we arrived in Sandymount than he bustled up to the garage-owner, engaged him in long and highly technical disquisitions on gaskets and valves and fan belts, tapped various rusty tubes and lengths of piping, drew in his breath from time to time or uttered a short and knowing whistle, took off his vibrant checked jacket to lie under the car and inspect its bowels, sprang to his feet – smoothing down his hair, which was shooting from his head in a wilder way than ever, with a simultaneous movement of both hands – and pronounced it a good car and an excellent bargain ('No problems there – no problems at all!').

Shore wrote out a cheque, we climbed into the district nurse's car – Mr Jawleyford humming a complacent air, a satisfied smile illuminating his unusual features – and, with an awkward jerking motion, we set off in the direction of Dublin. Ten minutes later, as we were speeding cheerfully towards Merrion Square, there was a sudden crash, and we ground to an immediate halt: the engine had fallen out and lay steaming in the middle of the road, while Mr Jawleyford, entirely unruffled by this unexpected development, was explaining in persuasive details how it had come about, slicing the air with his hands and fixing us in turn with his comical bright blue eyes.

I envied Mr Jawleyford his smooth and self-confident association with ffenella, in much the same was as I envied the middle-aged Copt, the French baron, the raffish Stoics and Salopians in their hacking jackets and tubular corduroy trousers, and all the other members of her multitudinous admiration society. As I wandered about Blackrock in the dusk, describing to Shore a most exciting dream in which the Mayor and Corporation of Dublin had, on bended knees, begged me to design for their city a Tube system comparable to London's, with special emphasis on the Circle Line, I found her features swimming up in my mind's eye, quite obliterating the finer points of a conception that had seemed so clear the night before, and so easy of operation; stumping about Phoenix Park – where, did I but know it, my future wife, then in her second year, was living in a set of windowless stables together with three other lodgers, an elderly Alsatian with false teeth and two horse copers from County Tipperary, both with wooden legs – I found myself quite blind to the beauties of Nature all about; taking tea with a group of jolly, rather dowdy girls on the lawns of Trinity Hall – the official accommodation for female undergraduates – I thought in an unworthy way of how much she would disdain so demure a gathering, and how out of place she would look among these fresh-faced, bright-eyed girls in their kilts and sensible shoes, like a panther let loose in a flock of sheep.

I lay and loped about the college in an ostentatious, late-adolescent manner; I hoped and believed that I looked soulful and interesting but found it hard, even then, to suppress a gloomy suspicion that the cumulative effect was unhappily buffoonish. I had no interest whatsoever in sport but wasted entire afternoons watching the races in College Park in the mistaken belief that she was bound to be there, my only relief afforded when a gangling, goat-like figure in horn-rimmed spectacles – the son of a rector from County Antrim, who had already achieved a modest fame by interrupting the visiting preacher in chapel on a point of doctrine – entered the half-mile wearing a moss-coloured tweed suit and orange brogues and carrying a walking stick in his right hand, and swiftly surged ahead of his more conventional rivals in singlets, shorts and shoes with spikes on the bottom.

Rigid with jealousy, I glowered in the most fatuous manner as she flung her arms about a bevy of chinless wonders at a party high above the Front Gate of Trinity, while all about us drunken undergraduates hurled glasses at the statues of Burke and Goldsmith down below, and prepared to be sick over the heavy wooden bannisters on the late arrivals as they surged up the staircase, bottles in their hands, a look of greedy expectancy lighting up their features. Hoping to surprise her – 'I happened to be passing' – I loitered for hours upon end on the steps outside the Dining Hall, reading and re-reading Yeats's hopeless musings on the similarly strong-featured figure of Maud Gonne, and watching the familiar figures of Trinity life shuffle past: the famous 'hanging judge' who, it was claimed, had, on his last day on the bench, condemned a man to death for stealing a bike, so achieving a lifetime's ambition of donning the dreadful black cap; the Professor of Philosophy, an expert on Bishop Berkeley, who had also written the definitive history of the College Baths; the bottle-nosed skip who spent his days, lavatory brush in hand, unblocking the college drains, and his evenings serving on High Table, helping himself as he did so to generous samples from the enormous white jugs of stout with which the undergraduates, courtesy of Arthur Guinness, washed down their evening commons; and the jazz critic of the *Irish Times*, a dark lop-sided figure, made more so after he had fallen down a manhole late at night, his muffled cries unheeded by his fellow-revellers.

And far away in the West of Ireland – for by now the district nurse's car had been kitted out with a new motor, and was capable of speeds of up to forty miles an hour – I waxed eloquent about her as Shore and I and my friend the Deaf Malvernian sat among the root vegetables in some lamplit grocery shop-cum-public house draining pint after pint of stout from a silver barrel that stood on the concrete floor, before swaying unsteadily home to the dainty bed and breakfast, aswirl with a mauve and black patterned carpet and antimacassars and sacred hearts and a frosted glass front door, where we had booked in for the night.

But all was in vain. The term ended; the undergraduates packed their trunks and boarded the Holyhead steamer or an Aer Lingus Viking at Dublin Airport; landladies cast reproachful looks at cigarette burns on mahogany dressers and the circular rings left by pints of beer on highly polished surfaces, shook out the blankets and prepared to replace their Trinity 'boys' with commercial travellers or the humbler kind of conference delegate; gowns, notebooks and all the paraphernalia of academic life at its most demanding were hurled into lockers, where they would moulder from July until October. Shore and Ian and I took ffenella out for a last drink in the back bar of Davy Byrne's, where I moodily gazed into my pint and wished that she and I could be left alone together, and still more so after we had been joined by Mr Jawleyford, who came ·bustling up in an particularly forceful set of tweeds, rubbing his hands together and swiftly taking command of the situation. Quite what I would have said or done under the circumstances was another matter altogether: we had, after all, never spent any time alone together, for even at the French wine tasting Shore had lain, unconscious, at our feet. After she had left for the airport, accompanied by Mr Jawleyford, we ordered another round, and then another, and ended the afternoon – and the term, come to that – in a state of gloomy insobriety.

Shore and I had decided that we would spend two months of the summer hitch-hiking to Istanbul – or, as I put it with undergraduate whimsicality, 'making a pilgrimage' to 'Byzantium' (I had been reading Sir Steven Runciman on the Byzantine empire, as well as taking my customary inhalations of Yeats). In a sudden and rather desperate burst of boldness, I had suggested to ffenella that if she wasn't doing anything she might like to come with us; and two weeks after the term had ended I received a letter from her saying that she would love to come, and would like to bring a friend with her. Could such a thing be possible? Was I a match for the middle-aged Copt in his ninth year reading agriculture, the Old Salopians, Mr Jawleyford and the large contingent of bloodies in the Bailey riffling through the racing pages of the *Irish Times* and making loud baying noises, none of whom (as far as I knew) had been asked to take ffenella as far as Torquay or County Wexford, let alone Byzantium? Had I been handed the opportunity of a lifetime, or would I – as seemed highly probable – make the most fearful hash of things and let it fall almost immediately through my nerveless fingers? Only time could tell; in the meantime, as I read and re-read her letter and rang Shore in Sheffield to tell him the news, I fondly believed that the most congenial year of my life was about to come to the best of all possible conclusions.

CHAPTER FOUR

The Storm-lashed Promenade

Passionate as I was about Ireland, and much as I missed it, I was never sorry to get back to our odd and ostensibly rather hideous corner of the English coast. We lived in what looked like, but was not in fact, a coastguard's cottage overlooking the sea. Ours was one of the middle cottages in a terrace of six; they were painted alternately black and white – with, when we arrived, a jolly-looking Oxo advertisement pasted to the end wall that faced the road – and stood in a desolate, lunar landscape of chalk and rough grass and twists of rusting iron and great chunks of concrete that had, at some stage in the proceedings, been mysteriously deposited in the waste land all about and had remained *in situ* ever since, neither earning their keep nor adding to the beauty of the scene. The cottages faced south-west, towards Newhaven pier, and only a road separated them from the front: during the equinoctial gales in particular the waves would crump against the Victorian esplanade, spray in great arcs across the road, batter against our front windows, which were smeared and streaked with salt, and bring pebbles rattling down the chimney.

I loved the cottage at all times of the year, but never more so than in a gale, sitting round our small black cast-iron stove in the back sitting-room while the cottage jarred and shuddered from the thump of the waves and the wind howled round the chimneys and through the telephone wires, or lying in bed in my room in the attic while the spray drummed against the panes of my dormer window. To the far side of the cottages was a shallow depression, full of ancient bicycles and long-abandoned prams: in the summer it was ablaze with tough little mauve flowers of a nautical cast of mind, but in the winter, when the gales were raging, it filled up with sea water and was known – to us at least – as Lake Lewis. Behind Lake Lewis was a railway line, along which trundled dark green Southern Region trains to Lewes,

Brighton and beyond; on the far side was a garage, a pub and a caravan or two, inhabited by red-faced women in Pirelli slippers, with wild blue eyes and unkempt white hair streaming in the wind.

Every now and then, when the gales were at their height, drivers would be forced to abandon their cars on the front. On one occasion my mother battled out in her nightie and a pair of gumboots, like a latter-day Grace Darling, and breathed life into an abandoned articulated lorry, which she then drove off to safety, causing some consternation when its owners returned during a lull in the storm to find their vehicle and its precious cargo gone. Even more rewarding was a mighty wave which sent a lorry loaded with Tizer hurtling out of control, covering the road with broken glass and foaming raspberry-coloured cordial. We rushed out with brooms and spades to help clear up the mess, and were rewarded with several bottles of the famous appetizer.

My parents had bought the cottage for about £750 in 1958, after some restless if interesting years in rented accommodation; we succeeded a hearty lady artist, who could stand the storms no longer and decided to return to Deodar Road in Putney. When we moved in the paint was peeling from the walls, which were made of shingle held loosely together with blobs of mortar, and furry with salt; for the first few weeks at least I slept in my attic room under a tarpaulin, with a bucket in the middle of the room and an open umbrella above my feet. We had no particular reason for coming to Seaford, but, as a family, we were enthusiastic swimmers, walkers and idlers in the sun; it was all very familiar; and, above all, the two old aunts were still ensconced in their large and highly polished tile-hung house in Blatchington, and Auntie Mary – clad more often than not in a pin-striped suit – was still to be seen moving slowly down the middle of the road in her pre-war Vauxhall, with a great snake of angry motorists filing away into the distance behind her.

Shortly after I went to Trinity, however, the aunts sold up and moved to Eastbourne, where they were joined in a flat near the front by another sister, Annie – the aunt at whose flat I had refreshed myself en route for Ireland for the very first time. Children of my generation grew up hemmed in by forceful or eccentric great-aunts – their numbers were accounted for, we were told, by the slaughter on the Western Front, which had left these remarkable ladies with no one to marry and energy to spare – and of all my great-aunts, Annie was the favourite. A wizened, bent figure, with an enormous curved nose like a Brazil nut and big round eyes like prunes – the family claimed, or at least my mother claimed on their unwilling behalf, a sizeable dash of gypsy blood – she had spent most of her life working as a nurse in the East End; but by the time I first knew her, in the early 1950s, she had retired and was living in a tiny flat in Onslow Gardens.

In those days, South Kensington was a land of grey brick and peeling stucco, heavily populated by maiden aunts, delapidated majors with watery eyes and damp, tobacco-stained moustaches, and elderly, ashen-faced City men who bore a strong resemblance to T. S. Eliot and went to work in black jackets and black-and-white striped trousers. Crouching over gas fires in Drayton Gardens in well-worn tweeds or sipping sherry out of tooth mugs, they were very much the sort of people who pop up in the stories of the excellent William Trevor, or gaze sadly out of the Distressed Gentlefolk advertisements on the inside pages of the *Daily Telegraph*; there was nothing remotely melancholy about Auntie Annie, but in the slightly down-at-heel gentility of that particular part of London she seemed perfectly at home. Winter or summer, she wore an aged fox fur slung round her neck – as children we spent a good deal of time examining the tiny, snarling face of the fox – and a bottle-green trilby clamped on her head, held firmly in place by one of those enormous, pearl-headed hat pins that played so important a part in mystery stories between the wars. She had legs like broomsticks in stockings, on the bottom end of which could be found a highly polished pair of brown 'sensible' shoes.

An enthusiastic amateur electrician and carpenter, she frequently fused the lights in the entire block of flats, and liked nothing better than to engage my father in technical debate about lathes and chisels and various types of wood. Though hospitable to a degree – I lived with her for several months after leaving school, while working as a packer at Harrods – she lived off diminutive chops or the occasional mackerel cooked over an ancient Baby Belling, the culinary equivalent of the upright Austin Seven. Despite her apparently proper demeanour, she was game for anything, tossing down the sherry at the least provocation and more than once – when far too old for such antics – joining my parents on various wild pre-war sprees, her fox fur and green felt hat remaining firmly in place as she scaled a six-foot wall or was lowered down a drainpipe into the garden of some unsuspecting party-giver. She must have been well over eighty when she eventually deserted her top-floor flat and moved down to Eastbourne to join her sisters. Away from her beloved London, from the peeling stucco and the winter smogs, she seemed a shadow of her sparrow-like self, and within a year or so she was dead.

Nor, it would seem, is South Ken any longer a natural haunt for the modern Auntie Annie: those once-familiar grey and white houses are reserved for the very rich, for Arabs and French bankers and South American businessmen. The maiden aunts have moved off to homes in Worthing or Bognor Regis, or upwards to meet their Maker, while their great-nephews and great-nieces are scattered round the rim of Central London in a great diaspora of Barbour jackets and green wellingtons, recreating the world of their forebears in the mugger-haunted groves of Clapham and Stockwell or the dismal slopes of Battersea Rise, or bicycling elegantly about the squares and terraces of Islington, or 'rescuing' fireplaces and panelled doors or eighteenth-century mouldings in Hackney or in Brixton while waiting – more often than not in vain – for their pioneer spirit to be rewarded (both socially and financially) as their 'up and coming' chosen land fulfills the excited prophesies of yesteryear and finally floats to the surface.

Only once, as a family, did we live in the vanished Eden to which these exiles will never return, when we left our enormous Battersea flat for a modern pink maisonette in a cul-de-sac near Victoria Grove, best remembered for the dreadful moment when a neighbour's child so aggravated the milkman's horse that it set off at a brisk trot and vanished round the corner to the musical clinking of glass, leaving its owner – who had unwisely forgotten to apply the brake – looking baffled on a doorstep; but whenever I spot the towers of the Natural History Museum, or Dino's spaghetti house on the corner by South Ken tube, or – my favourite eating-house in London – Daquise's Polish restaurant, with its elderly, stern commissionaires, exiles from Carpathia or the Russian Pale, and 1950s coffee-bar decor, I see in my mind's eye long crocodiles of schoolboys (of whom I was one) in caps of concentric blue and black, and mothers pushing enormous prams towards the park, and well-scrubbed children with impeccable partings and buttoned leggings and pale blue tweed coats with velvet collars, and, above all, my elderly, favourite aunt thrusting up the sash window of her top floor flat in response to our pealing of the bell and hurling her front-door key down to the street below, her great Brazil nut of a nose thrust forward, like a benevolent refugee from a Punch and Judy show.

Although the aunts had moved away, Seaford itself – and the cottages in particular – was rich in human interest. At the far end lived a wild and seemingly demented old woman, who emptied her pot out of the window every morning, fed the sea-gulls on bowls of cold porridge and, even in the height of summer, sat out in front of the cottages on a wooden kitchen chair wearing a motheaten fur coat held tightly about the waist by a length of baling twine, and the inevitable check slippers on her feet, with pale blue socks peeping up above. Next to us was a seadog and his sister, who had lived all their life there: he wore a gold ring in one ear and a singlet over a fine-looking paunch, and she played the piano; in the winter, when the storms were at their height, the sound of strumming and of voices raised in hymns came soothingly through the wall from next door.

To the other side of us lived Ben, a beaming, Pickwickian figure, and one of the kindest and dearest men I have ever known; he died, wretchedly and far too young, some years ago, and so we lost the best and staunchest friend a family could ever hope for. Ben was then in his mid-thirties; he had been at the LSE after the war, and on long walks along the front late at night I would pour forth – with the omniscience and smugness peculiar to people of that age – a torrent of half-baked ideas about literature and politics and the Meaning of Life, all of which he listened and replied to with a Jove-like patience. He worked in London, and came down to his cottage only at weekends; we all longed for his arrival, and nothing was more exciting than to hear his train rattling along the bank behind Lake Lewis, at which we rushed to put on the kettle for his homecoming cup of tea, and then went out to the front of the cottages to wait for him to come round the corner from Bishopstone Station, lit up by flaring orange lights, a suitcase in one hand and a bottle of whisky or some other surprise in the other.

In between the seadog with the vest and the paunch and the old lady with the bowls of porridge and the motheaten fur coat lived a very old and very engaging retired Mountie and his even older and equally engaging wife, who was bed-ridden for most of the time we knew her. We shared to an extreme degree the current middle-class snobbery about not owning a television set – as far as I remember, we acquired one only in the mid to late 1960s – and looked down on those who had succumbed as traitors and vulgarians of the lowest kind: nevertheless, my sister and I spent a good many evenings sneaking off before supper to join the Mountie and his wife in watching Cliff Michelmore, Derek Hart, Geoffrey Johnson Smith, Fyfe Robertson and the nasal Alan Whicker on *Tonight*. More often than not they addressed us through a Siberian blizzard, or showed us the tops of their heads only, or were edged off the screen by sudden convulsions of the set, which began to smoke if left on for more than an hour or so; the Mountie seemed oblivious to these alarming goings-on, and since we had no set of our own we were powerless to put things right. Beside us on the sofa lay the Mountie's elderly Yorkshire terrier: he was, like his owner, a friendly and likeable old gentleman, but various internal linings seemed to have perished, like the rubber in a hot water bottle that is nearing the end of its days, with the result that small canine farts puffed towards us, like sulphurous summer clouds streaming across the horizon, reeking of cabbage and the dog's equivalent of baked beans or onion sauce.

A year or two after our arrival the old lady in the motheaten fur coat was taken away to, I fear, a lunatic asylum where I like to think she was allowed to continue emptying her pot out of the window and feeding the gulls on bowls of cold porridge; and her cottage – which was, we were told in horrified tones, a slum of the *very worst* kind – was painted up and redecorated and let by its new owner to an eminent German composer, one of whose operas was being performed at Glyndebourne that summer. Although I was away for much of the time he was there, hitch-hiking round Spain with my kind friend Tom and brooding unhappily on the steady trickle of rejection letters received from Oxford and Cambridge Tutors for Admissions, my parents and my sister became – quite rightly – extremely fond of him: when he was ill they put him in my room in the attic, and he informed them later that the gurgling and knocking of the pipes had inspired him to some of his finest compositions. As a way of showing his thanks he invited us to a performance of his new opera at Glyndebourne.

Like many of my contemporaries I have come to opera in middle age, along with a general thinning of the hair and expansion of the waistline, and a far greater appreciation of the formal, the hieratic and the ritualistic in art as well as manners; I am as surprised by my love of Bellini and Richard Strauss as I am by my equally recent and equally unexpected relish for the lost, Arcadian landscapes of Poussin or of Claude – though all are, perhaps, pervaded by a combination of timeless beauty and a melancholy, autumnal touch of *lacrimae rerum*, that sense of man's frailty and impermanence that means so little to us when we are young, but both shadows and enhances our lives after the age of forty. As for Glyndebourne itself – to which, thanks to generous friends, we are invited far more frequently than we deserve or could ever begin to afford – it strikes me now as one of the few institutions that are all, and more, than they are made out to be: a sudden, momentary glimpse of Paradise, made all the more poignant and intense by the invariable act of truancy involved, by its bright irruption into the world of memos and photocopying machines and interminable office meetings.

Quite apart from the music and the gardens and the feelings of almost proprietory well-being, how touching it is to spot one's fellow-escapees, waxen-featured and baggy-eyed from worrying over the half-yearly figures or struggling with the small print in a contract, togged up in unfamiliar finery, friends and lady wives about them, bustling importantly to and fro with hampers and programmes and glasses of Pimms, or clutching in one hand a glass and a fork and a plate abrim with salmon or cold beef and in the other an enormous multi-coloured umbrella beneath which a little party shelters, standing rigidly to attention while the rain streams down with the force of a tropical storm! How ignoble yet how consoling the joys of sneering at the rich vulgarians in their apricot-coloured Rolls Royces, the wives agleam with gold, with skin the colour of caramel, their husbands, pot-bellied and waving large cigars, striding unashamedly about in maroon velvet jackets and sea-green shirts with ruffles foaming out in front and more gold about the wrist and even – oh culminating horror! – a giant lavatory chain worn about the neck from which hangs, it seemed, some intricate crest of office! And then, as picnic time draws near, to spot these same Veneerings (how welcome one would have been in one's own family, preferably a generation or two back, or discreetly concealed from view!) dining at heavily laden collapsible tables, complete with damask tablecloths and silver candelabra and a servile chauffeur clad all in grey in a peaked cap, breeches and high-collared jacket, bending low as he pours the party its restorative champagne!

But in those boisterous, far-off days - and, indeed, until shamingly recently - I derided opera as the most ludicrous nonsense, peopled by fat women making loud screeching noises and equally bulky male counterparts in over-tight trousers and false moustaches, like Tracy Tupman at Mrs Leo Hunter's poetical garden party. The plots struck me as absurd and implausible, the love duets the subject of high comedy as the overweight suitor sank slowly to one knee, his trousers stretched to bursting point, or strove to embrace his inamorata, like one barrage balloon bouncing off another. Not surprisingly, perhaps, I took particular pleasure in those disruptive scenes in *A Night at the Opera* when the Marx Brothers contrive to ruin a production of *Il Trovatore*, whisking the scenery up and down and swinging on ropes across the stage, like nimbler versions of the musclebound gym-master from my prep school days, while the pompous principals rush angrily to and fro beneath. Not surprisingly, too, I awaited the trip to Glyndebourne with a certain dread, deepened by the realization that, much as we all liked our exciting new neighbour, his music was decidedly modern.

Walking round the gardens at Glyndebourne before the performance began, I came face-to-face with W. H. Auden, who had written the libretto for our friend in the cottage so recently vacated by the lady with the pot and the bowls of cold porridge; apart from his famous facial lines, the thing I best remember about him - and, indeed, the entire evening - was that he was wearing one black shoe and one brown one, and that when I cast a furtive glance in the direction of his feet during the long interval, as the Pimms drinkers jostled all about us, I noticed that he had traded these in for a pair of brown-and-white checked slippers of the kind so popular in our particular part of Seaford. These looked very homely and extremely out-of-place amidst the encircling patent leathers, and since I was, in those days, all in favour of those who ignored the conventions and failed to dress for the occasion, my admiration for the great man - already at fever pitch - soared to unheard of heights.

Far from such excitements, the opera itself seemed to my untutored ear to consist of a series of unhappy lunar pings, interrupted from time to time by the crash of falling masonry and terrible, strangulated cries. Quite what Auden's words had to do with all this was not immediately apparent, and I could only assume that his musical tastes, like his footwear, were odder and a good deal more sophisticated than my own. (I suspect, looking back, that I did our neighbour's music a grave injustice, for although my hatred for modern music remains as fierce as ever, snatches of the opera I have heard since have sounded surprisingly melodious; and in those days, it must be remembered, I found it hard to sit through even Rossini or Donizetti, but squirmed uneasily in my seat as the singers shrieked unmercifully on, casting covert glances at my watch and wondering how much longer we would have to wait for a drink and a stroll in the grounds.)

We were taken to Glyndebourne again a couple of years later, in the long and lazy weeks between the end of the summer term and our departure for Byzantium. Although I much preferred Monteverdi to the lunar pings, what I really enjoyed were the picnic, the gardens, and the unashamed way in which many of the male members of the audience, overcome by alcoholic fumes and the good things they had just devoured on the lawns outside from heavily laden hampers, threw back their heads and ostentatiously snoozed throughout the second half of the proceedings. Their gentle snores could be clearly distinguished during the quieter moments of the drama, like the persistent drone of a bagpipe: every now and then a particularly piercing shriek from a soprano would awaken a slumberer who, with a cry of alarm, would gather up his belongings and prepare to make a dash for the emergency exit before being brought to his senses by calmer members of his party and assured that there was nothing to worry about; after which, if the mood were upon him, he might hum along with some of the more rousing choruses or tap out the rhythm with a well-heeled patent-leather shoe, to the intense irritation of the music-lovers all about, who rounded on him with the same beetle-browed ferocity that would otherwise be brought to bear on an absent-minded maiden aunt unwrapping toffees at the very moment that the heroine, singing lustily to the last, expires in the arms of her lover.

In the interval our jovial host unwisely insisted that I should open the champagne on the grounds that I was now at university, and should be well used to dealing with such matters: this proved a foolish move, since the cork shot suddenly between my fingers, glancing off the pate of a dignified City gentleman before embedding itself in a flower-bed with the force of an artillery shell, while the wine spent itself on the lawn in a tide of foam as I fought in vain to point the bottle in the right direction, like a small boy overmastered by a fire-extinguisher. Whatever Trinity's virtues, it seemed, such social graces were passing me by; it was time that I joined my own once more.

CHAPTER FIVE

To Byzantium with ffenella

Although Shore and I had announced our intention of visiting Byzantium and seeing for ourselves the home of our old friends the Palaeologues and Basil the Bulgar-Slayer - not to mention that potent figure, the Empress Theodora - neither of us had the remotest idea of how to get there, and had ffenella not decided to join the expedition it seems unlikely that we would have made our way more than a mile or so beyond Calais or Dieppe. As it was, she swiftly took command, revealing that she had arranged for us to be given a lift as far as Lausanne and ordering us to rendezvous at an address in North London towards the end of June.

I spent the weeks before our departure preparing anxiously for the great adventure that lay ahead. Eager to look my best, I swam several times a day, went for bracing walks over the Downs, and soaked up every available ray of south coast sun while reading improving works of literature in a deck chair in our midget-sized front garden. Ffenella had been to the most famous of all progressive schools, where she had consorted with the offspring of Hampstead potters, high-minded civil servants, eminent literary men and assorted vegetarians; since she had spent her formative years listening to string quartets sawing vigorously away in carefully restored mediaeval barns, dancing barefoot through flower-bedecked meadows, and discussing birth control and Eastern religions with bearded masters in spinach-coloured shirts and orange ties, I knew that she was both Arty and Progressive, and - as far as reading matter was concerned - almost certainly keener on important European thinkers than on the likes of Surtees or Sir Arthur Conan Doyle.

Drastic action was evidently called for if Shore and I were to sustain the level of intellectual repartee to which she was presumably accustomed, and to put matters right I hurried along to the Seaford

Public Library, returning heavily laden with novels by Camus, Kafka and J.-P. Sartre. From the depths of my deck chair I struggled to master these difficult writers, pausing every now and then to imagine myself discussing the finer points of existentialism with ffenella under an olive tree in Attica, while Shore looked on with a wild surmise; and in the intervals between taking violent exercise and confronting the great issues of our age, I fought hard (but in vain) to enjoy snatches of modern music on the Third Programme, and to brush up my knowledge of twentieth-century art. Every evening I gazed anxiously into the bathroom mirror, hoping that these endeavours would not only excite a much-needed improvement in my looks, but stamp me a masterful man of the world: to my distress my face seemed as featureless and as bovine as ever, like a huge lump of lard on which a pair of horn-rimmed spectacles had been uneasily balanced, and my jaw irremediably pendulous and granitic. All that could be done was to squeeze that day's crop of blackheads and hope that the next day would bring the changes of which I dreamt.

The evening before we left I carefully packed my rucksack – an enormous elephant-coloured affair made of heavy canvas, suspended from a mighty metal frame and set about with important-looking leather straps. In one of the side pockets I put *Pickwick* and *Mr Sponge's Sporting Tour*, and in the other a large supply of glycerine suppositories, which my father had received as a free sample. I had no idea of how to use these unwholesome-looking objects, and would have been quite appalled if I had, but it was widely – and correctly – believed that I would be rigid with constipation within minutes of spotting one of those old-fashioned French lavatories consisting of a hole in the ground and a pair of pedestals on which to place the feet, and my father thrust them on me as a possible solution to the problem. Under the flap of the rucksack I strapped my father's sleeping bag, in which he had snoozed fitfully in slit trenches from Normandy to the Rhine, while my passport, some loose change, £50-worth of travellers' cheques and a brand new Youth Hostels membership card were squeezed into an unusual money-belt made of linen, elastic and an elaborate system of poppers. This impenetrable garment was worn under my trousers, and was correctly believed by its inventor – my mother – to be impervious to the advances of brigands, pickpockets, confidence tricksters and the various riff-raff with which Continental Europe was so tiresomely aswarm.

Next morning I met my travelling companions outside a white terraced house in Primrose Hill. As I came down the road my eye lit immediately on ffenella, who had very sensibly taken command and was issuing instructions in a husky, voluptuous voice of the kind I associated with temptresses, gazing out at the audience through narrowed eyes and a fog-like cloud of cigarette smoke. She was wearing a navy-blue Guernsey that carefully followed the contours of her exciting-looking bosom, skin-tight white jeans, flat Greek sandals and a luminous cyclamen lipstick that seemed to my inexpert eye to blend in very nicely with her sunburnt features, strong white teeth and shoulder-length auburn hair. She looked, as she always did, strong and sensuous and pulsating with vitality, like a Nordic edition of Carmen, or the kind of saucy country wench one finds in eighteenth-century comedies skipping about with bare feet, a low-cut blouse and bits of straw attached to her skirt, embodying all that is fresh and natural in a stale and artificial world. At the sight of this radiant spectacle my knees began to tremble, but I quickly averted my gaze and concentrated instead on the other members of the party.

Shore, I was glad to see, was planning to travel in exactly the same clothes that he wore every day at Trinity, winter or summer, and which he was to wear in the years ahead on expeditions to Central America and the Middle East - a porridge-coloured tweed jacket, brown corduroy trousers, a Viyella shirt, a thick blue prep school jersey with a floppy collar, and well-polished brogues on his feet. In one hand he held a cigarette; in the other a rolled umbrella, which he waved from side to side with a curious shushing sound, as though he were cleaving his way through spiders' webs or foliage of a cloying and irritating kind.

The fourth member of the party, Jill —, was a school friend of ffenella's, and her opposite in every respect: the unkind might well have assumed that she had been specially selected to offset and highlight ffenella's fruity and flamboyant charms. My initial impression was of a thin, pallid girl with a flat chest and straight-up-and-down legs that lacked the normal swoops and bulges associated with calves and ankles, and were thrust into a pair of short fawn socks, which in turn led into a pair of sensible sandals with a floral motif carved into their uppers. She wore a gruel-coloured dress and wire-framed spectacles: her hair had been pulled firmly back from her brow, and was held in place by a rubber band at the nape of her neck. Her father was a psychologist with a carefully sculpted grey beard and a knitted tie, and could be spotted moving anxiously about behind the Swiss cheese plants in the bow window of a brightly lit first-floor room; between them they constituted, I suspect, my first sighting of that serious-minded and somewhat alien creature, North London man. Jill proved a likeable if – at least in my infatuated eyes – rather inconspicuous travelling companion; I have not seen her for over twenty-three years, but I like to think of her practising her skills as a librarian, reading the women's pages of the *Guardian*, marrying an earnest civil servant in socks and sandals and spending her days in a bright and eminently reasonable house in Clapham or Kentish Town, clad in a Clothkits dress and patiently explaining the facts of life to small children in disposable nappies with chocolate-smeared faces, sticky hands and dashes of tomato ketchup in their curly, uncombed locks.

When I arrived the little party was gazing rather gloomily into the boot of a small black and white Triumph. This, it seemed, was the car in which we were hitching a lift to Lausanne, and its owner appeared to be having some difficulty working out how to squeeze into it the four of us plus our rucksacks and his luggage and various accessories with which he insisted on travelling. I had met Nicholas A— several times in Dublin and while liking him a good deal – he was an unusually civilized man, with a strong interest in armorial bearings and a close acquaintance with the *Almanach de Gotha* – had been seized by spasms of jealous indignation at his whisking ffenella off on tours of antique shops just as I was inching my way round to asking her out to the pub. He was a bony, pale youth with thin lips and deep set eyes, in whom the aquiline features of Sherlock Holmes or the Duke of Wellington had been blended with a dash of a fair-haired Charles Addams spectre or a mournful Spanish grandee. A good deal more sophisticated than the rest of us, he was always very well and expensively dressed, and his two pigskin suitcases already looked ill-at-ease at the prospect of rubbing shoulders with my suppository-laden rucksack and its equally coarse companions. Apart from the pigskin suitcases, the boot was – to our alarm – heavily laden with several crates of Mackeson's stout, which Nicholas drank for his complexion, together with a wide range of deodorants, after-shave lotions and depilatory creams. There was nothing for it but to travel all the way with our rucksacks on our knees. Since I was far and away the largest person present, I sat in the front, and the other three squeezed in behind, muttering crossly about the depilatory creams; thus we set off on the long journey south.

Of the trip to Lausanne I remember very little – probably because, as the man in the front, I was far too alarmed by our host's unusual driving habits to notice the scenery as we flashed along the poplar-lined roads of northern France, from Beauvais to Paris to Auxerre, and from Dijon up into the mountains. Nicholas was an erratic and nervous driver at the best of times, much given to mounting the kerb, lunging wildly into the oncoming traffic, and advancing by fits and starts as the result of putting the car into the wrong gear or forgetting to take off the handbrake; faced with the extra temptation of driving on the wrong side of the road, his technique became spectacularly unsound. Every twenty minutes or so he would fall asleep at the wheel, tossing back his head and emitting a low and restful drone; and while the others in the back were enjoying the delights of the countryside, I kept my eyes firmly on our chauffeur, waiting to take the wheel and jab him in the ribs as sleep overcame him once again. Equally disturbing was his habit of foaming at the mouth while motoring at high speeds: although I knew from my reading of Surtees that choleric old gentlemen like Lord Scamperdale were much given to foaming – as were, one gathered, indignant or revolutionary mobs – this was my first experience of foaming at such close quarters. It seemed impolite to draw his attention to the foam, and since it seldom coincided with a bout of heavy snoozing I decided to let well alone and wait for the alarming symptoms to disappear. (Later I learned that – by a pleasing irony – the foam was due not to natural causes, but to our somnambulant driver's taking some kind of pep pill much favoured at the time by those who were working for their finals and needed to remain unnaturally alert.)

We took leave of our unconventional driver at Lausanne, where we stayed in a flat belonging to a fellow-undergraduate – one of ffenella's large army of admirers – whose father had made a well-deserved fortune from writing the words to old-fashioned popular songs. Also encamped was a team of bloodies from the Bailey; they had no intention of travelling rough, but seemed intent on whiling away the summer drinking heavily and sampling the fleshpots, such as they were. Among them was the large and fierce-looking scion of an ancient Catholic family, a belligerent giant with bulging red-rimmed eyes who spent most of his career at Trinity very much the worse for drink. At about two in the morning we were woken by a terrific crash of breaking glass to find this alarming figure standing in the middle of the floor, with blood on his hands, swaying dangerously from side to side and shaking his enormous head like a baffled bull pestered by flies: returning over-excited from some late-night revel he had walked straight through the plate-glass door that separated the hall from the sitting-room in which we were sleeping. The mildest of men before the pubs opened, he went on to achieve a certain notoriety in Trinity as a poker player and for throwing a fellow-reveller down his staircase, breaking both his legs in the process; and when, a year or two later, the cricket pavilion was burnt down, its smouldering ashes greeting the more industrious undergraduates as they hurried to a nine o'clock lecture, it was widely assumed that our bibulous fellow-guest was the guilty man.

Next day we decided to hitch-hike to the Italian lakes, en route for Milan and Venice, where we would find a boat to take us to Corfu. It was for some reason assumed that I would travel with ffenella, and Shore with Jill, and I had no intention of challenging this; and so we set out. Up to now I had, it seemed, spent the entire trip keeping an anxious eye on Nicholas A—, watching out for tell-tale flecks of foam or the sudden snore that heralded a wild lurch into the face of the oncoming traffic, and I had hardly exchanged a word with the object of my admiration: now that I had her to myself, surely the trip would come into its own, and my every wish be achieved? The trouble was that I had absolutely no idea how such wishes *could* be achieved - or even what they involved - and no experience of my own on which to draw. Torrid novels and the films of Brigitte Bardot were all very well, but could only take one so far; I had no intention of embarrassing old Shore by discussing such unseemly matters with him, but had I done so I am sure I would have found him equally short on both nerve and expertise, and eager to bring the conversation round once more to Romanesque churches or the less elevated but (to us at least) vastly entertaining flow of drivel in which, left to ourselves, we endlessly indulged, much to the disgust of our more sophisticated travelling companions.

However bold and jocular I might be when the four of us were together, once alone with ffenella I was not only tongue-tied to the point of oral immobility, but felt myself to be – as I undoubtedly was – lumpish, ludicrously gauche and utterly lacking in all those urbane qualities I had so assiduously set out to acquire in the weeks leading up to our departure. Far from proving the Lothario of my dreams, I found myself plodding stolidly along behind ffenella, her rucksack on one shoulder and my own on the other, the sweat plastering my shirt to my back in the most undashing manner, and misting up my spectacles as I cast entirely ineffective glances of adoration in her direction as soon as I knew she was looking the other way. I was, it goes without saying, far too taken up with my own boorish sensibilities to have any time to spare for hers; more than anything else I dreaded the embarrassment of making a false move or misreading matters, and – not for the last time in my amorous career – I found myself wishing that people like ffenella came provided with a system of flashing lights, unambiguously indicating whether the hesitant admirer should advance or desist.

Worse was to come. On top of one of those passes that separate Switzerland from Italy we were picked up by an Italian named Hector, who was driving a small cream baby Fiat. My heart sank as soon as I spotted him, for he was very smooth, very charming and extremely good-looking, with the saturnine, somewhat battered features of a young but worldly Roman emperor. He screeched to a halt within seconds of spotting ffenella standing beside the road, and reversed hungrily towards her, winding down the window as he went. His face registered a momentary irritation as I emerged puffing from the bushes, but he politely indicated that I should fold myself into the dwarf-sized seats at the back, along with his briefcase, our rucksacks and a large tailor's dummy which, for some reason, was his only travelling companion; ffenella – whose hand he had already kissed, raising imploring brown eyes to her face as he did so – was to be his guest in the front. Unlike those of us who keep both hands firmly on the wheel in the ten-to-two position, our eyes fixed unflinchingly on the road ahead, Hector belonged to the cool and dashing school of motoring: he took a series of precipitous S-bends with terrifying *sang-froid*, one hand loosely spinning the steering wheel – a cigarette clamped in place at the join between the first and index fingers in a way that, I remembered from Continental films, went with the kind of keen-eyed masterfulness I knew I could never attain – while with the other he continued to take ffenella's unresisting hand and raise it to his lips. As the Alps unravelled behind us, and the countryside became more recognizably Italian, he favoured us with a medley of arias from Bellini and Donizetti; and in the intervals between he addressed himself to ffenella in passionate, resonant tones. Although the gist of what he wanted to say was all too plain, he had no English and she had no Italian: I had once spent a couple of months plodding through *Teach Yourself Italian*, and to my alarm I found myself agreeing on ffenella's behalf that Hector would drop us at a youth hostel beside Lake Maggiore, and that we would meet him later that evening in an open-air restaurant beside the lake.

That evening, as we unpacked and prepared for the evening ahead – ffenella changing into a navy blue pleated cotton skirt, a broderie anglaise blouse and a thick black belt – I found myself wondering once again why it was that, in even the scruffiest youth hostels, Continental Europeans managed to emerge with immaculately creased trousers, pressed shirts with the sleeves rolled up just so between wrist and elbow, and highly polished slip-on shoes of the kind that, at the time, were calculated to drive apoplectic English majors wild with indignation; whereas the English male traveller was immediately recognizable by his bush-like hair, his red complexion, the sheet of sweat coursing down his features, his crumpled apple-green shirt, his orange Clarks sandals, and his fawn cotton trousers that, far from sustaining a crease, were invariably too long in the leg and baggy at the knee, and from which, despite interminable promptings, the apple-green shirt continually came adrift. Most telling of all was the uncanny way in which Continentals draped their expensive cashmere jerseys over their shoulders, with the same kind of studied elegance that they brought to smoking a cigarette: I had, from time to time, attempted this casual look myself, edging uneasily along like a man in an egg-and-spoon race, but my v-necked jersey had almost immediately slipped backwards off my shoulders or been carried away by a sudden gust of wind, and I had ended up angrily knotting the arms round my waist in the ungainly English fashion, like an umpire at a cricket match.

It was dark by the time we got to the restaurant by the lake, and the lights were twinkling among the trees between which the tables were set. Hector was already there, looking cooler and smoother and (or so it seemed to me) more repellently handsome than ever: I noted with some bitterness that he appeared to have no problem in keeping *his* cashmere jersey in place. He rose to greet us, kissed ffenella's hand more greedily than ever, drew back a chair for her and poured her a glass of wine, and indicated that perhaps I should find myself a chair and join them. It was at this point that my particular mortification began. During the day I had worn a pair of spectacles which doubled up as dark glasses, and which I normally replaced with my ordinary horn-rims as soon as it began to grow dark. This evening, however, I had rashly decided to keep on my dark glasses and wear them at night in the manner perfected only a year or two earlier by Marcello Mastroianni in *La Dolce Vita*, a film that I had been to see at least five times, and that seemed to embody the sinful *savoir faire* I strove for; I felt put out by Hector and his compatriots, and I felt the only answer was to beat them at their own game.

The only problem with this sudden sophistication was that I could now see virtually nothing of what was going on about me: without my specs I was too short-sighted to see more than a foot or two in front of me, but with my dark glasses on all was impenetrable blackness, pierced by the coloured lights bobbing among the trees and the bright white blur of ffenella's blouse. Moving my hands in front of me like a player of blind man's buff, I moved slowly away in search of a chair, stubbing my toes on stumps as I went and, as I ventured into realms of outer darkness, crashing uncomfortably into the trees that loomed unexpectedly out of the darkness. Eventually I found a spindly metal chair and – negotiating by sound rather than vision, like some gigantic fair-haired bat – I headed back towards my companions. As I approached them, the chair held before me like a blind man's stick, I noticed over the top of my specs that Hector was now holding ffenella's hand and gazing into her face with a rapt expression, oblivious of all about him – and that, to make matters worse, she was laughing in a way that she seemed not to employ when we were travelling alone together. Just at that moment I tripped again, this time on Hector's briefcase, laden as it was with order books and samples. I threw out my hands to stop myself falling, sent the table spinning and one glass of red wine all over ffenella's broderie anglaise blouse and the other into Hector's lap, toppled heavily to the ground and lay there, temporarily stunned, while they shot to their feet and began dabbing at their clothes in a frenzy of indignation.

Although ffenella was understandably vexed about the broderie anglaise, which now sported a large purple stain in mid-bosom, Hector was - for all his maddening aplomb - a friendly soul, and while he quite obviously wished that I was elsewhere, he was far too hospitable and polite to make his feelings plain. Instead he ordered another bottle, guided me into a chair, took ffenella's hand and continued to gaze ardently into her eyes. After issuing an elegant string of compliments which I loyally translated, wishing all the while that I was the principal and not the agent in this sorry business, since I so wholeheartedly agreed with every word he had to say, he asked me to ask ffenella if she would care to dance. I reluctantly interpreted this outrageous suggestion, bridling as I did so, and plumbing new depths of despair when she greeted his proposal with a relish that seemed to me to be wholly out of place. He took her arm and they disappeared in the direction of the band, leaving me staring glumly into the darkness.

I must have sat there for a couple of hours, wishing I had had the sense to change my specs and bring with me *The Pickwick Papers*; every now and then Hector and ffenella loomed out of the encircling gloom, hand in hand, at which I strove to look both animated, as though I were having the time of my life, and a bruised and sensitive soul. After a couple of minutes of desultory chatter - by now I had reached the limits of *Teach Yourself Italian*, and a certain repetitiveness was settling in - they disappeared once more, leaving me feeling particularly sorry for myself, and wondering in a peevish way why ffenella hadn't the decency to ask *me* to dance. Re-reading an account of this evening that I wrote shortly after our return to England, I find the pages suffused with indignation on this score: evidently it never occurred to me that, in those days at least, the asking was up to me.

Walking back to the youth hostel after Hector had finally driven away, I trailed behind ffenella like a sulky child, kicking stones and banging into the occasional bollard as it surged suddenly out of the night; ffenella was suitably unamused by my behaviour and strode on ahead, pausing from time to time to point out that it was time I grew up a little. Nor were my tribulations over. Not only had a brand-new shirt that I had hung out to dry been stolen by a fellow-hosteller, but when I vented my indignation by giving the youth hostel lavatory chain a particularly savage yank, the ballcock flew out of the cistern, striking me a glancing blow on the side of the head and sending me spinning to the ground for the second time that night. As I lay on the lavatory floor I thought – not for the last time – that travelling was only tolerable in anticipation or in retrospect, and that agreeing to ffenella's coming with us had merely multiplied the misery of it all.

As we travelled through Italy to Venice, down the Adriatic, through Greece and so to Istanbul, I soon realized that, apart from the regulation crones in black and jovial peasantry in waistcoats and handlebar moustaches, Mediterranean Europe seemed to be peopled almost exclusively by Hectors, all of them impeccably groomed and with cashmere jerseys slung over their shoulders, and all of them capable of transforming ffenella in an instant from the rather abstracted and impatient figure with whom I sat in silence at the side of the road, thumb imploringly extended, to the pleased and receptive embodiment of my dreams. Had my reading of Pasternak and Thomas Mann, my anxious perusal of literary magazines and the long hours spent listening to intolerable blasts of modern music on the Third Programme been all in vain? Would I ever command the *savoir faire* and the self-confidence to be able, like Hector, to hold her hand in the gloaming as a foretaste of heaven knew what ecstacies to come?

But not even the most adolescent and self-absorbed of undergraduates could devote his entire time to brooding on such matters, still more so since the trip itself was turning out to be rich in incident. In Milan my supply of suppositories melted in the sun, drenching my best pair of trousers in molten jelly and rendering transparent the pages of *Pickwick*. In Venice we spotted Nicholas A— looking as lean and grandee-like as ever, despite massive infusions of milk stout, checking armorial bearings in a dusty cat-infested grave yard. On the boat from Venice to Corfu ffenella and Jill were serenaded by dark-eyed, diminutive Greek sailors singing 'Never on Sunday', and in the morning these jovial songsters woke us as we lay on the deck in our sleeping-bags with a fine spray of synthetic rain as they bustled about us, hosing down. In Corfu, that most idyllic of islands, we stayed in a bat-infested youth hostel, and Shore had to damp down a small fire in the men's dormitory, brought about by his smoking in bed after a convivial evening spent downing bottle after bottle of retsina – that most magical of drinks – under a trellis of vines.

After a day or two in Corfu we crossed to Igoumenitsa, the swarthy brown Albanian mountains looming gloomily above us, and began to hitch-hike south. In those days Greece was relatively free of tourists and concrete holiday hotels, and the lorry drivers in particular made a great deal of us, insisting that ffenella and Jill clambered into the driving cab while Shore and I humped our luggage into the open back and climbed in after. On the first evening we stopped for supper at a remote roadside eating place consisting of a few upright chairs and tables standing in the dust, a string of bright bare bulbs, a trellis overhead – and, all about us, the great black mountains, the resonant tang of pine, the constant hum and chatter of crickets and the honking of far-off frogs. After we had eaten – and I found that I enjoyed the much-derided Greek food as much as I liked the Greeks, their country and their unusual but delectable national drinks, and greatly relished poking about the kitchens, pointing to this dish or that as it simmered and winked in a circular metal dish – we became uneasily aware of throats being cleared and stringed instruments being removed from their cases. The Greeks were, and no doubt still are, understandably proud of their music – half-European, half-Asiatic, and oddly similar, in its plangent melancholy, to the Irish music I had come to love so much – and once the plates had been cleared away and further bottles produced, our lorry drivers and the restaurant owner decided to treat us to a selection of Greek folk songs. No sooner had they struck up than they were joined by a surprising number of locals who mysteriously materialized from the seemingly empty countryside around, sauntering in from the darkness like actors strolling on stage, singing loudly as they advanced upon us.

All this was fair enough, if somewhat embarrassing, occasioning as it did a good deal of gazing at the toes of my blue and white Ted Heath sailing shoes, a fixed smile clipped firmly into place; but inevitably the moment came when our jovial hosts insisted on our repaying them in kind. I have had a particular dread of any form of community singing since my schooldays, when my housemaster forbade me to take part in inter-house singing competitions on the grounds that my tuneless drone would lead to our instant disqualification, and ordered me to stand at the back and mouth the words instead; and while ffenella and Jill and Shore struck up with 'Abide with Me' and 'The Old Bull and Bush' in tremulous, uncertain tones, I found myself overcome – as so often on that trip, since such singalongs cropped up with distressing regularity – by a sudden, incapacitating attack of coughing or by an urgent need to find a lavatory. Both these wheezes could, if cunningly deployed, be spun out long enough to enable our shamingly modest stock of songs to be depleted: but no sooner had my fellow-travellers wavered to a halt, enabling me to emerge from my hiding-place with an unconvincing nonchalance, than a fresh horror was upon us.

Separating into pairs, each couple joined by a handkerchief, or linked together like members of a rugger scrum preparing to take the plunge, the lorry drivers and the locals hurled themselves all at once into a display of Greek dancing, drumming their heels in the dust, their arms outstretched to either side and their fingers clicking with demonic glee. As the music grew ever wilder, and the dust rose like a miniature sandstorm, we consulted amongst ourselves in urgent, crisis-laden tones. How on earth would we cope when the music stopped and the time came round – as it inevitably would – for a display of English national dancing? Should we borrow some broomsticks to bang together in a simulated Morris dance? Ought we attempt a waltz or a fox-trot, conjuring up horrid memories of schoolboy bafflement on the dance floor, while all about me fresh-faced boys named Nigel and Julian glided to and fro with effortless mastery? Or could we pass ourselves off as improbable Irishmen and tackle the kind of jig that was so familiar a feature of the news in Gaelic in our favourite cartoon cinema in Grafton Street? For once our luck was in, for our lorry driver suddenly looked at his watch, gave a cry of alarm and, after draining his glass and shaking hands with the other lorry drivers, the locals and the mustachioed café owner, hurried us away.

We spent the next ten days or so trundling slowly round Greece in the kind of golden haze of which – and not only in retrospect – such student holidays are made: sleeping on beaches, inspecting ancient monuments, eating interminable meals and thinking ourselves quite exceptionally clever and waggish and lucky to be alive. In Delphi we spotted the Junior Dean of Trinity trotting rapidly towards us, clad in his customary uniform of heavy tweed, woollen scarf and charcoal-coloured fisherman's hat, his lips moving vigorously as he rehearsed his thoughts on Burke or the Act of Union; he greeted us politely, without in any way changing speed or deviating from his course, raised his hat with a courteous, old-fashioned movement, and vanished round a bend in the road, heading briskly off in the direction of Athens.

Later that same day I unwisely decided to emulate ffenella, who had discarded her sandals as part of a general rhapsody to nature; but whereas ffenella's feet appeared to be naturally calloused or impervious to harm, mine rapidly frazzled on the scorching tarmac, coming up in enormous orange blisters that made me look as though I were walking about on pieces of Pears soap. After a very short time I was incapable of even hobbling, and lay rigid on the side of the road while the others looked for a lift to take us to Athens, where I went straight to the hospital to have my blisters lanced. The hospital – to which we returned a day or two later to sell our blood – bore a strong resemblance to a battleground, and I found myself surrounded by groaning Greeks with their arms in slings and their heads swathed in blood-stained bandages, and jostled by trollies on which reclined the victims of horrendous car crashes or uncomfortable entanglements with various items of machinery; I hardly dared to produce my ignoble blisters – let alone explain the reason for their being there – which were briskly dealt with by a disapproving nurse with a black moustache, who dabbed them with an impressive mauve liquid and waved me away with a scowl.

Ffenella, on the other hand, was an instant success with the Athenians, and quickly made her mark with an army of hellenic Hectors; so much so that, after a very short time, Shore and Jill and I found ourselves effectively deserted. One good by-product of ffenella's appointments elsewhere was a temporary improvement in my normally excellent relations with Shore. Although Shore liked ffenella well enough, he was understandably irritated by the appalling effect she had on his old room-mate and travelling companion, and evidently believed that my behaviour in ffenella's presence was like that of a man under the influence of some damaging drug; his disapproval would, from time to time, manifest itself in the form of an occasional lecture aimed in our direction and accompanied by much wagging of the umbrella – which, I was glad to see, he was still carrying despite temperatures that were soaring into treble figures.

Such reconciliation, welcome as it was, was jeopardized once more as we left Athens on the last leg of our journey, following the coast round to Thessalonika, and so east to Istanbul. Only once on this long journey do I remember our all travelling together, when an antiquated lorry carrying crates of beer ground to a halt on spotting us sitting by the roadside, and its driver – a pot-bellied, hairy-chested figure in a sleeveless vest – insisted that Jill and ffenella should climb in beside him, while Shore and I perched among the crates behind. This unusual drayman had, ffenella later explained, conceived an overpowering passion for the pallid, reclusive figure of Jill and had spent more time than was wise taking his eyes off the road in order to squeeze her upper arm in an appreciative manner, like a housewife testing the ripeness of a melon, and explaining in incomprehensible English how much he admired the almost waxen whiteness of her skin. When night fell, he invited us to sample some of his wares, snapping off the crown tops with his back teeth and handing us bottle after bottle with which to wash down whatever food we had with us; after which he took Jill by the hand and pulled her unprotesting into some bushes, from which various puffing and grunting sounds soon emanated, leaving the three of us staring at one another in silence, too overcome by this sudden turn of events to speak – Shore and I utterly bemused by this sudden irruption of the physical into our world of virginal whimsicality, and ffenella slightly stunned that, for the first and only time, Jill's modest, more watery charms should be so obviously preferred to her own.

Although we met up in the evenings, sleeping on beaches as often as we could, the rather strained relations between our two groups merely excited still further my futile infatuation with ffenella – an infatuation that reached (or failed to reach) a climax one evening a mile or two from the Turkish border. After some row of a suitably childish kind, ffenella and I decided to leave Shore and Jill to their own devices – I hardly dared look my old room-mate in the face as ffenella picked up her rucksack and stumped off, leaving me trailing in her wake, making rueful and apologetic noises as I went - and find a place of our own in which to spend the night. We were about to doss down on the side of the road when a friendly policeman offered us the use of his cell, which was empty and - he optimistically assumed - unlikely to be needed that night.

The four of us had spent innumerable nights stretched innocently out in our sleeping bags side by side, like a team of elderly scouts and guides taking part in some wholesome and muscular weekend on the North Downs: the prospect of sharing a cell - alone! - with ffenella was not merely beyond my most fevered dreams, but threw me into an ecstasy of garrulous fear. As we laid out our sleeping bags, side by side and shockingly close, and began to unpack our rucksacks and even - oh heavens! - to take off our shoes, I found myself talking, very fast and with an alarming fluency, as though addressing a packed and appreciative lecture hall crammed with jam-making ladies from the WI, about apses and mosaics and the churches we had inspected over the last few days and the great heresies that had riven the early Church and why it was (here I began to fail a little) that the Greeks blessed with two fingers raised and the Romans with three (or was it the other way round?).

Looking up from unlacing my Ted Heath sailing shoes - by now I had moved on to the Monophysites, and my mind was racing ahead to encompass the Pelagian Heresy as well - I noticed with a start of dismay that ffenella had not only removed her shirt but, far from expressing any interest whatsoever in the Council of Chalcedon, was asking me in the husky, sultry tones associated with the temptresses of stage and screen whether her back - naked, and within inches of my trembling hands - had *really* caught the sun? This, surely, was the moment for which my entire life - or at least my life since I had first spotted her aboard the Holyhead-Dun Laoghaire boat in a Force Eight gale, a copy of *The Tin Drum* clutched firmly in one hand - had been but a prelude: I knew exactly how Marcello Mastroianni or Hector or the amorous middle-aged Copt in his ninth year reading agriculture or the great army of Salopians in their hacking jackets and tubular corduroy trousers would have proved themselves masters of the situation, and I could even envisage - oh horrid thought! - Mr Jawleyford advancing hotly upon ffenella, peeling off his mustard-coloured huckster's jacket as he went and rubbing his hands together, a curious twisted smile enlivening his unusual features.

As it was, I swiftly averted my gaze, fixing it firmly on the ceiling instead; far from answering ffenella's innocuous enquiry, I entertained her to a short lecture on the Emperor Justinian before stumbling away to the prison lavatory next door. There I was overcome by an attack of diarrhoea; and crouching unhappily over the porcelain hole in the ground, which was unpleasingly choked with aged melon rinds, I found it impossible to suppress an uncomfortable feeling that the trip – and my relationship with ffenella, such as it was – had reached some kind of inglorious watershed, and that from now on it would be downhill all the way. When I got back to the cell ffenella was zipped up tightly in her sleeping bag, asleep or feigning sleep, her face to the wall beyond.

* * *

Of the rest of that trip I need say little. After the gold and blue and white of Greece, Turkey seemed dour and grey; it was raining when we reached Istanbul, with great puddles in the streets and clouds massing over the Bosphorus. Shore and I were friends once more, and spent most of the time together, complaining about ffenella and Jill and burbling among ourselves in a familiar, comfortable manner. We visited the harem in the Topkapi Palace, and it seemed as dead and as dusty as everything else in this fabled city we had come so far to see; we drank a good deal of amber-coloured tea from tulip-shaped glasses; on a trip to the Black Sea coast we strayed inadvertently into a military zone and were arrested as spies, and Shore's umbrella was carefully dismantled by gloomy Mongolian-looking soldiers who, for some unfathomable reason, had reason to believe that it contained a hidden camera. Only the day before we took the long train home did we glimpse, in a tiny church out by the city walls, the Byzantium we had come for: the gold and black and white mosaics, the olive-eyed, melancholy saints, the hands raised up to bless, the incomprehensible words of terror and consolation.

* * *

Although Shore and ffenella and I remained in the same history set for the rest of our time at Trinity, snoozing through the same lectures on the War of the Spanish Succession and writing almost identical essays on the Blessed Oliver Plunkett or the Tribulations of Parnell, I saw very little of her after we had said a somewhat stiff goodbye at Liverpool Street Station, and gone our various ways – not because we ever fell out, but because the moment (if moment it ever was) had passed, and our paths led us in different directions, and into very different lives. And yet, as my time at Trinity receded ever more rapidly into the past, I found that I looked back on the months I had known ffenella with that particular, poignant nostalgia one reserves for the unattained, and for that drunken, delirious mixture of innocence and optimism that, once lost, can never be recovered. I gathered that she had married someone from Trinity immediately after leaving university; that she had gone to live in Hong Kong; that her children were at boarding school in England, and then – as time passed – at university themselves. And then, a year or two ago, the phone rang and a husky, familiar voice announced itself. 'Jeremy, it's ffenella here ...'

CHAPTER SIX

The Sporting Life

Among the many agreeable features of English films made in the 1930s are those scenes set in cosy-looking boarding houses somewhere in the inner suburbs. The landlady's favourite lodger – and, it goes without saying, the heroine of this mild, domestic drama – works as a secretary in an office full of curious, tubular furniture; her boss is invariably irascible and overweight, and wears spats, a frock-coat and pince-nez. Every evening her impulsive, clean-cut admirer – clad in an ankle-length overcoat, his large felt hat clamped to his breast as though he were about to burst into song – comes to collect her for a night on the town: this being an eminently respectable house, he is prevented from bounding up the stairs after the object of his adoration by the firm but kindly proprietress, who ushers him into the 'lounge', where the other inmates are resting their heads against the antimacassars, their pipes squealing and groaning as they struggle to digest Mrs B's evening meal of Irish stew followed by spotted dick and custard, and a nice bit of cheddar. These fellow-guests, most of whom are long-term residents, usually include a careworn clerk, bullied and underpaid at work but – like the key character in *Darts are Trumps*, my candidate for the finest film ever made – capable of an unexpected heroism; a dubious major with a carbuncular nose and a taste for the hard stuff; a disapproving frump of the school matron variety, who glares at the major and browbeats the clerk; and a jolly commercial traveller in dazzling tweeds, who joshes Mrs B, ignores the frump's withering glances, cracks jokes with the major of the kind associated with itinerant brush salesmen in half-timbered road-houses or 'four ale bars', and spends a good deal of his time rummaging in his case of samples for something to cheer up the heroine when she and the chap in the ankle-length coat have had a lovers' tiff.

Ever since I can remember I have, as a lover of South Kensington and Seaford, found boarding houses and small residential hotels – and particularly those that have come down in the world or have pretensions to gentility – wonderfully touching and comic; indeed, the only possible excuse for reading most actors' memoirs is the faint hope of hearing once again some legendary tale of the hazards of theatrical digs in Hartlepool or Birkenhead, of younger versions of Sir Donald Wolfit explaining to case-hardened landladies in rolling, resonant tones that remuneration, madam, is imminently antici-pated, whereupon all outstanding obligations will be immediately discharged.

During our second year at Trinity Shore and Ian and I inhabited digs of a near theatrical kind in Ballsbridge, a prim and respectable suburb of Dublin, the inhabitants of which were much given to twitching their lace curtains and exchanging disapproving gossip in low whispers, one hand raised to the mouth like conspirators of the old-fashioned variety. Unlike the traditional theatrical landlady, with her drooping cigarette, pink dressing gown, curlers and rolling pin at the ready, Mrs Brady was a bustling, apple-cheeked, house-proud little woman who spent her spare time applying Brasso to the stair rods and the gong in the hall table, and rearranging the plastic flowers that are so important a feature of boarding-house life. Mr Brady, on the other hand, was the soul of lethargy: after breakfast he would rouse himself to the extent of changing a light bulb or mending a fuse, after which he would sink exhausted into an armchair in a small back room, unseal a bottle of Jameson's, and watch the racing on television. Since Mr Brady was a retired bookie, this was – I hope – charged up to the tax man as some kind of professional expense.

The Bradys' house was a modest late-Victorian terraced affair of the kind one might find in Clapham or Fulham. Into this small space they managed to jam eight students, four 'regulars', a half-witted maid and their own four children: since every available room appeared to be crammed with lodgers of some kind or other, I could only assume that the Bradys slept in the small room under the stairs where Mr Brady, worn out by his labours, enjoyed the racing, while their children were laid out on racks in the kitchen, like apples in an attic. Shore and Ian and I shared a room with a mahogany wardrobe so enormous that the Bradys would have been well advised to leave it in the garden and fill it with additional guests; our fellow-lodgers from Trinity included a Woosterish Catholic peer and the heir to a whisky empire, and the presence of such grandees lent Mrs Brady's establishment a certain cachet. In a room by himself lived a lonely Wykhamist, who spoke to no one and was not spoken to in turn: when, one morning, the lavatory was blocked in a particularly obstructive manner, and Mr Brady had come hurrying to the scene carrying, for some curious reason, an axe in one hand and a saw in the other, it was generally assumed that the Wykhamist was the Guilty Man, and a hush fell over the breakfast tables as he made his furtive entrance.

Like the characters in the English films I so admired, we were assiduous in exchanging polite pleasantries over the breakfast tables, paying particular attention to the 'regulars'. Since the Trinity terms were so very brief, and some of the 'regulars' had been lodging with the Bradys for the last twenty years or so, they were – quite rightly – treated with rather more decorum than the tiresome and transitory riff-raff from Trinity College. They included the inevitable commercial traveller, replete with nicotine-stained fingers and a light drizzle of dandruff about the shoulder blades; a sad-looking elderly man with a livid purple birthmark and a nervous facial tic; and a stout, blousy chain-smoker in her early sixties who looked as though she stubbed her cigarettes out in her inexpertly peroxided hair. In those painful, embarrassing silences that descend like a freezing fog over even the most congenial of boarding-house meals, we listened agog as the commercial traveller – speaking, for once, in the discreet whisper that such solemnities demand – placed the inevitable order for orange juice followed by fried eggs, fried bacon, fried tomato, fried potato bread and fried puddings, black and white; watched with a horrid fascination as the cigarette-stubbing lady stubbed out her first of the day not, alas, in her hair, but among the remnants of bacon rind, and daintily dabbed her lips with a corner of her table napkin, leaving on it a bright vermilion smear; and waited glued to the edges of our chairs for the half-witted maid to skid up on a piece of bacon rind with a tray in either hand, or produce a pot of early-morning tea to which she had somehow forgotten to add any tea-leaves.

It goes without saying that we Trinity types thought ourselves wags of the highest order, and several cuts above the 'regulars', whom we derided behind their backs; no doubt they found us, as students almost always are, tiresome, arrogant and infantile to a wearisome degree. How boring it must have been to hear us stumbling about the flower-beds and knocking over milk-bottles and scrabbling ineffectively at the keyhole after a long evening spent in the Dublin pubs! How aggravating to have to listen to Shore's and my appreciative mirth as Ian appeared for breakfast wearing a gigantic pair of plasticine spectacles! How large and loud and oafish we must have seemed as we boomed about the house with a patronizing and proprietorial air, superior smiles playing about our lips as we beheld the profusion of doilies and cake-stands and dralon three-piece suites!

We soon discovered that Dublin landladies – with the remarkable exception of Mrs Todd and her television-watching husband with ancestral roots in distant Teddington – combined a garrulous charm with a flinty probity about money matters and an interest in portion control that went well beyond the kind of thing taught by men in white coats in colleges of catering. Mrs Brady kept a sharp eye on the comestibles, putting out brick-shaped individual items of butter so small that a magnifying glass was needed to track them down, and only reluctantly allowing the sauce bottles out of her immediate control (we were pleased to note that on this side of the water HP Sauce went under the name of TD Sauce – TDs being the Irish equivalents of MPs); like Mrs Todd, she was a keen believer in the six o'clock fry-up, but the sausages looked like tiny vessels adrift in a great white sea of china, the eggs must have been laid by chickens of stunted growth, while the slices of soda bread were sternly rationed to two apiece, topped up with a smudge of luminous raspberry jam. Nor was there any question of a late-night snack of the kind provided by Mrs Todd, and so ungratefully spurned: as we trudged round to the fish and chip shops after the pubs had closed, or tucked into a Brylcreem-coated banana split or a waterlogged hot dog in one of the heavily mirrored hamburger joints on O'Connell Street, lit up with puce- and lime-coloured neon strips, I thought with a twinge of regret of the fried egg I had tossed, with such cavalier disdain, over the Blackrock garden wall, and vowed that I would never refuse such offerings again. Luckily Shore was a modest feeder, toying with a grain or two of rice before pushing his plate aside with a sigh of satisfaction, while Ian was, from time to time, overcome by an urge to lose weight, struggling to avert his gaze as I tried to press upon him his fair share of soda bread and fluorescent raspberry jam; so with their pickings and a restorative trip to the fish and chipper, I managed to keep body and soul together.

Nor was Mrs Brady's managerial expertise restricted to the dining-room. As befits a busy and practical landlady, she had invested in a great many sets of nylon sheets, most of which were too small for the beds in question and – since these were pioneering days in the world of man-made fibres – extremely slippery, with the result that the pillow, similarly swathed in nylon, shot away from under one as soon as one laid one's head upon it, like a bar of soap in the bath, and needed ideally to be nailed or chained in place; while the restless sleeper – of whom I was one – could easily find himself sliding out of bed in the middle of the night, dragging the bedclothes with him as he crashed to the floor with a grunt. The blankets themselves tended to the threadbare and the undersized, and lacking in quantity as well: in winter we went to bed in jerseys and socks, carefully laying our overcoats, our tweed jackets and – if we happened to have them with us – our gowns on top of the blankets and the rose-patterned nylon eiderdown before retiring for the night.

Baths were a problem in most digs, in that a good many people – including, in our case, the commercial traveller, the man with the nervous facial tic, the blousy matron who stubbed cigarettes out in her hair, and the constipated Wykhamist – battled for possession of the bathroom at the same time; the hot water in the bath was measured out by feeding shillings into a meter, and two bob – the price of a pint of stout – seemed a good deal to pay for a hasty dip into four or five inches of tepid water while angry fellow-lodgers muttered and banged on the door outside, dancing up and down in their dressing-gown and slippers as they struggled to keep the cold at bay, and twirling their sponge bags round and round as they fought, in vain, to master their irritation. Instead, on two or three days a week we took our towels and our sponge bags with us into Trinity, and headed for the College Baths. After, perhaps, a 9.30 lecture on Mercantilism or the Blessed Oliver Plunkett (some part of whose anatomy, pickled, Shore and I had inspected in a Catholic church in Drogheda), we would refresh ourselves with coffee and a glutinous cherry or marzipan bun in Bewley's admirable Edwardian restaurant in Grafton Street, while all about us tweeded Dublin ladies in pork pie hats gossiped and guzzled, their shopping neatly stacked about their well-shod feet and their little fingers politely crooked above the cup; then we would stroll back to Trinity and spend the next hour or so, until it was time for a drink, wallowing in one of the gigantic late-Victorian baths, while all about us the rugger-buggers roared their dreadful refrains and described in gloating detail scenes of mass destruction and bovine drunkenness on the Rugger Club's recent tour of defenceless Home Counties or unsuspecting Oxford and Cambridge colleges, in the course of which hotels had been burned to the ground, glasses and crockery smashed, and rival teams of rugger-buggers debagged and coated in shaving cream.

Although I had never met any of the buggers, I had heard them shouting hoarse commands to one another on the playing fields outside as I dozed over Orpen's four-volume history of the Normans in Ireland in the well-heated Lecky Library on a murky winter's afternoon - the roars punctuated by the dreadful thwack of boot on leather and shrill blasts on the whistle by the referees, diminutive bird-like men in black, accompanied by a peremptory backwards hack of the heel and a matronly pointing of the finger in the direction of the crime. Later, as Shore and I made our way home through the dusk, we came across them trudging towards the changing-rooms at the end of the match - huge, slab-like men with tiny red-rimmed eyes, enormous tree-trunk legs the colour of spam and great square heads topped by tight, bull-like curls, their green and white shirts plastered to their chests and their arms draped round each other's shoulders, like soldiers returning from battle. Many, no doubt, were 'pinks' - the Trinity equivalent of blues - and members of the Knights of the Campanile, the exclusive sportsmen's club from whose rooms above Botany Bay (or so I liked to think, from my reading of *Decline and Fall*) could be heard, of an evening, the coarse strains of rugger songs and the crash of breaking glass.

Only a few years earlier such oafish cries - accompanied by the stinging flick of a towel in the changing-room, the rattle of studs on the tiles and the dangerous, uneasy sense of a pack in pursuit of its prey - would have filled me with a sense of dread and foreboding; as it was I felt - for the first and only time in my institutional career - immune from, and utterly unaffected by, everything I had come to hate about the team spirit and the cult of games at their most intolerant and oppressive. Yet even at Trinity I dropped my guard once or twice, and allowed myself to be persuaded to take part in an impromptu game of football or cricket, seduced and misled by comforting voices assuring me that it didn't matter how bad I was, that no one was taking it seriously anyway, that it was only a game after all, only to find that once on the field even the most jocular of friends became grim-featured and sternly competitive, fighting to get the ball, wildly hacking at one another's shins, failing to find my inability to kick or catch a ball forgivable, let alone comic or entertaining, and submitting me, as I trailed unhappily about the field, to scowls of ferocious disapproval and disdain. Much as I admired the elegance and even – without understanding in the least what they were up to – the technique of particular sportsmen, I combined, as I always had, utter incompetence with a bolshy dislike of anything that smacked of the team, and a fatal inability (later transferred to my professional life, for which team games are so astute a preparation) to understand how anyone could feel so strongly about what seemed to me to be such self-evidently unimportant matters.

For as long as I can remember I have had a blockage about organized games so severe that, to this day, if someone kicks a ball in my direction or invites me to join in a game of rounders I am paralyzed by ancient, atavistic fears and feelings of miserable unmanliness and inadequacy. My misery was aggravated by the assumption that, since I was large and blond and muscular-looking, with a granite jaw and bristling eyebrows of the kind sported by Mr Brezhnev and Denis Healey, I must by definition be a keen and proficient sportsman; from an early age it was assumed by the world at large that I must be an enthusiastic rugger player, so that parents stumped for something to say to this gauche and tongue-tied youth would ask me what I thought of yesterday's game at Twickenham, and look puzzled and rebuffed when – try as I might to let them off the hook and come up with an intelligent reply – it quickly became apparent that I had no idea of what they were talking about.

This assumption that I must be one of nature's scrum forwards was especially absurd, since I had a particular horror of the game, and never began to understand the rules or what was going on all about me. My kindly interrogators were right, however, in assuming that at school I was invariably put in the scrum, where my ears - already numbed by an arctic wind - were wrenched from my head, the man in the row ahead farted rudely in my face as, grunting with effort, he strove to drive the enemy backwards, and all around me sweating spam-coloured tree trunks lunged and hacked. Once the scrum had broken up, I found myself more adrift than ever: because I had no idea of the rules beyond a vague and baffling belief that, for some unexplained reason, one was not allowed to throw the ball forward (was that it?) I was overcome with terror if the ball bounced in my direction, and passed it as quickly and as politely as I could to someone else to look after. This usually turned out to be a member of the rival team, provoking cries of outrage from my team-mates, all of whom were, by now, hot-eyed and heavily besmeared with mud, and rabid with the urge to win.

Sometimes, to my relief, the game moved away from me while I pretended to be retying my bootlace or conscientiously guarding our end of the field from sudden attack: yet even then I was not safe, for all of a sudden, when I was gazing peacefully in the wrong direction, the ball would rocket out of the sky like some ancient, misshapen cannon ball, striking me a terrible blow on the side of the head and bringing me crashing to the ground with a grunt of surprise and annoyance. Seconds later, as I was rising unsteadily to my feet once more, I was invariably overrun by a horde of enemy players sweeping victoriously past to score yet another try, and was crushed to the ground once more; and once again I was subjected to the rage and derision of my fellow-sportsmen, who shunned me as we trailed dejectedly off the field after a massive defeat for which, it seemed, I was almost entirely to blame, and pursued by withering glances as I crept into the noisy cameraderie of the changing-room, hoping in vain to escape detection. Although I was, by the time I was sixteen, one of the largest boys in my house, I had, to my relief, been banned from house matches as too great a liability, and stood instead along the touchline in an overcoat with tiny new boys of twelve or thirteen, their heads barely reaching to my elbow and their thin treble voices mingling with my fruity bass, rising in mighty clouds of steam into the icy afternoon air as we cheered our team to victory of the kind they would almost certainly have been denied had I been shortsightedly picking my way about the field and pointing in the wrong direction.

Although I was equally inept at soccer, it struck me as an altogether superior game, for all the horrors of the tackle – elegant, simple and, apart from the offside rule, vaguely intelligible. All the same, it was something best avoided; and towards the end of my undistinguished school career two friends and I enrolled on a refereeing course. We were the only boys in the entire school to volunteer our services, and our tutor – a lugubrious, literal-minded man in a brown blazer who travelled especially down from Wolverhampton to teach us the mysteries of the game – assured us that by the end of the course we would be quite well enough qualified to referee at Wembley, and he hoped that at least one of us would consider taking up refereeing as a career after leaving school. He little suspected, poor man, that we were only taking the course because it coincided with the games period, and so kept us safely away from the field of play; either way, we must have seemed, even to the most optimistic eye, unpromising material. My fellow volunteers were my closest friend, an excitable youth with a great bush of rust-coloured hair, a twitching, pointed nose and the swooping volubility of an old-fashioned Oxford don, who was quite as bad as I was on the games field, but made up for it by a kind of ferocious bravery – the result, perhaps, of spending his winter holidays hunting in Devon – which was quite beyond my cowardly powers, and won him a grudging, jocular respect; and a small, soft, rather worldly Jewish boy from Golders Green, whose amused disdain for the rites and ranks of public school life I always found extremely congenial and sympathetic, alien and abhorrent as it was to most of those about us.

For several weeks we spent the games period sitting comfortably indoors, leaning up against the hot water pipes in a lofty mid-Victorian classroom, while the man from Wolverhampton drew earnest diagrams on the blackboard and asked us searching questions about the offside rule. Eventually the great day came on which we were to be examined. Another man from the Midlands materialized, also wearing a brown blazer, and clutching important-looking papers; and the testing time was upon us. What shape, he asked us, was the ball? Was the goalkeeper allowed to wear a cap? How many men made up a team? Who or what was Stanley Matthews? Much as I would have liked to fail – for I dreaded having to put theory into practice, and a near-miss might have enabled us to spin the whole happy business out for a further few weeks – I could not; nor could my friend with the shock of rust-coloured hair, nor even the boy from Golders Green, who certainly *hadn't* heard of Stanley Matthews and had difficulties in remembering which was the goalkeeper and which the centre forward. At the next school assembly the headmaster announced with pride that the three of us had distinguished ourselves by becoming the first fully qualified referees in the history of the school, and that he fully expected to see one of us refereeing the Cup Final in the years to come; after which he produced three certificates with our names engraved upon them, and a stunned silence fell upon the school as three of its most unsporting inmates filed eagerly forward to receive this highest of professional distinctions.

Sad to say, nemesis was lurking – as it always did – on the games fields that stretched away at the bottom of the windswept granite hills on which the school was set, like Colditz amidst smiling lawns and rose-embowered gardens. Because my hunting friend was something of a licensed jester, and an altogether more forceful and colourful character than his fellow-referees, he managed to escape lightly: but for the two of us further sorrows were in store. The boy from Golders Green set off for his first – and, as it turned out, his only – appearance as a referee in a smart navy-blue blazer with the school crest on its bosom, and below his knee-length footer shorts he sported a pair of white colonial officer's socks held neatly in place with a pair of garters; I came down to see how he got on, and what tips I could pick up from so experienced a practitioner. It became obvious within minutes that he had lost control of the game: his every decision was greeted by roars of indignation, his tentative peeps on the whistle were rudely ignored, a terrible baying sound rose like a mighty wind – and then, to my horror, I noticed that one of the school's three professional referees had been seized by the heels and was being dragged backwards through the mud before being dumped on the touchline, half-conscious and gasping for air, his blazer and trim white socks now chocolate brown, while the game went on without him. Normally matches were refereed by the chaplain or one of the three geography masters – one of whom had played for Pegasus and as an amateur for England, flashing about the field in voluminous black shorts and a white flannel shirt with the sleeves rolled up – so until now referees had been immune from persecution; but as I looked at the prostrate form of my friend – who appeared to have lapsed into a coma, moaning and tossing his head from side to side, and foaming slightly at the lips – I wondered what humiliations lay ahead, and whether qualifying as a referee, for all its short-term benefits, had not been one of our graver miscalculations.

Next day I too donned my blazer and pocketed a whistle, and set off trembling for the footer fields. No sooner had the game begun than I realized that a great gulf was set between the man from Wolverhampton's neat, immobile diagrams on the blackboard in the soporific classroom and this turbulent, muddy arena peopled by fast-moving, fierce-looking seventeen-year-olds intent on victory, all of whom were hearty, aggressive lovers of changing rooms and showers, thoroughly at home in the brutal, virile world of jockstraps and shin guards and jars of dubbin, and far more knowledgeable about the game than I would ever be, for all my certificates signed by the headmaster and counter-signed by the man in the brown blazer.

As the game surged up and down the pitch I puffed heavily along behind, wishing I could see through my specs, which had rapidly misted over and were plastered with tiny spots of mud, and wondering whether I could, unnoticed, clip a quarter of an hour off either half, and so reduce the torment of it all; and then, all of a sudden, a great cheer went up from one of the teams and its touchline supporters, and I dimly discerned an aggrieved goalkeeper retrieving the ball from the back of the net. I knew at once what I should do: I blew a confident blast on my whistle, and pointed, with a swivelling motion of the body, to the middle of the pitch to indicate that a goal had been scored, and that the game should restart in the middle. As I strolled back to supervise the kick-off, I felt a sudden surge of confidence: plainly there was nothing to this refereeing business so long as one kept one's nerve and blew the whistle in a determined and unequivocal way.

Alas, I had relaxed too soon; for hardly had I blown the whistle before the losing side were pressing all about me, angrily waving their arms in the air and pointing out that the scoring player had, in fact, been blatantly offside, and that it was quite wrong of me not to have noticed this, let alone awarded a goal. They so obviously felt very strongly about it, and seemed so terribly cross and over-excited, that in order to keep them happy I blew another blast on my whistle and announced that, after all, a goal had not been scored: at which the other team – which until then had been beaming and rubbing their hands together – rounded on me with equal ferocity and insisted that I reinstate their goal. It seemed I could not win, however hard I tried, and that I had a friend in neither team; in my eagerness to satisfy both teams, and avoid the fate of my colleague from Golders Green, I suggested that I award an honorary goal to both sides, but this only drove them to further ecstacies of rage. All this time the minutes were ticking away, and before we could settle the matter I had blown the whistle yet again to announce half time and the bearing on of oranges to restore the tired and indignant players. During the interval the two captains went away to complain to the geography masters, one of whom promptly appeared in full refereeing kit, as though he had been expecting a call, and I was summarily dismissed. My career as a professional referee had run its course, and I knew with a sinking feeling that, like the boy from Golders Green, I would never tread the sacred turves of Wembley or White Hart Lane.

Some weeks later I got it into my head – for a quite inexplicable reason – that if I volunteered to serve at Communion this might somehow enable me to miss some footer games. This involved going to see the junior padre, who was altogether more high church than the pipe-smoking senior padre, for whom serving a Communion was the thin end of the wedge and far more remote from the injunctions of Our Lord than a brisk bit of refereeing followed by a hearty singalong in the showers. The junior padre was a kind, much ridiculed figure with a nose like a root vegetable, spectacles bound up with tape, and straw-coloured hair, and he carried with him an odour not simply of sanctity but of damp hay, as though he too had spent a night or two in the manger. He seemed surprised to see me since, though good at scripture, I had never evinced any signs of especial piety, and most of the boys who volunteered for this kind of work were of the simpering 'pretty boy' variety who enjoyed dressing up as choir boys and, no doubt, applying a dab or two of rouge or even mascara before making their impressive entrance. (I hasten to say that this had nothing whatsoever to do with the junior padre, who was not in the least that way inclined, but was rumoured to cast longing looks in the direction of one of the younger matrons.) Despite the ridicule of my friends, and the somewhat louche company I was compelled to keep at unreasonably early hours of the morning, I rather enjoyed banging importantly about behind the altar rails, carrying enormous silver salvers of the kind held aloft by champion darts players or rose growers and brimming flagons of delicious-tasting wine, the filling of which was preceded by a companionable popping of corks.

Not surprisingly, none of this won me a moment's reprieve from the world of sport; nor did it - as I had half-hoped - translate me from my endemic doubt and agnosticism into a true believer. Neither of my parents had (or have) any time for religion, which my father dismissed as the most fearful bosh and self-delusion; I had (and still have) a strong religious urge, based more on a strong sense of the sad impermanence of things than on the intricacies of faith, and a great love for the symbols and stories of Christianity, but remained far too much of an old-fashioned rationalist, and far too depressed and overawed by the longevity and immensity of the universe, and the unimportance of our part in it, to be able to accept formal religion as anything other than a form of spitting in the wind, beautiful, consoling and wonderfully wise, but sadly all in vain. For all my doubts, however, I loved no language better than that of the Authorised Version - greatly preferring it to Shakespeare, with whom I never quite got to grips - the 1662 Prayer Book and the great eighteenth- and nineteenth-century hymns (and regarded their demotion a few years later, and their disappearance from the language and the culture of our children, as a work of philistinism comparable to striding into the National Gallery and ripping up all its contents, or dynamiting Durham Cathedral); and few moments in life have ever been more magical than the final chapel service of the summer term, when we sang 'The day Thou gavest, Lord, has ended' in a darkened chapel, and the shadows lengthened on the lawn outside, and eight long weeks of freedom lay ahead.

On the games field, however, the summer term brought only the mildest of improvements. I loved the sight and the sound of cricket (provided others were doing the playing) and found the toc of bat on ball and the smell of linseed oil and the spectacle of vicars and men in blazers striped like Joseph's Coat of Many Colours loafing in deck chairs as magical and as redolent of summer as any other right-minded boy: but I had more than once suffered the disapproval meted out to those who go in to bat for the house as the last man in, with only one run to win, and are promptly bowled out first ball. I disliked the speed and the hardness of cricket balls, and the way in which they stung the palms or caught the end of one's fingers but-end on, sending a terrible judder through one's frame; and since I had never owned a jockstrap or worn a protective batsman's 'box' I had, more than once, been caught amidships by a flying ball and lain groaning in front of the stumps while my fellow-cricketers urged me to get a grip on myself, and the assembled parents and visitors sternly averted their gaze.

My suggestion that cricket should be played with tennis balls was disdained by the sporting set: however, I discovered several other cowards and incompetents who shared my heretical views – some even going so far as to prefer French cricket to the English variety, a solecism similar to taking a dab of French mustard in preference to the English sort – and we would, from time to time, take along with us to matches a tennis ball which, after an over or two, we craftily substituted for the real thing. This excited a good deal of irritation among the serious-minded players present, disconcerting in particular grim-featured batsmen who, after spending a good deal of time consulting with the finger-wagging umpire and digging great holes in the pitch and gazing severely around the field, were thrown entirely off balance when a tennis ball came slowly loping through the air towards them, bouncing a good deal on its way to the stumps or being carried quite off course by a sudden gust of wind. Sometimes we were in luck, in that the rival team were only too relieved to play with a tennis ball and, equally importantly, to forge the results in the large green scoring books; my fellow incompetents included the Jewish boy from Golders Green (who was even more enthusiastic about tennis balls than I was), a most likeable boy with a high-pitched, quavering voice who was unkindly known as 'Grandma' (he has since made a name for himself as a choirmaster specializing in mediaeval and Renaissance music, and quite right too), and my Parsee friend with the unusual underclothes, who was later expelled from his Oxford college after falling through a greenhouse from a great height.

On those afternoons in winter in which we were spared soccer or rugger we had to go for house runs over the granite hills, in the course of which the Parsee and I were always firmly to the rear, walking whenever possible and breaking into a slow jog – more akin to running on the spot – whenever we saw a games-loving prefect hovering bossily about to chivvy the laggards and make sure that no one took a short cut home. I disliked those runs intensely, both for their own sake and for the drastic effect they had on my bowels, immobilized for much of the week by the fact that many of the house lavatories had no locks on the doors, which we sensitive souls found binding to a degree. This sudden urge to go to the lavatory usually overcame me in a built-up area, presenting me with an almost insoluble dilemma: if I continued running I would almost certainly unleash my load into my shorts, which would be embarrassing and disagreeable to say the least; if I dropped back to our customary walking pace, my legs crossed and my buttocks firmly clamped together, I stood in immediate danger of attracting the attention of a sporting prefect, who would lash me into action and so bring about the state of affairs I was above all anxious to avoid. I'm glad to say I struggled through my running career without fouling my shorts, but it was a close shave.

In the last winter of my career the Parsee and I both decided to take part in the annual cross-country race. This event was one of the high points of the school calendar: caps were awarded to the first ten arrivals – the winner was at once acclaimed a hero of the school – and junior boys and the masters were expected to turn out to watch the ninety-odd competitors come puffing onto the main games field in the direction of the final tape after a strenuous eight-mile run, much of it over and along the famous granite hills. Although my father had won a cap some twenty-five years before, I saw no point in trying to compete and decided instead – in a perverse and childish way – that I would do my best to come in last. Unfortunately the Parsee shared this ignoble ambition, and since he was spindly almost to the point of emaciation and devoid of any visible muscles, he stood a better chance than I did of carrying off the prize.

We were taken by bus to the starting point in the middle of a muddy field, where we found our fellow-runners eagerly jumping up and down on the spot and bending at the knees and massaging their thighs in readiness for the ordeal that lay ahead; others were peeling off jerseys and track suits and climbing into spiked running shoes which left neat round holes in the earth, like those in a pepper pot. Rather reluctantly, since it was a wet and blustery day, I removed my jersey and trousers and added them to the great pile of discarded garments that were to be taken back to school in the bus to await our return in an hour or so; the Parsee, I noticed – with a tremor of alarm – was making no effort to disrobe, and was evidently planning to compete in grey flannel trousers, a thick cricket jersey and a long red woollen scarf; and whereas I was running in gym shoes, he appeared to be wearing a pair of regulation black leather lace-ups. Behind us the three geography masters strode eagerly up and down in gum boots and duffel coats, flapping their arms and blowing on their hands to keep them warm; and then, all of a sudden, a whistle blew and we were off, streaming uphill across the open field towards the distant hills, like a hunt in pursuit of a fox.

At the far end of the field was a small wood; once we had reached this, and were safely out of sight of the geography masters, who had climbed gratefully aboard the bus and were heading we knew not where, the Parsee and I lent against a tree to recover our breath – for we had felt obliged to run across the field at least, in the course of which we had already dropped well behind the rest of the field – before proceeding at a gentle, civilized stroll, chatting of this and that and deriding our ludicrous fellow-athletes, the last of whom could be seen trailing away in the distance ahead of us. But, laugh and joke as we may, we knew that, before long, one of us would have to break away and make a serious bid to be last; and, as we came over the crest of the hills and saw the lights of the school twinkling below us – by now it was getting dark, and our nearest rivals were showered and changed and preparing themselves for a celebratory supper of battered spam and eggs – we fought for mastery with all the cunning of which we were capable. The Parsee would sit in silence on the only available rock in the midst of a desolate mountain bog until, from sheer discomfort, I was forced to forge ahead; I then sheltered from the rain under the only tree for miles around, and watched with satisfaction as the Parsee edged uncomfortably ahead with all the speed of a man enmeshed in treacle. In the end, though, the weather got the better of me: clad only in my football shorts and a rugger shirt, I was less well equipped than the Parsee to withstand the rain and the cold, and as we started the steep downhill stroll for home I reluctantly took off the brakes, my rival padding triumphantly behind.

It was quite dark as I passed the winning post, and the bell for supper was ringing as I turned the corner into the yard of my house, where my fellow runners were engaged in their familiar pursuit of kicking tennis balls about. My housemaster was waiting to receive us; he denounced us in ringing tones, his voice trembling with anger and indignation, and once again I found myself wondering – as I wondered whenever he lashed himself into a frenzy of fury over a defeat on the football field, or the failure of our house to produce a single cap for cricket – how it was possible for a grown man to take such matters seriously.

Only once did I gain my housemaster's approval in the sporting arena, and that was when I reached the finals of the heavyweight boxing competition. Although I had – or so it seemed to me – a mild and retiring disposition, with no wish whatsoever to strike anyone on the nose or in any other part of the anatomy, my iron jaw and beefy frame steered me firmly in the direction of the boxing ring in much the same way as they had set me down in the second row of the scrum, only with slightly more success. I was completely indifferent as to whether I lost or won, but I found that if I kept both arms fully extended in front of me, like a sleepwalker advancing down a flight of stairs, administering the occasional polite prod with the left hand, I could keep the enemy at bay and survive the three obligatory rounds without too many blows to the nose of the kind that sent the tears springing to the eyes, or terrible gasp-inducing thrusts to the stomach; and now, to my alarm, I discovered that by these means I had not only vanquished a whole string of opponents, some of blue-jawed and hairy-chested ferocity, but was due to appear in the finals, to be held in the gym before the entire school at the end of term. The boy from Golders Green and the Parsee – neither of whom had ever set foot in the ring – attributed my success to two further peculiarities of style, both of which, they claimed, disconcerted the opposition while provoking a certain amount of sympathetic merriment among the onlookers: whenever I was struck, I let fly an inadvertent fart, and whenever I lashed back I did so to the accompaniment of profuse apologies, so that the familiar grunts and hisses of the ring were replaced and over-ridden by staccato, booming cries of 'Oh Gosh I *am* sorry' and 'Are you sure you're all right?'. Both these keen sportsmen volunteered to be my seconds, and busily set about preparing me for the Great Night.

My opponent was a huge, placid boy from Solihull with big, bovine blue eyes, a heart of gold and a remarkable shortage of intellect. I knew he took his boxing career seriously, and that he longed above all to be able to bear the heavyweight cup home to the parental mantelpiece; and that he was stronger, fiercer and a very much better boxer than I could ever hope, or want, to be. Shortly before the day of the finals, I drew him aside and – speaking very slowly and hyphenating my words like the characters in *Rainbow* or *Tiny Tim*, and carefully avoiding any puzzling or ambiguous turns of phrase – I made it clear to him that I was more than happy for him to win, that the important thing was to avoid actually hurting one another, and that we should, while providing a full and persuasive display of ducking and feinting and weaving, exchange entirely bogus blows, sending one another reeling against the ropes with punches that, to the innocent eye, carried the clout of a Marciano, but in effect struck home with the power of a powder puff. As I explained my stratagem he nodded in a slow, benevolent way, and we spent some minutes practising fraudulent upper cuts and straight lefts to the body, jabbing and banging and bopping one another like fair-haired versions of Randolph Turpin or Sugar Ray Robinson. I felt greatly cheered by my opponent's thoughtful and cooperative approach: so much so that, far from tossing sleeplessly in the dorm, I slept soundly on the night before the fight, ate a hearty school lunch instead of toying listlessly with my toad in the hole and tapioca pudding, and set off for the gym, accompanied by my seconds – both of whom had equipped themselves with white roll-necked jerseys and carried sponges and a towel – with a cheerful, self-confident smile, and the springy, elastic gait of the natural athlete.

The heavyweight bout was, as it always seemed to be, the climax of the evening; we waited our turn in the wings, where all about us bantamweights and featherweights and middleweights and whole armies of other weights whose names escape the memory lashed at hapless punchballs in a frenzy of pugilistic fervour or drew on their gloves or sat, trembling, with their heads in their hands or, the battle over, were carried back from the ring by their seconds, blood pouring from their noses and their eyes the colour of prunes. As we sat there, I continued to impress upon my opponent my willingness – indeed my eagerness – to concede defeat in exchange for the avoidance of black eyes and bloodshed of the kind we saw all about us – had tomato ketchup been available I would have hastily pressed it into service – and, as before, he continued to nod and smile and offer me every reassurance.

Eventually our time came; our names and weights were announced, we stepped smartly into the ring, and a great cheer went up from the assembled boys and masters. I noticed with a sudden spasm of unease that whereas I was lounging in my corner with my legs crossed, stifling a yawn with a giant padded hand and jesting lightly with my sporting seconds, my opponent was flexing his knees and bouncing up and down and taking wild swipes at the air with his fists; but I could only assume that he was a far better actor than I had given him credit for. The bell rang for the first round; we touched gloves, I whispered 'Don't forget', and we were away. Within seconds I realized that something had gone badly wrong: my patient tutorials had been quite forgotten in the excitement of the hour, and the prospect of carrying the trophy home to Solihull had driven all else from a mind that was, at the best of times, ill-suited to dealing with too many things at once. My opponent's eyes were no longer bovine and benign, but blazed with a terrible, cross-eyed lust for blood: his mighty left hook swung out and sent me spinning against the ropes so hard that my fart – usually so mirth-provoking an aspect of my life in the ring – was quite silenced by a cry of dismay; and this was followed by a demon swing from the right which caught me sharply on the side of the head, and sent me reeling back in the direction from which I had just come. I tried to remonstrate and to remind him of our pact, but my words were cut short by an upper cut of the kind that, in comics, is accompanied by a giant star enclosing 'Wham' or 'Biff'; and no sooner did I look in his direction again – tempted as I was to turn and run – than he unkindly jabbed his fist at the end of my nose, which buckled beneath the blow like a concertina in mid-squeeze.

I crept back to my corner feeling bruised and extremely cross, and my rage and indignation were shared to the full by my two seconds, who considered my opponent's behaviour to be unsporting to a degree. For the two rounds that remained, I realized, there was nothing for it but to fight back for the first and only time; and that is what I did. The final bell rang; when we met in the middle to shake hands, my enemy's face had resumed its look of dreamy benevolence, and I knew it was useless as well as far too late to remonstrate. Dodging the issues was all very well, but I had had my comeuppance at last.

★   ★   ★

Such were the recollections that flashed through my mind as I lay in the enormous Edwardian bath, occasionally adding a dash of boiling water from one of the huge brass taps at its far end, and listening to the voices of the buggers uplifted in song. For another three years or so I would be immune from all that they embodied and were in training for :- from an aggressive and competitive world in which the honours went to those who, from an early age, had learned to play the game and pull their weight and be members of a team, more than anxious to believe that what seemed to me - from a position that combined timidity, envy and a fatal, undermining sense of the fragility and the futility of most forms of human endeavour - to be matters of supreme indifference were, in fact, of serious and compelling importance. I was - and have remained - absurdly uncompetitive, and my scepticism and detachment manifested themselves in the kind of derisive commentary peculiar to those who see themselves as spectators rather than participants, and doubters rather than true believers; later on I was to learn that detachment can all too easily slide into evasion and escape, that jocularity has its limits, and that the rituals and forms and institutions I so disliked and derided had, after all, their virtuous as well as their vicious aspects. In the meantime, as I towelled myself down on the wooden duckboard and climbed into my green corduroy drainpipes and my wasp-waisted tweed jacket and combed my hair in front of the mirror on the white tiled wall and prepared to set out for Davy Byrne's or the International Bar, I felt myself to be a wag of a particularly fortunate kind.

CHAPTER SEVEN

Clip-on Tudor Beams

At about this time I conceived, for the first and only time in my life, a deep dislike and resentment of London. It was composed, I suspect, more of fear than of moral or even aesthetic disapproval: whereas Dublin seemed homely, familiar and amenable, a private world of irresponsibility and gratifying self-esteem, London had become an ugly and alien monstrosity. To my diary I confided a Savonarola-like fury at what I quite suddenly considered a vile and meretricious city, the inhabitants of which were insincere and irremediably compromised. Like most students, I reserved my especial disdain for those Londoners who, selling their birthrights for a mess of pottage, were so compromised and so brought low as to have to go to work; I had yet to read the young Marx on Alienation – a heady brew that lay in store – but as I watched the grey-suited figures hurrying to and fro, briefcase in one hand and an umbrella in the other, I saw them not for what they were, but as perverse, contemptible characters who had, almost wilfully, exiled themselves from Paradise or refused a place in Arcady.

Travelling home by train from Victoria one evening, I found myself sharing a carriage with seven tired, middle-aged businessmen, with faces the colour of pumice and bowler hats on their heads and a dusting of ash on their waistcoats, and as their heads slumped across their chests, or they struggled with the *Telegraph* crossword or joshed one another with heavy camaraderie, I smiled a superior smile and vowed that I, at least, would remain a free spirit, unable to sink so low. Twenty-five years on, I salute those fellow-spirits; I mourn, too, the sudden passing of the bowler hat, that noble item of headgear which – at least as far as London office workers are concerned – lingers on only in the minds of cartoonists and advertising men, along with

Frenchmen in berets and striped vests and curled mustachioes, or Irishmen with ape-like upper lips.

The London I grew up in as a child was, of course, rigid with men in bowler hats, along with small boys in grey flannel shorts and fairisle sleeveless jerseys, ex-soldiers with pudding-basin hair cuts and tight-waisted demob suits, policemen with snake-clasps to their belts, charwomen with turbans on their heads and flower-patterned pinnies with strings at the back, and all the much-loved familiars associated with Ealing comedies, every frame of which I scan for a fleeting glimpse of the London I dimly remember – innocent of tower blocks, the public buildings mercifully uncleaned, the taxis upright and hooded, soot and peeling stucco all about.

It went without saying that my mother was – and still is – a firm believer in that great and famous divide that separates Londoners north of the Park from their fellow-citizens to the south of that mightiest of natural frontiers. From an early age I remember being told that 'no one' lived north of the Park. Were those endless houses stretching away on either side of the Edgware Road but empty façades, a vast Potemkin village erected to persuade gullible foreigners that London was indeed – as we were so often informed – the largest city in the world? Or were those people I spotted hurrying about their business, for all their apparent normality, close relations of *Homo Sapiens*, similar but not the same? Such were the speculations aroused by my mother's stern, exclusive words.

Indeed, even now I find myself worried and ill-at-ease in Islington or St John's Wood or Highgate or Kentish Town, peering anxiously over my shoulder as I walk and exhaling a sigh of relief as the tube whisks me back to more familiar pastures. Of course I tell myself that it's all nonsense and prejudice of the most foolish kind, and the rational me is constantly pointing out that North London is hillier and more handsome than the dingy south, its inhabitants generally brainier, more alert, more avowedly altruistic and altogether more cosmopolitan; the irrational me, however, continues to find it alien, hostile territory, like a fiercer version of North Oxford, peopled by gloomy, long-suffering lady novelists, ambitious northerners, assorted herbalists and all too many equivalents of Peter Simple's Mrs Dutt-Parker and her appalling offspring. Of course I *know* that the stuccoed buildings of Belsize Park are far finer than those of South

Ken, that Camden Town is every bit as elegant as Campden Hill, that Hampstead *must* be the most agreeable part of London in which to live; but none of it *feels* right, try as I may to eradicate an ancient bigotry. Maddened by the horrid realization that most of Dickens's Londoners spent their lives in Clerkenwell or Islington or Camden Town, I struggle to ignore the evidence or - defying authorial instructions - shift the action to Pimlico or Putney or some more congenial area.

Shortly after the war we moved into a large, homely flat in one of those enormous red Edwardian blocks that run, like a string of amber beads or sombre frontier forts, along the south side of Battersea Park. Such blocks were, it seemed, haunted by retired admirals, spies and literary men of a lugubrious cast of mind. To get into the entrance hall one pushed open heavy mahogany doors, with inlaid windows of bevelled glass; to the side of each doorway was a noticeboard - such as one might find in a boarding school, listing enviable sporting achievements and long-forgotten scholarships - on which the name, rank and flat numbers of the inmates had been carefully painted in letters of gold and black. A maroon carpet ran the length of the hall, with gloomy mosaics on either side; at the far end, a lift shaft stood encased in an elaborate black metal cage. To get into the lift one had to wrestle with a pair of trellis doors, like diamond-pane windows suddenly sprung to life or the parts of an old-fashioned camera, which lunged and savaged the unsuspecting traveller, striking him sharp blows about the shoulder or nipping his leg. Since we lived on the first floor, we had little reason to ride this ferocious if torpid beast of burden, but I think of it still with a curious affection, and whenever I hear the 'Harry Lime Theme' - the music I best remember that period by - I see in my mind's eye that dark, melancholy hall and the ancient trembling lift slowly descending to do its duty, preceded on its downward plunge by swathes of blackened, grease-encrusted rope, like an ashen-featured elderly retainer shuffling dimly forward with a faint, pneumatic hiss.

The flats were built round a well, at the bottom of which lay a grey, forbidden world of pipes and dustbins and subterranean tunnels: this was the domain of the janitor, a kindly Guardian of the Underworld in a faded blue boiler suit and a tweed cloth cap. At night the well was peopled by loud and lovesick tom cats; so vexatious were they that, temporarily ignoring ration books and post-war shortages, the inmates stood on their small kitchen balconies and hurled potatoes at the offending beasts in a vain attempt to drown their cries. By each of these balconies was an outside lavatory, and a small lift, worked by ropes, on which the dustbins travelled up and down; I dreamed sometimes of sitting on this lift and hauling myself aloft, but was altogether too timid and too law-abiding to make the attempt. Still more daunting was the long, dark corridor that ran from our frosted glass front door – which stood in the middle of the block, by the aged, wheezing lift – to the main body of the flat, which looked out to the brightness of the world beyond; I used to close my eyes and make a dash up this interminable alley, for I believed very strongly in the existence of the devil – a red, rather jovial figure equipped with the regulation horns and pointed tail – and was quite convinced that, when in London, he lived above a wardrobe in the small room to the right of the front door, and that he would one day spring out at me on his unpleasant cloven hooves, waving a red-hot toasting fork in one hand and straining eagerly forward to grab me with the other.

Although the flats along Prince of Wales Drive were – and, no doubt, still are – ferociously middle-class, we felt that we were living in dangerous border country, like Anglo-Norman inhabitants of the Irish Pale, or lonely Teutonic knights adrift in a sea of Slavs. Before us stood the park, with its quota of prams and nannies, and beyond that the safety of Chelsea and the river; behind us stood row upon row of small grey back-to-backs, stretching on and on as far as the eye could see, to the heights of Clapham and still beyond, with every now and then a railway line lifted up above the back yards, as in Gustave Doré's famous engraving, or a dirty red brick church, or one of those neo-Georgian early twentieth-century schools which, with their great white painted mullioned windows and Dutch gables and slatted belfries, seem to me now to be among the finest public buildings of the last hundred years or so.

These low, dark streets – many of which were swept away to make room for great dripping slabs of concrete in the 1960s – were inhabited by what seemed to be an almost alien race, of men with collarless shirts and women in checked slippers and flowered pinnies and the dreaded 'dirty boys', hurling wildly to and fro in boxes mounted on roller-skates, and clad in an ominous uniform of black plimsolls, rolled down socks, baggy grey shorts and sleeveless jerseys with a diamond pattern embroidered on the front. On occasional dangerous forays to the shops in the street behind we gazed at these savage beings with a fearful tremor; no doubt my sister and I looked unforgivably prim and tidy and neatly brushed, and far too good a chance to miss, and one day as we were walking back from the shops – I had on a pair of jeans from America, a rare and enviable acquisition – we were (or, rather, I was) set upon and belaboured by a team of public-spirited 'dirty boys'.

Very far from such horrid goings-on was the day school in Queen's Gate to which I was sent at the age of five. My father took me there every morning, since he worked in a clinic at the other end of the street (every now and then he brought home, like a trophy from the wars, a bladder stone, a marble-sized object with the consistency of pumice): it was an excellent and thoroughly pleasant school, despite which – being an unusually tremulous youth – I found it hard to suppress the sobs when I was dropped off at its whitewashed portico. I remember little of the school beyond marching round the corner into the Cromwell Road for institutional lunches, and having grave difficulties in spotting the blackboard: towards the end of my career I wet my pants for some ridiculous reason, and the headmaster's wife – a most jolly, practical woman – wrapped me in the school carpet until my mother arrived to take me home.

On Sundays we often went for a walk in Kensington Gardens to watch the model boats on the Round Pond and climb about a large statue of a naked, musclebound figure on horseback waving a sword. A diversion of a gloomier kind was provided by an elderly man in a brown overcoat who came to feed the ducks with crusts from a brown paper bag. Every week an ambulance stood on duty; every week he had an epileptic fit by the side of the pond, and dropped his brown paper bag, which was whisked away by a gust of wind; every week he was promptly and punctually spirited away by the waiting ambulancemen; and every week he returned with a fresh supply of crusts, and the sad ritual was repeated once again. I found a terrible pathos in the sight of his brown paper bag and its scattering of crumbs – very similar to that excited, in later life, by a pair of worn and highly polished shoes set out in a lonely bedroom, or other people's sponge bags, or the small, endearing items of private pride and self-esteem.

Sunday lunch was something of an ordeal, involving as it often did the sluggish mastication of mutton fat and gristle. We were brought up, quite rightly, on the assumption that polite feeders ate what was placed in front of them, and since my mother is a quite excellent cook – though perhaps, in a robust old English way, almost too contemptuous of messy foreign food and dubious items such as avocados – this usually presented no problem, and we were taught to look down on snivelling, dainty children who couldn't cope with brains or tripe and onions or tapioca pudding. Even so, certain types of fat and gristle and meat jelly tested our powers to the utmost, and long after my parents had washed up and retreated to the sitting-room my sister and I could be spotted sitting glumly on either side of the kitchen table, listlessly stirring the remains of Sunday lunch – by now congealed and cold – about our plates, and bracing ourselves for that dreadful, conclusive gulp that would settle the matter once and for all for another week at least. Unknown to the grown-ups, the kitchen table had a small shelf underneath, on which we could secrete strips of bacon and hunks of gristle; when, in the early 1950s, we moved from Battersea to South Ken, and the kitchen table was rudely upended by a team of removals men, a dusty shower of discarded items of food – not unlike the desiccated pieces of bread and withered grapes that surround the mummies in the British Museum – rained down on the kitchen floor.

Unfortunately we had no animals to whom we could feed these recalcitrant gobbets. We had, for a short time, a tabby called Dakin – named, I never knew why, after a grocer's shop on the corner of Oakley Street – whose career was cut short after an attack of diarrhoea in the airing cupboard; just as, much earlier, a dalmatian had received his marching orders for eating my sister's gumboots. For a time we had a pair of hamsters in a wooden cage, but life turned sour after my mother sucked up several of their babies in the hoover, mistaking them for Rice Krispies, with the result that the mother hamster – until then a most benign and placid creature – turned on the remains of her brood and gobbled them up.

This shortage of livestock was more than made up for by a steady stream of visiting 'uncles', many of them old friends of my father's from Cambridge or St Thomas's; one such 'uncle' had lost an eye in the Western Desert, and a particular excitement of an evening was to be allowed to tap its glass replacement with the back of one's fingernail before saying good night to the grown-ups and settling down for the night. My parents seem to have lived lives of unbridled merriment in those halcyon days before the war; my sister and I sat agog for hours listening to stories of night club life and swinging from chandeliers, and when, in due course, we became old enough for that kind of thing ourselves but stayed instead at home, reading books or going for long walks and affecting to disdain the company of our peers, all of whom seemed alarmingly bright and dashing and self-confident, I felt that, beside our parents, we must have seemed dull dogs indeed.

Especial jollity was excited by my mother's entirely frivolous attitude to work and her accounts of her professional life: of her being retrieved from employment in an unsuitable hotel in Russell Square by an elderly aunt clad all in black, gazing sternly at the proprietor through her pince-nez and wagging her umbrella as she demanded her niece's immediate release; of my father's regular arrival in an enormous red false beard at the publishing house in Soho where my mother was guarding the fort while the partners enjoyed an extended 'working lunch' (the firm went bankrupt shortly afterwards, brought low by a celebrated obscenity case, and my mother's giving away most of their stock to her friends); of climbing in and out of St George's Hospital, and battling with the matron, and – we shouldn't have laughed, but alas we did – a terrible scene involving the disposal of a dead baby in a dustbin. Equally gripping – to me at least – were my father's rather less flamboyant accounts of his experience with the Guards Armoured Division during the war; I found it impossible to believe that, under the circumstances, I would have done anything other than run away, and to this day I look on those who went through the war with respect and a curious envy, like a race of men apart, or the end of a particular line.

For some reason or other, both Julia and I greatly enjoyed throwing things out of our second-floor window into the street below. On one occasion the blue-boilersuited janitor had cause to complain after we had been spotted emptying our pots out of the window, like figures from Hogarth or our elderly neighbour-to-be in the motheaten fur coat with binding twine about the waist; and some months later the same windows came into their own on the evening of Julia's birthday party. It was, I'm sure, a decorous, well-mannered affair, with a fire blazing in the nursery grate (and a brass-topped fireguard firmly in place), the mothers chatting in the sitting-room next door, and the children looking neatly brushed and shining and scrubbed, the girls in pale blue smocked cotton dresses and little white socks and black patent leather button shoes, and the boys in clean white shirts and well-pressed corduroy shorts – a world away, it seemed, from the terrible sooty streets beyond, in which the 'dirty boys' prowled like grey and hungry wolves.

Since this was the Age of Austerity, the range of goodies available in the shops was severely restricted, and, to our alarm, we quickly realized that every guest had brought an identical birthday present in the shape of a small blue rubber doll's hot water bottle. Acting with unusual initiative and determination, I raised the nursery window, and as each new hot water bottle was unwrapped to cries of surprise and delight, its predecessor was hurled into the street below. Next morning, we went down and gathered up some twenty dolls' hot water bottles: since we both detested dolls, submitting those rash enough to enter the nursery to terrible punishments, and even decapitation or a burst of machine-gun fire, we rationed the bottles out among our large and appreciative retinue of teddies and stuffed animals – some of whom were, quite coincidentally, feeling the cold, having mysteriously failed to grow fresh hair after a seasonal trim with the haircutting scissors – and all was well once more.

Far more than my sister, I was, in those days, a stuffy, indoors creature, delighting in the spectacle of rain drumming against the window-panes and – like a bespectacled swot of the grammar school variety – much preferring an afternoon spent examining dinosaur bones in the Natural History Museum to boyish outdoor pursuits. At weekends in summer, though, we often drove out to Richmond Park, picking our way slowly through the low grey streets of Wandsworth and Putney before entering the park by the Robin Hood Gate. More often than not we took a picnic with us and spent the whole day there, tunnelling through the bracken, climbing into the same hollow oak trees that my daughters sampled some thirty years later, and illegally swimming, or pretending to swim, in the Pen Ponds, one hand sculling the water while the other remained firmly in the soft black slime on the bottom, before returning home for a late high tea, tired and itchy from too much sun, our bare legs pricked and stabbed by the bracken, and our feet encased in a thin layer of London clay that had a dry, delicious, nutty smell.

An additional perk of these trips was sneering at the houses on the Kingston Bypass, with their clip-on Tudor beams and dainty net curtains in the windows and – though this was hard to verify as we motored slowly past – the strangulated voices saying pardon in the lounge. Most of us keep in reserve the ultimate deterrent in pejoratives – to be unleashed on the big occasion only, when the final anathema is to be pronounced, friendships blighted for ever and a last stand taken against the powers of wickedness and night. In our family this not very secret adjectival weapon took the form of the word 'suburban', occasionally preceded by 'utterly' when extra emphasis was required. 'Loathsome', 'vulgar' and 'vile' were as nothing beside this oral mark of Cain; only 'common' – that most brutal of middle-class epithets – offered any competition, and even that had a rugged, jovial ring to it that saved it from plumbing the lowest depths of moral and aesthetic turpitude.

For as long as I can remember, the suburbs and those who inhabit them have been the subject of derision and disapproval, scorned and unloved with equal fervour by snobs and socialists alike. Hovering uneasily between the city and the countryside, suburbanites were – and still are – scorned by the inhabitants of both. Who but a clerk of the dimmest kind would *choose* to live in Purley or Petts Wood – lifeless, unsociable, petty-minded places, lacking the dash of Chelsea or Campden Hill or the working class vitality of Hackney or West Ham, offering up in handkerchief-sized gardens aswarm with red-coated gnomes a pale, pathetic echo of the fields and meadows that lay beyond the endless lines of identical houses? As avid readers a few years later of Nancy Mitford's *Noblesse Oblige* – how we rubbed our hands over 'toilet' and 'pardon', while bridling over 'chimneypieces' and 'looking-glasses', which were surely taking things a bit too far – we shared with so many of our fellows a keen and ferocious interest in those tell-tale slips of accent or intonation, or furnishings and clothes, that revealed the true suburbanite. Utterly untinged by the slightest qualm or doubt, we derided the vulgarities and the pretensions of suburbia with a terrible relish and indignation: two-tone chiming front door bells and flying ducks in the hall and fur-covered lavatory seats formed an integral part of the unkind but fiercely funny English comedy of manners, visual equivalents of the Veneerings or Mr Pooter or those pompous City tradesmen, so savagely mocked by Surtees, who papered the walls of their newly acquired country houses with bogus family portraits bought in bulk.

Little did I guess, in those far-off days of the early 1950s, that I would live much of my adult life in those same suburbs, near my beloved Richmond Park. Unlike the mechanized, blighted country-side – de-hedged, wired-up, littered with the ghosts of ancient elms – or the tatty inner cities, suburbs have, by their very nature, a sense of expectation, embodying in brick and mortar that old truism about it being better to travel hopefully than to arrive: in one direction lies the promise of the city, in another the wide open spaces, and in between is a way of life that is agreeable, spacious, sociable and mild. I continue, like most of my kind, to use 'suburban' as a pejorative; deep down it's a song of praise.

* * *

Shortly after the war, my parents bought the kind of car that would be looked on with deep disapproval by the safety-conscious motorist of today. At some stage in its career it had done service as a Macfisheries delivery van: the bonnet (a truncated version of the old MG), the wheels (spoked) and the front seats (bucket and stuffed with horsehair, which curled out of cracks in the leather) were those of a pre-war Morris; an enterprising previous owner had replaced the back seats and the boot with a mock-Tudor shooting-brake rear end of the kind that lingered on into the 1960s in sportier versions of the district nurse's car (as recommended to Shore by the ingenious Mr Jawleyford). The windows on either side of the front seats were made of yellowing perspex, and were fitted into the door with a couple of short spokes; beneath the perspex was a canvas slot of the sort that would prove irresistible to the modern burglar, but was harmlessly deployed in the execution of hand signals. There were no seats in the back of the car: where once kippers and mackerel and great gaping cod had basked on blocks of ice, my sister sat on a stool, while I perched on the hub of one of the two back wheels. We were both of us very proud of this unusual vehicle, in which we were driven to school every day, trundling over Chelsea Bridge on our way from Battersea to South Kensington; every now and then we would make a longer journey, flashing through the countryside at nearly forty miles an hour, our hands tightly gripping the aged leather backs of the seats in front in case we were dashed to the floor by the sudden application of the brakes. Most enjoyable of all were summer expeditions to a tiny, whitewashed coastguard cottage in West Wittering, lit only by paraffin lamps; we disliked the elsan, which stood in a shed at the back and was emptied once a week into a nettle-bed beyond, but I loved the great muddy estuaries and the high, mysterious trees filled with flapping crows and the large white 1930s houses with their thatched or green-tiled roofs and impenetrable, well-trimmed hedges from behind which – or so I liked to imagine – one heard the clink of ice in cocktail shakers and the laughter of over-dressed women and retired stockbrokers in faded tan trousers and blue and white check shirts, nautical-looking jerseys and canvas sailing shoes.

About once a year we would go and stay with my grandparents in Gloucestershire. This invariably proved a rather daunting business, partly because although our grandmother and an aunt who lived there as well were all that grandmothers and aunts should be (i.e. kindly, jolly and an endless source of first-rate cakes and puddings), my grandfather was a quite terrifying old gentleman, much given to shouting and banging about the house with sticks; and partly because – even making allowances for the sluggish nature of our car and the fact that a short spin for an adult seems like eternity to a child – Gloucestershire was a very long way off in those innocent days when motorways were a distant gleam in the eye of some demented civil servant. Slowly we picked our way down the Western Avenue, past 1930s factories of the kind that nowadays have preservation orders slapped upon them, through traffic so thin that on one occasion, when a mattress we had tied to the roof flew off and landed in the middle of this busiest of arterial roads, we were able to drive back in a leisurely manner, pick it up and lash it back on again without causing the mildest disruption to the traffic. Hour succeeded hour as we inched our way westwards, through West Wycombe with its gold-topped church on the hill above, down the other side of the Chilterns, over the top of Oxford, and through Witney with its blanket factories, where the buildings began to assume a distinctly – and dauntingly – Cotswold look.

At Burford we turned left down the road that led through Lechlade to our destination, and as we did so the mood of the travellers changed from merriment to glum foreboding. Hands became suddenly clammy, followed by intimations of diarrhoea and a sinking of the stomach; the landscape, with its dry-stone walls and windswept trees and gaunt, embattled farmhouses looked suddenly fiercer and gloomier and altogether less benign than the cosy commuterland we had rattled through earlier in the day. Townees through and through, accustomed only to London parks or mild, domesticated seaside streets, my sister and I found ourselves in an alien world of mud and bulls and cart-horses and raw-boned agricultural labourers in flat tweed caps, heavy flannel shirts with collar-studs (but no collars), waistcoats and manure-stained unmentionables with ties of string below the knees. More often than not the night seemed to be closing in as we chugged the remaining mile or two, crunched across the well-raked gravel and ground to a halt with a sighing of springs in front of a large, square and entirely unembellished farmhouse, which stood in the middle of the town, with the yard and the buildings all about it. Bracing ourselves against the inevitable cacophony of shouting voices and barking dogs and *The Archers* blasting in the background, we pushed open the hall door and went in.

Whenever I read the novels of that most cynical and entertaining of men, R. S. Surtees, and look at Leech's gloomy, ill-lit engravings of his bleak, draughty, sparsely-furnished hunting men's country houses, I am immediately transported back to the grandparental house – to the long, stone-flagged hall, the dark stained bannisters and doors, the acres of brown or blue-green lino, the fox's pads and hunting scenes on the walls, the saddles drying in front of the fire, the gigantic wardrobes that always seemed, to a child's eye, to be on the point of toppling down on one, the clean scrubbed kitchen table, the game hung up from hooks in the scullery with its shallow porcelain basins, the dim lighting that left the tops of the rooms in darkness and seemed to light up faces from below, like characters in *grand guignol*.

As for my grandfather, he would have been immediately and happily at home in Surtees's brisk and hard-boiled world of bottle-nosed squires and wintry, weather-beaten tenant farmers like himself. He looked like a leaner, fiercer version of the Duke of Wellington, with an enormous, razor-thin aquiline nose, small grey eyes jammed rather close together, a leathery farmer's skin and a body that carried not a spare inch of flesh upon it. Only in his old age do I remember him wearing conventional trousers: otherwise, perhaps wrongly, I think of him always in breeches and boots or gaiters, plus a flat cap and a tobacco-coloured tweed jacket. Like Mr Sponge, he was always neatly turned out, striding about the farm in impeccably polished boots; on his rare, disdainful trips to London he would pace the streets in a voluminous cream riding mac, so stiff that it could, like my Nigerian fellow-students' trousers, quite easily have stood up by itself, and a flat-brimmed hunting bowler with a ring in the back; he was irritated by my parents for choosing to get married on a day he was hunting, and photographs show him striding crossly into the church in his hunting gear, a whip clutched firmly in one hand. He had a thin, lipless mouth of the kind one associates with Red Indian chiefs; he hummed as he moved about the house, producing a curious droning approximation to song that alternated with the kind of hissing sound produced in the stable outside by Bennet the groom when adding that extra sheen to his employer's highly polished hunter.

Humming apart, a great deal of shouting went on, most of it addressed to the ladies of the house, who bustled to and fro when he came in at midday or in the evening, setting out his slippers and his whisky and his copy of the *Wilts and Glos*, serving up enormous lunches on the dot of half-past twelve (these always included a choice of at least three puddings), and making sure that no one disturbed the great man as he enjoyed his afternoon snooze before the fire, a blue and white spotted handkerchief shielding his face as he slept. An afternoon rest was *de rigueur* for every member of the household, so much so that a great stillness descended over the entire farm, and my sister and I were the only people apparently awake from two to half-past three; my mother has continued this admirable tradition, and until I was in my teens I assumed that most people were sensible enough to doze off after lunch. If I had my way most offices would have let-down beds (or even dormitories) so that tired executives could enjoy some shuteye after an exhausting lunch or the rigours of a morning spent dictating internal memoranda.

Everyone – farm workers, family, the odd local in the street – was terrified of 'the Guv'nor', and not without reason. He came from a family famous for its rages. His father, a benign and popular figure, had once run down one of the farm hands in a fit of irritation, leaving him with a 'bent' leg for life but apparently bearing no lasting grudge against his short-tempered employer; his mother – a battle-axe of a woman, from whom he inherited the thin lips and the beaky profile – was said to have remained at home on the day of her husband's funeral, filing her nails as the coffin was carried out of the house.

The Guv'nor himself was much given to gnashing of the teeth: so much so that, shortly before his death, he attacked the elder of our two Gloucestershire uncles in the course of a ferocious argument over why the Aga had gone out, bringing him crashing to the ground and biting him severely in the leg – a heartless act, for my uncles always seemed to us a most jolly and cheerful pair, much given, my mother told us, to blowing hunting horns from the tops of their tanks while advancing on the Nazi hordes. My grandfather reserved his particular rage, however, for my mother, the most defiant of his children. She used to tell us how, as a child, she regularly sought refuge in the top of a tree as he stormed towards her with a whip in his hand, climbing back into the house after dark once my grandmother had given the all clear; and our annual visits were often enlivened by the sound of shouting drifting up the stairs to where we lay in bed and, on one turbulent occasion, of the old gentleman's footsteps disappearing down the hall as he went out to fetch his gun to brandish in my mother's face while ordering her to leave the house by dawn the next day.

By a pleasing irony, incidentally, my mother was the only one of his children to inherit his ferocious cast of mind, if not his disconcerting readiness to match theory and practice. In later life she liked to tell us how she had maintained discipline by rapping us so severely about the shins with a wooden spoon that both my sister and I had to wear old-fashioned leggings to cover the bruises and the running sores, and how she had taught me to swim in the Chelsea Baths by standing on my hands as I clung to the edge, so forcing me to strike out for the other side. I have no recollection whatsoever of these dreadful goings-on, and since she was in fact the most kindly and protective of mothers I suspect they are both fine examples of her powerful rhetoric and fierce imagination; either way, they were useful and – particularly when told in her forceful and comical way, to the accompaniment of great gales of laughter and much dabbing of the eyes – highly entertaining additions to the folklore of the family.

Not surprisingly, guns loomed large in my grandfather's life. The Guv'nor was as good a shot as he was at fly fishing and riding to hounds with the VWH or the Cotswold, and spent as much of the year as possible indulging in these congenial pursuits. Every morning he would drive very slowly round the farm in his funereal black Vauxhall, the back seat of which reeked of leather and hot labrador, ordering us children to jump out at every field we came to, open the gate to let him drive sedately through, and close it up behind him. Each gate seemed to have a different and yet more complicated form of latch, and our clumsy efforts to wrench them open excited loud and scornful shouts from the old gentleman as he sat behind the wheel, one elbow propped out of the window and his great nose plainly visible from half a field away, like an Arab dagger shining palely in the sun. From time to time a rabbit would scurry across our path as we steadily bumped along, or a particularly succulent and pie-worthy rook would wander by; unable to resist these delicacies, my grandfather would seize his gun from the seat beside him and blast angrily away from the car window. These dreadful explosions invariably took us townees by surprise, and the roar of the twelve-bore – magnified a million times, it seemed, within the narrow confines of the elderly Vauxhall – not only made us leap from our skins with fright but left me with a dislike of bangs so intense that, even now, I rush from the room with my fingers in my ears when the balloons are blown up at a children's party, or tiresome small boys start to twist them in their hands or trample them underfoot.

It was always a relief when these tours of duty were over, and we were free to climb the straw bales in the barns and inspect the bulls from a reasonable distance, safe from the tyrant's eagle eyes and fierce, sardonic tongue, or wander into the famous church where my aunt could be found explaining to interested visitors that the fifteenth-century glass was over a hundred years old and had been taken down and hidden during the Civil War. On summer afternoons, once the rest was over, we would walk through sleepy pre-Raphaelite meadows and swim in the river, my mother once exciting gasps as she plunged fully clad into a boiling weir to rescue a drowning cousin, pausing only to remove her watch; and when it was wet we would creep up the back stairs and steal about the forbidden attic rooms, with their magic hoards of 1920s *Tatlers*, sweet-smelling apples on racks and dry, dead flies on the windowpanes, plus a Nazi flag captured by one of the horn-blowing uncles, a Sam Browne belt, a model of Sir Donald Campbell's record-breaking car, a rocking horse, a gigantic black Bible with nightmare-inducing engravings by Gustave Doré, and the copy of Sassoon's *Memoirs of a Fox Hunting Man* that was used to prop up one corner of the ever-gurgling water-tank.

It is one of the sad ironies of life that ogres often inspire stronger feelings of pride, and even affection, than the dutifully good; and so it was with my grandfather. For most of the time I knew him I was too afraid of him to feel a great deal of affection; I had no interest whatsoever in fishing or guns or horses, with whom I only felt at ease if they had been mounted on rockers, or moved smoothly about on castors; but I admired his caustic tongue and his fierce intelligence, and – like other members of the family – I liked nothing better, once safely back at home, than to boast of his terrible deeds to friends with milder, more civilized and altogether more conventional immediate ancestors. Unlike my grandmother – who was for ever subverting the tyrant's power, whispering and laughing behind his back – he was, I'm sure, always pleased to see the back of us, mightily relieved as we packed our cases into our unusual shooting-brake, cranked the starting handle, and set out on the interminable journey back to a world he held in profound contempt.

He died some fifteen years ago on a night of terrific winds, in the course of which two trees were brought down in the garden, and the church lost some of its elaborate, leering gargoyles. The house he lived in has been converted to flats, while the yard – once crossed by heavy herds of cows on their way to the milking machines – is full of weekenders' cars, and the barns and cattle sheds boast carriage lamps and white painted porticoes and panelled teak doors with fanlights cunningly inlaid; the Guv'nor himself, I like to think, is warming the seat of his pants before some celestial fire, discussing the day's events with Facey Romford, Soapey Sponge and the mighty Earl of Scamperdale, a hunting man at home in the company of his peers.

★   ★   ★

Sometimes, instead of heading back to London, we drove in the opposite direction, towards my father's family in Wales. Although my mother looked askance at the Welsh, blaming our failings as a family on Celtic gloom and general evasiveness, my sister and I found life on the other side of the border wonderfully peaceful and undemanding after the stridency of Gloucestershire. My grandparents lived in a large, red-brick Edwardian house full of Turkey carpets and mauve and red stained glass and massive, dark-stained items of furniture, at the foot of the hill in Bedwas. My grandfather was a successful local businessman: he seems to have spent a good deal of time in Constantinople, and the house was full of Turkish memorabilia and pieces of Ottoman coinage, rubbing shoulders with mayoral trowels and similar emblems of office. He was a Welshman of the dark variety, with – or so I seem to remember – firm black eyebrows with a touch of the Groucho Marx about them, and an equally black (though genuine) moustache. He was a small, compact man: at some stage in the 1930s he was made High Sheriff of Monmouthshire and when, some twenty years later, my father, though then living in London, was picked for the job in his turn, he turned it down since there was no way in which he could squeeze himself into the diminutive black velvet jacket and breeches, white ruffled shirt, black silk stockings, Captain Hornblower hat and tiny black patent-leather shoes with silver buckles that he had inherited from his father in a neat tin trunk filled with tissue paper. Only the sword could be used again; and it would hardly do, it seemed, to wait upon the Queen or precede a heavily bewigged procession of judges to the local assizes wearing a tweed jacket and corduroy trousers, even if one was wearing a sword of office in a belt about one's waist and carrying an impressive-looking wand or rod of office in the right hand. Sad to say, I remember very little of him, since he died when I was eight or nine: I heard the news at prep school in Seaford, and – with a schoolboy's callousness – referred briefly to it in my weekly letter home ('I was very sorry to hear about Grampy. Please will you send me ...').

My grandmother was descended from a long line of Welsh clergymen, and claimed to be related somehow to John Morley, the biographer of Gladstone, and Sir Oliver Lodge, a celebrated Edwardian scientist who liked to dabble in the occult, tapping excitedly on tables and consorting with clouds of ectoplasm. She was a large, gentle, dreamy woman, very magical to children; she spent a lot of time strumming hymns on the piano and, like my Gloucestershire grandfather, she kept up a constant humming as she moved about the house, albeit of a more melodic kind. Her regime was benign if somewhat austere: she rose early, was sparing with fires and, rather to our alarm, ate prunes or apple purée with her All Bran and tried, in vain, to convert us to this practice. The house was full of books – Andrew Lang's fairy books, with their terrifying illustrations of hump-backed dwarves with enormous noses and untrimmed finger nails luring diaphanous maidens into bramble bushes, or dreadful wart-encrusted monsters that dwelt in bottomless pools, or many-headed serpents that lived, as serpents so often do, in great palaces with shimmering marble walls; and Arthur Mee's *Children's Encyclopaedia*, crammed with useful information about eclipses of the sun and the tribesmen of Turkestan; and volume after volume of Harmsworth's *History of the World*. The clocks ticked; the furniture gleamed; my grandmother hummed in the background; life was peaceful, and quiet, and safe; it seemed like a home from home.

CHAPTER EIGHT

Trundling about in the West

Halfway through my second year at Trinity I met and became friends with three girls whom Shore and I – with wearisome whimsicality – collectively entitled 'the Damsels'. Whereas ffenella – whom I occasionally spotted, with a terrible pang, striding into other people's sets of rooms in black boots, tight black trousers and a matching black fur coat and hat, as though the principal boy from a pantomime had wandered onto the set of Eisenstein's *Ivan the Terrible* disguised as a scheming if beardless boyar – seemed the very embodiment of a wicked, sensuous sophistication, the Damsels, by contrast, had the wholesome, smiling qualities I associated with cheerful suburban tennis clubs and dimly-remembered novels about girls from the Home Counties called Jill or Jennifer who wore jodhpurs, yellow polo-necked jerseys and their hair in plaits, were mad about ponies, and successfully thwarted plots laid by girls in glasses and men with thin moustaches to deprive them of the rosettes that were rightly theirs at the local point-to-point or pony club gymkhana; and whereas ffenella liked to spend a sunny afternoon drinking double brandies in the company of poker-playing Old Harrovians with trembling hands and black bags under their eyes, the Damsels – while occasionally stretching to a sinful bottle of Spanish wine at 7/6 a bottle – were eager exponents of cocoa, home cooking and games of ludo in front of the fire. Ffenella might have stolen my heart, but I felt safer with the Damsels; it seemed as though I had moved from the world of Balzac to that of *Cranford*, and what my new world lacked in excitement and urbanity it made up for in a cosy, uncompetitive domesticity.

All three Damsels were from the English upper middle classes, and all three were likeable and good-looking in a fresh, straightforward way, being much given to hairy checked tweed skirts, bottle-green twinsets, fur-lined suede boots and the bulky sheepskin coats associated with labradors, Land Rovers, point-to-points and the touchlines of rugger matches; they moved about with unaffected, hockey-players' strides, had firm handshakes, and looked as though the wind had caught their cheeks, which glowed with a ruddy fire. With one of them – a jolly, pretty girl with bright blue eyes and her fair hair cut in a fringe, whose parents ran a prep school on the south coast – I soon imagined myself in love. I remained quite as gauche and incompetent as ever when it came to expressing this sudden passion: Shore and I – occasionally accompanied by a reluctant Ian – used to go round to their flat for supper, and after we had eaten, and were sitting on the floor in front of the peat fire, I would – greatly emboldened by generous samplings of the Spanish red wine – advance in a snail-like way upon the one I loved as she sat darning a pair of socks or doing some crochet-work. So slow was my advance, and so fearful was I of seeming over-impetuous, that by the time I had edged my way to within striking distance – a matter of six inches or so – the evening was over and it was time to leave, or she had sprung up all of a sudden, dusting down her skirt with both hands, and moved off to the kitchen to put on a kettle; when she eventually returned to her seat, and had handed us all our cups of tea or cocoa, it was time for the elaborate, unregarded ritual to begin all over again, as I bore down upon her with all the speed and dash of a glacier.

One evening – spurred on by I know not what – I decided to adopt a more drastic strategy, and take her out to dinner. I had never been to a nightclub in my life, though my parents had long entertained us with tales of wild pre-war nights in the 400 Club and reporting to work in full evening dress, an empty bottle in one hand; Dublin was hardly famous for its night life, but I knew that there was a place in Westmoreland Street, much patronized by Trinity students who wanted to eat and drink and even dance till the small grey hours of the morning, and to it we bent our steps. The 'night club' occupied several floors of a building; each floor boasted its own restaurant and dance floor; the walls were clad in a virulent yellow pine, and plastered with signed photographs of long-forgotten North Country comedians and men disguised as nigger minstrels and sad-eyed songsters from Galway and County Cork looking ill-at-ease in their clip-on bow ties and heavily Brylcreemed hair.

As I picked my way to our table through the Yorkshire travelling

salesmen and the parties up from the country and disdainful groups
of Trinity students, many of whom were preparing to be loudly and
horridly sick before the night was out, I felt very much a man of the
world: this was not, perhaps, the ultimate in sophistication – the hot
blast of frying chips and the ketchup bottles disguised as outsize
plastic tomatoes hinted as much – but to be taking a girl out on my
own to one of Ireland's leading night-spots was surely a step in the
right direction, and exactly the kind of experience I needed if I were
to make my mark as a man of the world and the kind of Mastroianni-
like lover I had dreamed of being before Hector and his great army of
well-groomed lookalikes with their slip-on shoes and jerseys draped
about their shoulders had made me all too aware of the mighty gulf
between aspirations and actuality.

No doubt we ate yet another enormous fry-up or some Dublin
version of spaghetti, stiff with tomato sauce and served up with huge
hunks of white bread and marge; either way, we filled in the evening
with agreeable chat about this and that – whimsical on my part and
sensible on hers, with not a mention of the Palaeologues or
Constantine Porphyrogenetus – until, at about one in the morning,
I decided it was probably time to leave rather than run the risk of
having to step smartly onto the dance floor, the experience I abhorred
above all else. It was a fine, cloudless evening, and I suggested I
walked her home to Rathmines, a distance of two or three miles. By
now the wine and the heat and the absence of Byzantine complica-
tions had done their worst: I loved her – or so it seemed to me – quite
as much as ffenella, and in the marvellously straightforward and
manly way I associated with iron jaws and the sensible smoking of
pipes; hardly had we reached Trinity before I had clasped her to my
suede-clad bosom and was raining kisses on her upturned lips, just
like the masterful characters in Continental films. Although I had
never kissed anyone before outside my immediate family – and even
there we were none of us at all given to kissing, which was regarded
as a dubious Continental business – it seemed an easy enough
business, and very pleasant too; we moved at a slug-like pace in the
direction of Rathmines, our arms locked round each other's waists,
stopping every fifty yards to test the waters once again; it must have
been half-past three by the time we reached her door, and rather than
go in and wake her unwitting fellow-Damsels – for the three of them

shared a room – we leaned against the garden wall to steady ourselves, and set off once again, like an old-fashioned stopping train, on our amorous tour of the Dublin suburbs.

It was dawn by the time we returned once more to her garden gate, by which time I had, as far as kissing was concerned, more than made up for what I had failed to achieve with ffenella and the pouting, Bardot figure whom I had so admired behind the canteen cash register in my days as a trainee tycoon; I tried, and failed, to buy a six-shilling bottle of unspeakable wine from an early morning grocer with which to celebrate these unexpected triumphs before limping back to Mrs Brady's, where I furtively turned the key and stole upstairs in my socks to snatch an hour or two of sleep before we joined the commercial traveller, the man with the nervous tic, the lady who stubbed her cigarettes out in her hair, the sprigs of the nobility and the constipated Wykhamist in the dainty delights of the breakfast table.

As I lay in my large double bed – Shore and Ian tossing fitfully in their narrow bunks at its foot – I felt I was now very much one of the boys, on a par with those self-confident bloodies I had so envied and half-admired the summer before, and more than a match, potentially at least, for those overcharged undergraduates who, or so we were led to believe, were overcome by feelings of abominable lust when confronted by the girls in the Swastika Laundry, and hurled them to the ground behind their counters with terrible grunts and rending of undergarments, bringing down upon them as they went a deluge of freshly pressed jackets and trousers in their protective paper wrappings. Who could tell what the summer term would bring?

* * *

Rather than head straight back to England at the end of term, I decided to spend a few days on the Aran Islands with my old friend the Deaf Malvernian. The Deaf was – as his name suggests – a trifle hard of hearing, and would sometimes sit looking distressingly blank as the conversation raged about him, before suddenly cutting across a surprised-looking speaker with a remark of alarming irrelevance or inconsequentiality; he was, at the same time, a mine of gossip and useful information, since he seemed quite capable of hearing what was of interest to him, still more so since his simple-minded fellows tended to let fly indiscretions in his company which might otherwise have remained unspoken. He was the idlest man of his year, and lay in bed most mornings till well past midday, the shutters of his bedroom clamped firmly shut and a low snoozing sound wafting under the door. He shared a large and airy set of rooms in New Square with another old friend of mine, who went on to become the world's leading expert on the caddis fly – an expertise that was hard won, since, according to the Deaf, it involved lying naked in the Nubian Desert while the caddis flies stung the persistent researcher, or laid eggs all over him, or did whatever unpleasant things caddis flies do when the mood is upon them. I had – and still have – a great deal of time for the Deaf Malvernian, and when he suggested that we should travel together to those most magical of islands, I hurriedly agreed.

The Aran Islands consist of two small and one slightly larger islands in the middle of Galway Bay: to the north, on a golden, Grecian morning, one can see the Twelve Pins of Connemara, to the south the sheer grey cliffs of Moher in County Clare, and away to the west, over the endless Atlantic, great grey stormclouds that suddenly boil up and come howling in, turning day to night in a matter of seconds and passing on as quickly as they came, leaving the islanders, bathed in a watery sunshine, to watch the waves and the rain lash down on the mainland away to the east. Made famous by Synge, who had spent much time on these low-slung, windswept islands with his ear jammed to the floor of his bedroom listening to the locals gossiping below, and by O'Flaherty's film *Man of Aran*, with its turbulent seas and tossing curraghs and wild heroics on the cliffs of Dun Aengus, they were legendary for their remoteness and as a kind of heroic, lingering embodiment of de Valera's romantic dream of a devout, unmechanized, Gaelic-speaking peasant Ireland – a pleasingly Irish state of affairs, since the islanders were widely reputed to be descended in part from one of Cromwell's oppressive English garrisons which, by some unhappy oversight, had never been relieved, with the result that the homesick East Anglians or West Countrymen intermarried with the islanders and returned en masse to the Church of Rome.

Before we left, the Deaf Malvernian went across the road from Trinity to Fox's, the celebrated tobacconists whose Provost's

Mixture featured a drawing of the Campanile on the tin; the Deaf had read – in Synge, I think – that the islanders, like old-fashioned pirates or toothless varmints in Westerns, were greatly given to chewing quids of tobacco, deftly spitting the soggy detritus from the corners of their mouths. He hoped to ingratiate himself with the locals by offering them individual portions of chewing tobacco, and to this end he caused to be brought up from the vaults of Fox's great blocks of sticky black tobacco, which he then cut into small cubes and wrapped carefully away in the bottom of his suitcase. Sad to say, he had little luck with this ingenious ploy, since all his intended beneficiaries turned ungratefully away, mystified or repelled by the unpleasant and unfamiliar objects he brandished so eagerly before them.

Since Shore's district nurse's car was unavailable to us, we decided to hitch-hike to Galway, where we were to pick up the weekly boat to the islands. We got a lift most of the way with a travelling salesman, the boot of whose car was filled with bags of fertilizer and colourful brochures in which beaming farmers in waistcoats and tweed caps gazed happily into the camera against a background of emerald hills and cloudless Wedgwood sky. As we trundled through the grey, soggy Midlands and down the main streets of drab, rainswept little towns made up of white or flint-coloured matchbox houses, he told us with gusto of how Roscommon – Ireland's answer, it seemed, to the Isle of Ely – was the most inbred county in Ireland, of its alarming lunacy rate and the prevalence of webbed feet, and whiled away the long hours with lurid tales of rural incest of every conceivable permutation, and of sex-crazed, lonely farmers ravishing sheep, goats, dogs, rabbits and even – when overcome by uncontrollable tides of lust – turkeys and Rhode Island Reds.

The rusty cargo boat from Galway was full of knobbly, red-faced islanders in flat caps, grey tweed suits and blue flannel shirts; puzzled German philologists in metal-rimmed spectacles making earnest observations in slim, efficient notebooks bound in soft black leather (at the approach of one of these ponderous scholars the islanders helpfully broke into the Gaelic, bringing him to a fever pitch of excitement by casual, passing references to heavily bearded and musclebound heroes of Celtic antiquity); and a gloomy Mancunian couple – he in a maroon-coloured jersey, fawn trousers and sandals with orange socks peeping underneath, she in a patterned dress and a turquoise anorak – who told us with some pride that they had been visiting the islands for the past eighteen years, but had yet to step off the steamer. Two hours later we anchored off the dazzling white sands of one of the two small islands, and to the whiff of brine and diesel oil and salt sea air was suddenly added the sweet, evocative smell of burning peat, the gentle, pervasive reek of which drifts over Ireland like a pall of incense, and nowhere more so than in the far, romantic west.

Leaning over the rails with the glum Mancunians, we watched the islanders hurrying down to the beach from their thatched and whitewashed cottages, the children leading donkeys, the women rolling empty pale blue calor gas drums, the men pushing their dark, thin curraghs into the surf and leaping nimbly aboard as the waves rolled and crashed about them. Within seconds the curraghs were nosing all about us, like black, sharp-featured sharks, taking passengers and provisions on board and dropping off the empty calor gas tins, more earnest German professors who had completed their field studies, and islanders who had decided to spend a day or two among the bright lights of the mainland. Every now and then a brown and white cow, looking pop-eyed with embarrassment, was winched overboard with a system of straps and pulleys, its legs dangling ignominiously down and a stream of cow-pats raining onto the deck below; once in the water, its halter was seized by a man from the nearest curragh, the straps and pulleys were undone, and the cow – showing surprising skills as a swimmer – was gently towed to land.

Although the Deaf and I had decided to spend our week on Inishmore, the largest of the islands, it seemed a pity not to set foot on the others; and, bidding farewell to the Mancunians, who promised they might think again next year, we lowered ourselves into a wildly swaying curragh, and were rapidly rowed ashore. The curraghs were made of canvas stretched over a wooden frame, with a great pointed prow in front, like the nose of some terrible fish; the oars seemed to consist of little more than long, and apparently bladeless, four-sided poles. Our oarsmen had large, bony faces, long fang-like yellow teeth and bright, pale-blue eyes; like the men of the Outer Isles, they spoke in soft, almost Welsh voices, and they wore on their feet pampooties – soft, rather dainty black leather shoes that tied about the ankle and looked oddly out of place, as though their beefy, weatherbeaten occupants would, upon arrival on the strand, suddenly spring away across the sands on tiptoe and execute a flawless *pas de deux*.

During my time at Trinity I spent a very great deal of time poking about the West of Ireland, striding across mountains, sitting in empty, whitewashed pubs and examining ancient abbeys where the cattle moved sluggishly about among the ruins and a rash inspection of a raised sarcophagus would, more often than not, offer an alarming glimpse of its bony occupant, grinning through the cracks at the windswept world outside; and the best of all these trips was the week I spent with the Deaf on Inishmore. We stayed with an elderly widow in a square, isolated farmhouse some miles out of Kilronan; we slept in large brass beds, with horsehair mattresses and coiled springs of the school bed variety; the lavatory consisted of an elsan in a shed at the end of a garden consisting entirely of rocks, and the door with its serrated top banged and flapped in the wind as we fought to go about our business with the help of neatly torn out squares of the *Connacht Sentinel* that hung from a spike; our landlady gave us the familiar fried breakfast, and at half-past eight every morning she drove us out of the house, each equipped with a large wheel of soda bread, and sent us on our way.

It was the coldest, as well as the windiest, place I had ever known: I wore two pairs of trousers, two shirts, three jerseys and some kind of anorak, and I was still cold and drenched by the sudden Atlantic storms that in an instant blackened the sky and quite blotted out the sun; I wore out my only pair of shoes on the rocks after four days, cunningly – if ineffectively – soling them with discarded sardine-tin boxes. In the tiny, whitewashed pubs – consisting of a pair of benches, a table, and a couple of silver barrels of Guinness on the floor – conversation ground to an awkward halt as we appeared, looking waterlogged and cheerful, to be resumed in very obvious Gaelic; the Deaf – like some Victorian trader bringing out his glass beads and brass rods in darkest Africa, or a pork pie hatted commercial traveller snapping open his case of samples – rummaged about in his oilskins for the placatory quids of tobacco, and was met with puzzled rebuffs; when we did eventually fall into conversation with the islanders the Deaf distressed them once again by failing to hear what they said, gazing blankly ahead of him with not the faintest flicker of interest lighting up his features, or cutting sharply across a long and eloquent description of island life, rising brusquely to his feet, looking keenly at his watch and telling me it was time we were on our way.

I assumed, in my patronizing, ignorant way, that few of the islanders had been to Galway, let alone Dublin or even England, for their distinctive, handmade clothes and shoes, their unusual bony looks and their quiet gentle speech seemed to set them apart even in the west of Ireland, as though they were – or should be – a protected species or dwellers on some kind of Celtic reservation. To my surprise, I found that many of the old-timers to whom I had been speaking in slow and measured tones, wondering whether they had heard of trains or aeroplanes or television sets, had, in fact, spent most of their working lives in Boston or New York, returning in old age to the islands they had left in their teens. Every now and then we bumped into large, middle-aged Americans in grey herringbone jackets and button-down shirts and huge flat-bottomed brogues and even – if the day was unusually warm – a blue and white seersucker jacket and candy-coloured spectacles; they too were expatriate islanders who had returned to their native patch at last, to end their days among the dry-stone walls and tiny, grudging fields strewn with seaweed and the great black cliffs with the seabirds wheeling overhead and the Aegean blue of the sea and the great sweep of the horizon and the sleepy, inescapable tang of peat. As we said farewell to our apple-cheeked landlady and boarded the boat for Galway (together with a Gaelic scholar from Heidelberg and a policeman from Galway) I felt I was leaving somewhere unique and precious and – for all our brief acquaintance – very dear to me. Since then, I learn, they have built a golf course and an airstrip on Inishmore; and I know I shall never return.

*   *   *

Although I found it hard to summon up quite the same intensity of emotion that I had once spent (in vain) upon the person of ffenella – about whom I had confided, to my diary, swooning speculations about her lips and bosom and Titian-coloured hair – I now fancied myself to be keenly in love with the fair-haired Damsel in the sensible tweeds, and eagerly looked forward to an ecstatic reunion at the beginning of the summer term, in the course of which I hoped we could pick up the threads of this curious business of kissing. Sad to say, the exciting preliminaries of the term before were to lead no further, for within a few days of our return to Dublin she had found a new and far more suitable admirer in the shape of a large, contented undergraduate with the sleepy, benevolent look of a bibulous hamster who was – unusually for a hamster – given to reading the *Daily Telegraph* in front of the fire in a cardigan and a pair of leather bedroom slippers of the kind carried about in the mouths of labradors.

I learned of my loss the day after I had returned from an important visit to the Mullingar Music Festival. The annual Ard Fheis, or Music Festival, was usually held in some remote outpost of the Gaeltacht in West Cork or Connemara, but this year it was to take place in Mullingar, a small grey town in the Midlands within easy reach of Dublin. Despite my incurably English looks and fearful stiffness of feature when confronted by any kind of song and dance routine in which I might conceivably be expected to participate, even to the extent of tapping my foot or, still worse, clapping my hands together in a hearty, uninhibited way, I nursed a most unEnglish passion for Irish music, for the plangent wail of uilleann pipes and shrieking fiddles and rattling spoons and the jaunty melancholy of tin whistles, and had spent many enjoyable hours in the rooms of the Deaf Malvernian listening to the dirge-like laments of the MacPeake Family of Belfast. Pipers, fiddlers, and red-faced accordionists, nimble-footed dancers in saffron kilts would, we gathered, be converging on the little town from all over Ireland, along with solemn, bespectacled Gaelic schoolmasters and ardent nationalists in Aran jerseys and hairy woollen hats; the pubs would be open, by special dispensation, for twenty-four hours on end; it seemed in every way far too good an opportunity to miss, and within minutes of reading about it in the *Irish Times* Shore and the Deaf and I were speeding towards the west as fast as the district nurse's car could take us.

By the time we arrived in Mullingar in the early evening the entire town seemed to be in a state of advanced intoxication: the doors of the pubs were flung wide open, and from within there came a confused roar of squeezeboxes and song and counter-song and cries and the sound of breaking glass and, above it all, the insistent ping and crash ·

of the cash register; men and women were staggering about the streets, bottles pressed keenly to their lips, and scattered here and there were unfortunates being sick in the gutter or being ministered to by their friends or peacefully snoozing in some neglected corner; in the middle of the bulb-lit town square, surrounded by a seething mob of puce-faced farmers and waxen-featured nuns and tight-lipped officials and hot-breathed policemen, stood a ribbon-bedecked podium, on which a group of Irish dancers were soberly and gracefully going through their paces to the accompaniment of an elderly ceilidh band.

We eagerly joined in the revels, fighting our way to the bar and draining a confusing mixture of stout and beer and Jameson's; at some stage in the proceedings we were swept along in a mass invasion of the podium and landed, to my shame, on a soft mat of giggling, portly nuns, who dusted me down and kindly helped me onto the podium once more; as dawn broke on a glinting sea of empty bottles and half-eaten bags of chips, and the musicians trailed unsteadily away, we climbed back into the district nurse's car and wove slowly back to Dublin. We found a nautical pub on the quays where we struggled – in vain, it seemed – to keep up our momentum and sustain the jollity of the night with several glasses of hot whiskey or mulled wine; it was a brilliant, sunny summer morning and, feeling by now both seedy and sorry for ourselves, we limped into Trinity via the side gate, while eager, ambitious undergraduates with gowns over their arms and bulging briefcases swinging by their sides streamed all about us in a purposeful way towards libraries and lecture halls; at the far end of College Park we came across the still smouldering remains of the cricket pavilion, ignited – or so I liked to believe – by the bull-like undergraduate who, the summer before, had disturbed our sleep in Lausanne by striding through a plate-glass door.

In the afternoon, still sweating and clutching our brows, and good for little else, we drove out to a beach to the north of Dublin, and lay slumped among the sand-dunes in porcine, repellent slumber, unshaven, unbrushed and foul of breath. In the intervals between these fitful bouts of snoozing I noticed, squinting my eyes against the sun, that the fair-haired Damsel and my friend the cardiganned hamster were not merely exchanging glances, or even modest pecks on the cheek, but sat or lay with their arms wrapped firmly round each other. By the end of the afternoon, as we motored gloomily back to Dublin, my head pulsing and throbbing as though it had been taken over by a troupe of malign Wagnerian dwarves banging their anvils with uncalled-for ferocity, I realized that another short and inconclusive episode in my life as a Lothario had drawn peacefully to its close.

★   ★   ★

It was about this time that, rather to our surprise, Shore decided to take up painting, and on weekend trips to the West he held up proceedings no end by unrolling large sheets of paper which he then proceeded to cover with drawings of dry-stone walls or gigantic piles of rock. He was extremely secretive about his work, fighting off the inquisitive with a lunge of his badly-furled umbrella, shielding his sketches from us with a curved, protective arm, and hurriedly stashing them away in a large canvas bag once he had, to his satisfaction, covered the paper with a series of large grey ovals; he invariably smoked as he worked, the ash growing ever longer and eventually tipping into his black Assyrian beard, or singeing a hole in the work in progress. Shore was, we were quite sure, a gifted painter of rocks, and seemed to produce innumerable variations on this rather restricted theme with tireless enthusiasm; but fond as I was of my friend, I had to admit, whenever I dodged the umbrella and sneaked a furtive glance, to finding his rockscapes a touch lugubrious, lacking in colour and human – or even vegetable – interest. As the weeks went by Shore became ever more reclusive about his painting; but interest in it soared to fever pitch when the Deaf Malvernian, employing some highly ingenious feint, surprised the artist at work on an ambitious oil painting in which, the Deaf assured us – his blue eyes popping with excitement, and his orange hair shooting from his head in a panoply of flame – Shore had, for the first time, introduced some animation into his lunar landscapes in the unexpected form of naked women – very fat, and very pink – bursting out of eggs identical in shape and colour to the oval rocks for which he had so strange a partiality. The Deaf's astonishing revelations excited a frenzied buzz of excitement and speculation about our unpredictable friend, whom we regarded all at once with fresh interest and respect.

We knew that, when not on a tour of Western Ireland, Shore painted his unhappy rocks and naked ladies bursting out of eggs in the Art Rooms at Trinity: he was a member, we were not, and he could paint his unusual masterpieces free from prying eyes other than those of the Deaf, who had smuggled himself into the Art Rooms in heavy disguise, and had been quickly ejected by Shore, waving his umbrella before him and making curious chuffing sounds as he drove this unwelcome intruder to the door, down the staircase and out into Botany Bay. A few days later we discovered where Shore kept his completed works. One dank and tedious evening as we lay on our beds after a heavy supper of fried bacon and black pudding, our pipes squealing like prep school plumbing, rehearsing in a desultory way for some forthcoming exam the activities of Rinucini, the Papal Legate to Ireland in the 1640s, I was suddenly so maddened by the tedium of seventeenth-century Ireland that I leapt from my enormous double bed onto Shore's more modest put-me-up in order to rouse him from the heavy slumber into which he had fallen. To my horror, there was a terrific crack and crunch of breaking glass; Shore gave a cry of shock and despair: beneath his mattress, we now learned, were at least half a dozen rockscapes (but, to our disappointment, no naked ladies bursting out of eggs), carefully framed and wrapped in brown paper and laid above the springs, safe from prying eyes but not, alas, from flying feet.

Mrs Brady was very Irish in her abhorrence of fresh veg, and whereas her modest fry-ups tended to make my pipes squeal and churn, they threatened to close down Ian's altogether. Within a week of the beginning of that particular term he was rigid with constipation, so silted up that neither syrup of figs nor All Bran nor any of the patent medicines advertised in the Dublin evening papers could send even the mildest tremor through his intestinal system. I told him from my long experience of these matters – constipation seems to have been an occupational hazard among my contemporaries when young – that an enema and plenty of exercise were the only answers to this horrid problem. Since he refused to do so himself – confining his activities to leering like a satyr through the bevelled glass of the chemist's shop at the critical moment of purchase – I bought him an enema from a shop at the bottom of Grafton Street: he packed it carefully away in his briefcase, where it remained for the rest of our time at Trinity, rubbing shoulders with the likes of Hugh Trevor-Roper and Christopher Hill, attending lectures on Isaac Butt and Hooker's *Ecclesiastical Polity*, and making occasional appearances – much to the surprise of the onlookers – on pub tables or in genteel households as its owner, having mislaid some sheet music or a gramophone record, emptied out the entire contents of his briefcase in his search for the missing object.

As an exercise, we persuaded him – for all his hatred of the countryside – to join us on an occasional stroll around Powerscourt or along the quays to Phoenix Park; while trips to the municipal baths were curtailed only after the discovery of an unpleasant, cork-like object floating in the water (not everyone in Dublin, it seemed, was in need of an enema). He seemed to get special pleasure, though, from a large silver chest-expander. Every morning, and again before jumping into bed, he would stand in the window wrestling with this diabolical device, occasionally adding an extra coil as his biceps grew ever larger and more masterful. Years before I had, in my early teens, written off in facetious mood for a Charles Atlas course, as a result of which I was deluged with a steady stream of pamphlets showing how balding, six-stone weaklings with limbs like knitting needles had been converted in a matter of days into iron-jawed musclemen, and including a photograph of Charles Atlas himself pulling a string of railway carriages with his teeth in a casual, self-confident way; even so, I found I was quite incapable of opening the expander more than six inches or so, after which it lunged back into position with a ferocious snap, catching my hair or my specs or the end of my nose in its shining coils and exciting a cry of pain and indignation. Like the enema, the chest expander ended its days in Ian's large and hospitable briefcase, soon becoming – like its new neighbour – something of an expert on constitutional history and the various Balkan Wars of the later nineteenth century.

To offset Rinucini and the vindictive chest-expander, we decided to investigate the possibilities of going to America for three months during the long summer vacation, buying a student flight from Dublin for £50 and travelling as much as we liked on Greyhound buses. A friend of mine – a cheerful, rather grand girl whose uncle was the current Father of the House of Commons – excited us greatly with her account of a student flight the year before, which had cost her a mere £30.

She and her fellow-passengers, many of them Trinity students and all of them, avowedly, committed carnation-growers, had met under the clock at Victoria Station. At one point in the proceedings they were joined by an extremely drunken Irishman with a carbuncular nose, wild-looking hair and a whisky bottle peeping out of one pocket of his shiny gaberdine mackintosh; he had to be helped on to the train that was to take them to Gatwick by a couple of equally empurpled cronies, who successfully prevented him from dashing himself to death on the rails or sliding from his seat and bruising his head on the floor of the compartment, and laid restraining hands upon him when he sought, with much pleading, to refresh himself further from the bottle in his pocket. All the way down to Gatwick, my friend assured me – her voice sinking to a shocked, conspiratorial whisper – the drunken Irishman broke into maudlin snatches of song before slumping, in mid-melody, into a gap-toothed stupor, during the course of which the carriage resounded to his porcine snores. Imagine my surprise, she told me – by now she was warming to her theme – when, as the train drew into Gatwick, the drunkard, swaying on his feet like a palm tree and struggling to hold himself upright with one hand on the luggage rack, suddenly pulled from the second pocket of his filthy gaberdine a gold-embroidered peaked cap, which he balanced on top of his boisterous fuzz of hair, and a pair of string and leather motoring gloves which, after a good deal of fumbling and misplacing of fingers and thumbs, he drew on. He then announced in a slurred and over-heated voice that he would be driving the party of carnation-growers to New York, and that they should follow him to the aeroplane, which they dutifully did.

According to my informant – normally the most reliable of girls – the flight was as alarming as might have been expected: some of the carnation-growers had to stand all the way, like strap-hangers on the tube, while others perched on crates marked 'Fragile'; still inflamed by drink, the red-nosed pilot shot off in the wrong direction – he seemed to think that New York lay vaguely in the direction of Egypt – and had to be recalled; in the frozen wastes of Gander he disappeared once more in the direction of the bar, and the journey was held up for several hours as efforts were made to fan him down and soothe his heated brow for the last, crucial leg of the journey, in the course of which he could all too easily overshoot the mark and drive straight into the Empire State Building, scattering anxious carnation-growers all over Fifth Avenue and Forty-second Street. Armed with this cautionary tale – the truth of which, of course, I never doubted – I quickly set about buying our tickets.

★　★　★

My parents never expressed any interest in paying a visit to Ireland, or seeing Trinity for themselves; years before, my mother had been to stay with some friends in a house near Cork, and though she had found them as convivial as ever, she was – as a tidy farmer's daughter, much given to energetic dusting and hoovering and polishing of surfaces – sternly unamused by the plaster raining from the ceilings, the springs shooting unexpectedly out of the chairs, the unkempt state of the garden and the grass sprouting out of the drainpipes, the wild-looking children with uncombed hair, jam-encrusted faces and a notable shortage of shoes, and – a familiar complaint from English visitors – the hairy, fierce donkeys, whose often untrimmed hooves lent them the appearance of ill-conditioned skaters.

Later, I often wondered what she would have made of the elegant late Georgian house in Sandymount, belonging to one of Dublin's most distinguished writers, and a most civilized and congenial man, in which the legs that had fallen off the family beds had been replaced with piles of books, while the walls around glimmered with Jack Yeats's cobalt Dublin scenes and the somnolent chestnut-coloured cows of Nathaniel Hone; in the meantime, much as I would have liked to have shown my parents my beloved Dublin, I found it hard not to feel an unworthy sense of relief. Dublin was a part of my life I could keep entirely to myself; and being still at an absurdly self-conscious and embarrassable age, I dreaded what horrors might be perpetrated and what indiscretions unleashed were they suddenly to appear on the ten o'clock plane from London, striding disdainfully into Front Square or down Grafton Street, scattering loud and unflattering comments on Shore's beard and Ian's trousers (about both of which I felt, all of a sudden, bristlingly protective) and the clothes, accents and general demeanour of those whom they encountered on their way.

Embarrassment, it seems to me, is one of the over-riding emotions of youth, and I was prone to it to a ludicrous degree: so much so that although from an early age I was greatly haunted by the brevity of life, and found it hard – at least in the small hours of the night – to view the world, and our part in it, in other than the gloomy, reductive perspectives of the astronomer or the geologist, I thought about my own death almost exclusively in terms of inconvenience caused or some fearful social blunder of the kind that would almost certainly excite frowns of disapproval or murmurs of reproach from those assembled all about. How embarrassing, I thought, to gasp one's last at a dinner party, sliding beneath the table with a terrible terminal grunt, casting a blight over the pudding stage, and quite baffling my hostess as she turned to address me with a bright, enquiring smile, only to find my chair mysteriously void! How awful the pathos of a massive coronary in Act Two of *Rookery Nook*, causing the actors to falter in mid-speech as all eyes swivel like one from the goings-on on stage to the second row of the stalls, while theatre staff hurry anxiously forward as my giant frame is manhandled into the wings, like an enormous sack of swedes, obliterating the view of those in the rows behind and, quite possibly, spoiling the evening for the other members of our little party! Such were the long-term worries that creased my brow and left me hollow-eyed in the morning; a more immediate cause for concern, however, was always much nearer at hand – as it so often is among those of that age – in the form of family and friends determined, it seemed, to say the wrong thing.

Years earlier, on my first day at public school, my father – stunned at my gullibility and, though always the kindest of men, unable to resist – had persuaded me to take up knitting and take with me a long, pale blue sample of my work on the grounds that, however bad I might be at conventional games, my expertise would almost immediately win me a place in my house knitting team; within seconds of my arrival I had fathomed the depths of his deception, and the pale blue knitting – along with an elderly teddy bear, who had come on my own initiative – spent the rest of the term unhappily hidden away in the bottom of my black tin tuck box, never to reappear; who knew what comparable crimes might not be perpetrated were they to be let loose on my side of the Irish Sea?

Although my sister and I were extremely fond and very proud of our parents, finding them well above average in terms of informality, dash and youthful good looks – early on in my prep school career a precocious and rather fat Indian boy had informed me that my mother was 'a very good-looking woman', rolling his prune-like eyes and describing invisible egg-timers in the air with his outstretched hands – we had both suffered agonies of embarrassment on learning that they were planning to descend on the school for half term to take us out. How inevitable it seemed that they would refer loudly to our nicknames in front of our friends, or call us collectively 'the children', so undermining – in my case at least – all my hard-won (and seemingly futile) efforts to establish myself as one of the boys! How I envied those sensible boys whose grey or rapidly balding fathers wore quiet lovat-coloured suits and professed an interest in the cricket scores, and whose dowdy, matronly mothers sported white gloves and absurd hats like puce-coloured almond whirls and made modest clucking sounds in the background! Instead of camping out in a small ex-army tent – within sight of the school grounds! – and pumping up paraffin stoves and shaking out sleeping bags and unscrewing thermos flasks of soup, why couldn't they behave like regulation parents and book in at one of the old-fashioned chintz-covered family hotels in which the town abounded? Much as I enjoyed deriding *nouveau riche* scrap metal merchants from Wolverhampton who staggered importantly about the grounds on open days in brown or silver suits and silver ties, clutching outrageously large cigars between bejewelled and manicured fingers, while their spouses trailed along behind, ablaze with diamonds, peroxide and swathes of leopard skin, I sometimes experienced an ignoble pang as our half-timbered former Macfisheries delivery van – so dear in its proper context – came gasping and rattling up the drive and took its place among the cigar-puffers' immense white Jaguars and important-looking family saloons.

My mother, in particular, seemed to have little respect for or understanding of the codes and traditions of school life, of which I found myself – much to my own surprise – a sudden and temporary enthusiast. On one particularly dreadful half term she left me holding her handbag in front of a surging and startled mass of sportsmen and scoffers (in a photograph recording this unfortunate incident, I look – in my boater, black jacket and sponge bag trousers – like a muscular grandmother who has been suddenly, and painfully, turned to stone); and then, to make matters worse, she made off with the matron's dog. A year or two back my parents had owned a small white whippet; it was a friendly enough beast, but – like many whippets – it seemed to devote a good deal of time to trembling and suffering from indigestion, so much so that it had once been sick on the shiny green lino outside my housemaster's study. Showing great presence of mind, my father scooped up the sick in one hand and hurled it out of the window into the housemaster's garden, where other parents were milling about clutching cups of tea and fixture cards. This particular whippet had been summoned to the great kennel in the sky, and was still sorely missed. The matron in my house owned an almost identical white whippet, a spirited animal which was extremely popular with the boys – and with non-sportsmen in particular, since it had an admirable habit of rushing onto the cricket field and carrying off the ball, or holding up play at a critical moment by bearing onto the pitch a twig or a tennis ball, which it then expected, with many imploring looks and much wagging of the tail – a serious-minded batsman or demon bowler to throw for it. Since I never seemed to be ill, I had very little to do with the matron except by proxy, for I ate up off the end of a ruler all the radio malt that she distributed to allegedly weedy or undernourished boys whose anxious parents thought they needed building up, or whose bones were in need of reinforcement; but thanks to the whippet, my mother and the matron were friends in an instant. It turned out that the matron could no longer keep the dog and was looking for a new home, and when my parents left that evening the whippet was happily seated in the back of the converted Macfisheries van, its tongue lolling out and a cheerful smile lighting up its features. This damnable deed was instantly blamed upon me by hearties and aesthetes alike; and I thought again with a purely provisional envy of those sedate, conventional parents who would no more have made off with the matron's dog than shaken out their bedding within full view of the entire school, masters and boys alike.

As we grow older we delight in the unusual; children prefer to read about such matters or describe them at second-hand, and exhibit in everyday life – in front of their friends at least – a terrible urge to conform and not be the odd man out. How sharply, and how unworthily, my sister and I disassociated ourselves from our mother when she skidded up on a dog's mess outside Peter Jones and lay laughing on the pavement while we stared stonily ahead into a windowful of underclothes, pretending that the unseemly goings-on behind us were none of our concern! How we strove to ignore the rude intruder when, at a rather grand party full of alarmingly sophisticated sixteen-year-olds, to none of whom we had addressed a word, she arrived to pick us up and, seeing us looking bored and gloomy and alone, had roared out in a voice so loud that the band stopped playing and all heads swivelled scornfully in our direction, 'I should come home now, kiddies, if you're bored!' Little did I guess, in those far-off, unduly anguished days, that in a surprisingly short time my wife and I would be embarrassing our daughters in exactly the same sort of way, and that they would live in dread of her turning up at school in a pair of bedroom slippers or an overcoat thrown over her nightie, or of my clapping too loud and too long at a school speech day, or waving from the audience at a daughter on the podium with such vigour and such enthusiasm that, once again, all eyes swivelled in my direction. In the meantime, and in Ireland, I was more than happy to get on with the business of growing up, unobserved and on my own.

CHAPTER NINE

South of the Border

Rather to my disappointment, the student flight to New York from Dublin turned out to be a tame, well-ordered affair, with none of the high drama or eccentric piloting offered to the carnation-growers the year before; I was, however, pleased to note that at least three-quarters of the students on board consisted of nuns, elderly countrymen in brown tweeds who wrung their flat caps in their hands all the way across the Atlantic, like old-fashioned washerwoman battling with a particularly stubborn stain, and young labourers in jeans and donkey jackets and mud-encrusted army boots, second cousins no doubt to those stout-swilling figures I had encountered two years before on the Holyhead-Dun Laoghaire boat, who were off to earn an honest bob digging drains in Brooklyn or the Bronx, and strolled off the plane with the easy nonchalance more fitted, I felt, to a trip on the Bakerloo line from Kilburn to Charing Cross. I had been lent a flat somewhere in the East Sixties; as I trundled into New York aboard the airport bus, and strolled about the canyon-like streets of the great city, I thought it the most thrilling and the most beautiful place I had ever visited – and, with Chicago, far superior to those mildly European cities, like New Orleans or San Francisco, of which the Americans seemed so inordinately fond.

In New York I met up with my two travelling companions, Messrs Shore and Rivers. New York felt like the hottest room in a Turkish bath, causing my spectacles to steam up at the slightest provocation and plastering my shirt to my body in unseemly swabs of sweat, and encouraging the well-versed locals to move about the streets with the unhurried tread of a film run extra-slow: Shore, I was glad to note, was wearing exactly the same clothes as he had worn in Greece the year before, including the thick blue jersey with the turn-down collar, swatting the air with his umbrella as he hurried us off to examine the paintings in the Frick or the unicorn tapestry in the Cloisters.

Rivers was a huge, friendly fellow who looked as though he must have had a touch of the Hereford bull somewhere in his background, for he had the same breadth of nose, the same look of rather baffled ferocity, and the same top-knot of tight fair curls: only the horns and the hooves were missing, and they could well have been concealed about his ample person. Rivers's great virtues as a traveller were conviviality and audacity: whereas Shore and I were brave in principle and on paper but timid and law-abiding in practice, Rivers had the qualities of a jovial bulldozer, brushing aside form-waving customs men and tiny Central American soldiers toting outsize machine-guns, and enabling Shore and I to sail through in his wake. These qualities were much in demand in the weeks ahead, since we had decided to make our way down to Mexico, and see what happened after that.

In Mexico City we took care to avoid eating fresh veg (we had read distressing articles about the use of human manure), admired Diego Rivera's angry murals of apoplectic Englishmen in bowler hats, and booked in to the Hotel Monte Carlo, in which for some peculiar reason cars were parked in the sitting room and guests picked their way between the bonnets and propped their drinks among the luggage racks; we had to share an enormous bed in the attic, and prepared ourselves for sleep by lying in a row, like the bearded aviators in *A Night at the Opera*, drinking Mexican brandy tasting of burned sugar out of toothmugs. In Guatamala, the most beautiful country I had ever seen, with its green misty mountains the shape of tongues and Indian peasants in costumes as bright as the parrots that flapped from tree to tree, we camped by the bottomless waters of Lake Atitlan with its ring of tapering volcanoes, and were worshipped as gods from the East by some over-excited Indians in Chichicast-enango who had been busying themselves sacrificing chickens in their Spanish colonial church.

In El Salvador we were given a lift by a government minister, whose enormous car, flanked by out-riders on motorbikes, screeched to a halt in a village of straw huts and clucking hens and empty petrol tins; his ideas about contemporary England owed much to an extensive reading of Henry Mayhew, and as we sped along he quizzed us keenly about costermongers and flower-girls and those unfortunate individuals who – some hundred years before – haunted the sewers of London searching for missing valuables. In Tegucigalpa, the capital of Honduras, I disgraced myself by passing out in the downstairs lavatory of a hospitable South American ambassador. We had eaten nothing all day but bananas; our host, who had recently been posted in London, was wretchedly homesick for that city and had everything he needed sent out from Harrods in crates of the kind that I had spent the autumn after leaving school hammering together in their warehouse on the other side of the Brompton Road. His garden was full of bibulous, red-nosed fellow diplomats, including an excitable American shouting 'Gunga Din', and before the evening was out, his whisky had done its worst. Desperate for news of Anglo-Saxon life, the ambassador and his wife put us up for the next three days while I recovered from my hangover, after which they pointed us in the direction of the coast, where we hoped to find a boat that would take us across the small slice of the Caribbean that lay between Honduras proper and its British namesake.

The road to Puerto C— was the colour and consistency of hot corned beef, and ran through large, sweaty hills that looked as though they had been draped with over-cooked spinach. We travelled for the most part in enormous grey lorries with chimneys, wheels at least five feet high, and a cab at about the level of the second deck of a London bus. We stopped the night in one of those diminutive Central American towns that seemed to be peopled entirely by juvenile shoeblacks, strollers and soft-drinks salesmen pushing barrows, and to be lit by strings of bare bulbs looped among the trees; we slept on benches in a small public park, and during the night an enterprising townsman unlaced Shore's shoes, removed them from his feet, and made off with them into the darkness.

Next morning we arrived in Puerto C—. It seemed custom-built for Graham Greene, including as it did some motheaten palm trees, a greasy sea with rusty banana boats anchored off shore and dead dogs bobbing about closer to, men with straw hats and no teeth, and lavatories suspended on posts over the water, below which brightly coloured fish circled eagerly about, waiting for manna to rain from heaven. Much of the main street, it seemed, had burned down some twenty-four hours earlier, and smoke was still drifting across the town; all that remained was row upon row of metal hospital bed frames, for every other house had been a brothel, and since all the houses were made of clapboard, only the bedsteads had survived the conflagration.

Feeling very English and out-of-place, we lugged our rucksacks into the nearest bar and sat down, hoping – in vain – to be able to order a wholesome breakfast. Being nearer the waterfront, this particular bar had survived the flames; it doubled up as a brothel, and even at that early hour customers were stumping solemnly upstairs, unbuckling their belts as they went, like early commuters hurrying to catch the train. After a few minutes we were approached by a friendly Jamaican without any shoes on, who tried to persuade us to invest in a gold mine further down the coast, most of the produce of which appeared to have ended in his teeth: when we demurred, and explained that we would rather go to Belize instead, he was all anxiety to help. 'No problem,' he assured us. 'I'll take you there in my boat. It's only a mile or two across the bay.'

We spent most of that day sitting in the bar-cum-brothel and strolling disconsolately along the waterfront, eyeing the dead dogs and wondering whether we would ever emerge from this dreadful place intact. Towards the evening, our Jamaican friend summoned us, and took us down to the sea to inspect his boat.

'Are you sure it's only a mile or two away?' I asked him as we tramped towards a rotten-looking jetty from which most of the planks were missing: for according to my map Belize was at least sixty miles away.

'That's it over there,' he insisted, pointing to a line of clouds on the horizon. 'Ten miles – maybe twenty – nothing more.'

Shore and I took one look at the Jamaican's boat and for the first – but by no means the last – time we decided that, whatever Rivers might think, this was going too far. We had expected something with an outboard motor, or at least a small sailing boat: drawn up on the beach was a hollowed-out tree-trunk of the type I associated with the cannibals in *Coral Island*, with the odd plank lashed to the end of a stick serving as a paddle. Hating to hurt the kindly Jamaican's feelings, we politely but firmly refused his offer; Rivers, on the other hand, leapt enthusiastically aboard, told us that he would see us in Belize, seized a home-made paddle and vanished into the dusk, his rucksack behind him and the genial Jamaican to the fore, his voice ringing out over the water as he denounced us for our feebleness of spirit.

As we strolled back along the smouldering main street, Shore and I wondered how on earth we were going to explain our abandonment of Rivers to his parents in Reigate, for we were convinced that our intrepid fellow-undergraduate had paddled off to meet his Maker. Rivers's father was of the peppery colonel school, while his mother was given to twittering anxiety; both, it seemed, were likely to take a dim view of the proceedings, and might well be unamused when they learned that we had allowed their only son to set out to sea in a hollowed-out tree-trunk under the command of a toothless gold prospector. By now it was dark, and the greasy waters of the bay suddenly sparkled with reflected lights, and the dead dogs and abandoned oil drums were mercifully shrouded in darkness. With our innocent English faith in the rectitude and reliability of men in uniforms, we approached a stocky individual with a large revolver dangling from his belt, from whom gold braid sprouted like some exotic fungus. He assured us – rightly, as it turned out – that the only way we could get from Puerto C— to Belize was to retrace our steps to Tegucigalpa and climb on board an Air Honduras Dakota; there were no buses till the morning; as for where we could stay the night – his eyes glazed over, and he waved one hand in a large, dismissive way towards the streets beyond, which were suddenly aswarm with sailors, dockers, confidence tricksters and banana salesmen, all (or so I nervously assumed) working themselves up into a frenzy of ferocity with glass after glass of fortified rum, and preparing to lash out to left and right with their machetes once the mood was upon them.

We sat in various bars for most of the evening, keeping our backs to the wall and watching the locals with keen suspicion, waiting for the first signs of machetes being drawn from their scabbards: from time to time stoutish girls with faint moustaches and compressed bosoms foaming over the top of tight and tubular dresses would try to invite us upstairs but were met with a polite refusal ('No, thank you very much indeed'). Towards midnight we picked up our rucksacks and tramped tiredly along the quayside, dimly hoping to come across the Honduran equivalent of the kind of windswept family hotel one finds in Seaford or Skegness, replete with black and orange swirly carpets, sauce bottles, a highly polished brass gong, plastic flowers and the sound of *The Archers* drifting down the hall. Such places seemed impossible to find; instead we eventually banged on the door of a delapidated verandahed building made of corrugated iron.

A grill was opened in the front door, and a rather bad-tempered woman looked out. Realizing that we were foreigners, she muttered morosely about 'girls' and tried, in a lacklustre fashion, to interest us in the various services available in the corrugated iron shack, and the cost of each particular item. Eventually we persuaded her that we wanted nothing more than a bed for the night: looking surprised and rather cross, she led us down an unlit corridor, showed us into a room in which there were, for some odd reason, two beds of the prep school variety, and left us to our fate.

It was far from the pleasantest place in which I have spent the night, and a long way from the doily-festooned bed-and-breakfast of our dreams. The mattresses on which we laid our sleeping bags were strained and streaked with heaven knew what hideous exudings; we were separated from our neighbours by partitions that were made of plywood up to six feet or so from the ground and chicken wire above that, and our rest was interrupted all night by horrid puffings and deathly groans as over-excited seadogs and banana salesmen made full use of the facilities we had so ungraciously disdained; gigantic brown cockroaches flew busily about the room, landing on our faces with disturbingly sticky feet, and when we could stand it no longer we chased them about with our shoes and smashed them against the walls with a satisfying if repellent crack.

Early next morning we set out on the long haul back to Tegucigalpa, where we were put up by a homesick employee of the Bank of London and South America who wanted to talk about life in Worcester Park and the pleasures of commuting to Waterloo. The airport – like the bus station – was full of legless beggars pushing themselves about on flat trollies mounted on wheels, and holding out stumps for hands; on the elderly Dakota we were each handed a bottle of Coca-Cola daintily wrapped in a tissue, and a straw to suck it up through. In Belize there was no sign of Rivers; we waited there for a couple of days, fanning ourselves on the verandah of a tumbledown white wooden hotel, left messages, and moved on.

Thumbing a lift through the Yucatan, we were enshrouded by a sinister, sticky cloud of vast black and yellow butterflies, made to feel thoroughly ill-at-ease by disagreeable-looking iguanas, and attacked by an army of heavily armed mosquitoes in Meridan. Back in the cooler, drier mountain air, and sleeping in scrub by the side of the road, we were wakened in the middle of the night by theatrically attired Mexicans in ponchos and broad-brimmed hats carrying a paraffin lamp and leading a cow; lit from below, like a candlelit scene by Georges de la Tour, they proceeded to cut its throat - catching the blood in an enormous jug - before slicing the unfortunate animal into a series of cleanly dissected joints, which they put into sacks before extinguishing the light and disappearing as quietly and as quickly as they had come.

Back in Mexico City we left more messages at the Hotel Monte Carlo, together with a spare pair of shoes and various items which Rivers had been unable to squeeze on board the hollowed-out tree trunk; and I began - with a great deal of scratching out and tearing up of sheets of air mail paper - to write the dreadful letter to Reigate in which I would, as tactfully and as tastefully as possible, break the news to his sorrowing, elderly parents that their only son and heir was, even as I wrote, lying on the bottom of the Caribbean with a toothless Jamaican gold prospector having his bones picked clean by assorted sharks, sting-rays and piranha fish.

Two months later we were standing about in Harvard - the letter, still uncompleted, lay in my rucksack beside me - when I spotted a large, jovial figure with the looks of a Hereford bull loping across the Yard towards me. He had had the time of his life, he assured us: the hollowed-out tree-trunk had run aground on a coral reef some miles off the coast of British Honduras; Rivers had done dreadful things to himself on the coral, and had contracted some kind of tropical fever; somehow the kindly gold prospector had refloated his tree-trunk and taken his babbling guest to some obscure settlement where he had left him, sweating heavily, with the locals before heading home to Puerto C— to resume his prospecting business. Having set our minds at rest, Rivers hurried away to board a Greyhound bus, saying that he'd see us in Ireland in the autumn. With a cry of relief, I burrowed in my rucksack and tore up the letter to Reigate. Next year I would find myself writing, or preparing to write, a very similar letter from the Jordanian desert; but that is another story.

★   ★   ★

Back in the United States, we spent the next two and a half months travelling frenziedly about the country in Greyhound buses: since we could only afford to spend one night in five in a YMCA or a cheap boarding house, we spun out as many nights as we could on the road, jumping on whatever bus happened to be going in vaguely the right direction from eleven o'clock in the evening onwards, our faces lit a curious underwater green by the night lights, and our bodies clammy with frozen perspiration as a result of the air conditioning. Being nothing if not English travellers, we spent a good deal of time complaining about the sealed-up windows and wondering in loud and puzzled voices why American buses - unlike their Southdown equivalents, which hurtled along the coast road between Eastbourne and Brighton at all of twenty-five miles per hour - were unequipped with windows which, by dint of a great deal of winding on a handle, would open a good six inches, so introducing a gust of turbulent seaside air, blowing newspapers inside out and causing elderly ladies with enormous white handbags on their knees to clutch at hats made of straw and decorated, for some inexplicable reason, with artificial cherries and other varieties of fruit and veg.

We saw, in this way, a very great deal of America. I have always been a physical coward of the most ignoble variety, dodging behind my wife at the sight of a drunken Glaswegian reeling down the road towards us, a half bottle of whisky peeping from his jacket pocket, a tin of lager waving in one hand and a terrible approximation to song bursting from his lips, or keenly averting my gaze when large men with shaven heads and eyes like malignant sultanas and outsize boots and gigantic stomachs hanging over their trousers start to abuse mine host, or lingering longer in bed than I should at the sound of a crash downstairs in the middle of the night: although I loved America - and not only because it spared one the excruciating pains of trying to communicate with foreigners, forcing unnatural sounds from one's lips to uncomprehending stares and twisting the features in a permanent, ingratiating grin - it had, even in those days, a reputation for ferocity, and I spent more time than I should crossing the road whenever I saw anyone under the age of sixty-five heading in my direction.

Apart from New York, I particularly relished the Deep South, with its tongue-and-groove shacks and great trees dripping with spanish moss and Georgian fanlights and white porticoes half-glimpsed through the foliage and general air of indolence and decay: whereas the great deserts of Arizona and the West - which I knew I was supposed to admire - looked to me like a waste land full of clinkers, and not a spot in which to linger. Since the South was known to be a sink of iniquity and a source of national shame, I kept my preferences to myself when talking to those we met along the way.

Not being at that time sufficiently given over to nostalgia, or particularly interested in my own immediate past, I quite failed - to my lasting regret - to take the opportunity of revisiting the interminable, wheat-laden acres of the Canadian prairies, in the middle of which we had, somewhat incongruously, spent a sizeable slice of 1954.

* * *

We had travelled out to Canada on a rounded, friendly Canadian Pacific boat that had, we were informed, spent part of the war years lying on the bottom of the sea, and had only recently been hauled to the surface, given a lick of paint, equipped with its full complement of deck quoits, bar stools, heavily eyebrowed officers and jocular ship's doctors, and pressed into service once again, its brass fittings gleaming in the pallid sun and the ship's library full of middle-aged women reading the novels of Rosamond Lehmann. My father had gone on ahead, and my mother, my sister and I travelled as a threesome, sharing a cabin, the porthole of which was soon festooned with teddys' undergarments hung out to dry in the stiff sea breeze. My mother brought with her several enormous and very elderly wood and canvas suitcases, one of which contained - carefully wrapped in sheets of tissue paper - some brand new breeches and a pair of highly polished riding boots, for she expected to fit in a good deal of riding on the prairies, and was anxious to set the cowboys a good example.

Of the trip out I remember little beyond the excitement of spotting our first iceberg off the coast of Newfoundland - the housey-housey players and the bogus majors propping themselves up on the rail to watch it passing by, before hurrying back to enjoy an even larger gin-and-It - and the little, red-roofed houses peeping through the mist on the green and sloping sides of the St Lawrence estuary. In Montreal the boys of my age looked alarmingly bright and up-to-date, their crew cuts and jeans and sneakers and shiny blue or red satin baseball jackets a dazzling contrast to the knee-length grey flannels, concertina'ed socks and fairisle sleeveless sweaters of post-war English youth. Dimly aware that we were in - or at least adjacent to - the land of the horror comic and the teenage gang, I suspected the apparently mild sons of the family with whom we were staying of concealing flick-knives and bicycle chains about their persons, and to keep them at bay I offered them some English pennies I had in my pockets; once my supply of Danegeld had run out, I felt entirely at the mercy of this mighty continent.

In Regina - the capital of Saskatchewan - we lived in a variety of different houses, including a hotel near the railway station, where I slaked my insatiable appetite for cowboy comics, comparing and contrasting the techniques and adventures of Gene Autry, Roy Rogers, the Lone Ranger and a thousand others, many of whom tended even in comic form to double chins, expansive waistlines and a certain thinning at the temples, and looked as though they would be more at home in the company car, a case of samples by their sides and their jackets neatly suspended from hangers behind the driving seat, than on the back of a wild-eyed Palomino. Other abodes included a wooden house in the suburbs, in the basement of which I discovered a cache of ancient *Life*s, that included an arresting view of Jane Russell's bosom surrounded by straw; and a boarding house run by a benevolent Chinaman with an interesting if restricted vocabulary.

It was while we were living with Mr Tom Maw Dot that my sister and I made the unwise decision to go and see a film called *The House of Wax*, which was driving audiences around the world beserk with fear, and was currently showing at one of Regina's leading cinemas. The commissionaire made no attempt to stop us, let alone issue us with any kind of health warning; we hung about outside, wondering whether or not we dared go in and half hoping that something would prevent us from doing so; then suddenly made a dash for it, bought our tickets and our red and green 3-D spectacles and - wishing by now that we had gone for a walk in the park instead – took our places in the auditorium.

The villain of the piece was a sinister gentleman whose face had been hideously disfigured in a fire; so dreadful were his looks, and so unappealing to the ladies – most of whom wore low-cut satin 'gowns' at all hours of the day or night – that he had, by some miracle of plastic surgery, built himself a detachable second face, complete with pointed moustache, black goatee beard and the full range of mobile features. Sad to say, the fire had had a deleterious effect on our hero's character, too; charming and suave by candlelight, clad always in tails and a white bow tie, by night he became the terror of the Paris streets. He was, it seemed, an important and ambitious figure in the world of waxworks; and rather than go to the expense of employing full-time workers in wax, he preferred to wait until he came across someone who looked surprisingly similar to Julius Caesar or Marie Antoinette, quietly put them to death, lightly coat them in wax, and prop them up in his museum, suitably dressed for the part.

All this was unpleasant enough, though not too horrific to one who had read, with horrid fascination, the trials of Neville Heath and of the fiendish Haig with his acid baths, and had peered nervously under his bed in case the clerk-like figure of Reginald Christie, the Monster of Rillington Place, had sought refuge there from the massed policemen of England, and had breathed a great sigh of relief on learning that the master criminal had been arrested by Putney Bridge; altogether intolerable, however, were the scenes in which Paris was swathed in purple and mustard-coloured fog, and the normally urbane waxworks proprietor, his terrible features hidden by the collar of his cape and the inevitable top hat, prowled out in search of his victims, swinging nimbly from wall to window on the end of a rope and grinning unpleasantly into the faces of his lightly-sleeping victims, most of whom – like the French actresses whose toes got stuck in the bath – seemed to wear a great deal of make-up in bed and nighties even more low-cut than the 'gowns' they wore by day.

At moments such as these we lowered our 3-D specs, converting the dreadful doings on screen to a blissful blur, then peeked again with a gasp of horror at the sight of his scalded, beetroot features and enormous bloodshot eyes. Confronted by his subterranean laboratory, rigid with wax-encrusted corpses and seething retorts, my sister gave a sudden cry of fear, dashed for the exit and ran all the way home; I decided to sit it out to the end, but could stand it no more when the heroine, suddenly realizing that she was alone in a laboratory with a man who was not all that he claimed to be, beat upon his handsome, saturnine face, and cracked the mould so that his false face fell away, exposing the puce and twisted features we had come to dread so much, like an enormous foetus driven mad by drink – at such a sight I too turned and ran, sprinting half way across the city and never stopping till I'd reached our Chinaman's homely clapboard house and my bed on the verandah.

For years afterwards I was haunted by the waxwork-owner's terrible features, so much so that even to hear the film's name made me sweat with fear, and my dreams were racked by this lurid embodiment of evil; and although I imagine that – to an adult – *The House of Wax* would seem a creaking, overblown affair, redolent of pasteboard and hoary props and make-up over-lavishly applied, when they showed it on television a year or two ago I dared not watch it in case the old horrors renewed their ghastly power.

That summer my mother took us camping in the Rockies. We drove west across interminable prairies through Moosejaw and Medicine Hat and out towards Calgary; every now and then we came to a railway line and were held up by a goods train so long that it was hard to remember how and when it had started when the guard's van eventually trundled into view; and all about us the land stretched on and on in shimmering waves of gold. Beyond Calgary we suddenly spotted the Rockies, and rushed towards them like sailors starved of the sea. In Banff we went riding; my sister and I approved of the cowboy saddles, with their comfortable backs and enormous pommels to cling on to, but they excited a certain derision from my mother, as did the cowboys' habit of riding with low-slung stirrups and legs straight out, rather than with their knees about their ears. That night we pitched our tent in a camping ground, with a lake on one side and the pine trees all about. In the middle of the night we were woken by the rasping sound of a grizzly bear sharpening his nails on a nearby tree. My mother shot out of the tent in her nightie and spoke sternly to the bear, who slunk away looking sheepish and ashamed; and after that our nights were undisturbed.

*   *   *

After Shore and Rivers had left to go back to England – with what a terrible pang of envy I saw them go! – I took a bus down to Washington and went to stay with a friend of my parents, a jolly divorcee who looked rather like Marilyn Monroe and had two small children and a middle-aged admirer. The children, though beautiful to look at, had voices like characters from a Donald Duck cartoon and spent more time than was good for them wrenching open the door of a fridge the size of a sentry box, from which they emerged clutching vast kegs of fizzy drink and gigantic slabs of ice-cream, which they ate in a loud and messy manner while striding about the house; as a well brought up Englishman, taught not to eat between meals or while moving from room to room, I viewed such behaviour with a censorious, maidenly eye, flinching convulsively back should their sticky features lunge too close and wincing at their sudden cries of rage.

On my second night there the admirer, with much winking and leering and nudging of the elbow, lent me a knee-length white tweed jacket and a Texas-style string tie – for, he assured me in resonant tones, we had to be properly dressed for the occasion – and took me into Washington to a striptease club where, to my disappointment, the dancers wore chaste if spangled G-strings and twirled tassells from their bosoms, each revolving in opposite directions with such force that I expected the dancer to be lifted from the ground at any moment and whir away over our heads into realms of celestial cigar smoke, lit for ever by strobe lights. After a couple of days I began to feel *de trop*: I told my hostess that I needed a swim, and that I would take a bus to Miami for that purpose.

Deprived of my friends and no longer bold, and increasingly short of cash, I found myself whirling about America like a headless chicken in trousers, or a bespectacled Flying Dutchman weighed down with a terrible freight of dirty underpants and American paperbacks and a gigantic, razor-sharp knife which our kindly host in Tegucigalpa, fearing for our safety but quite mistaking his man, had pressed upon me in the firm belief that it alone stood between me and immediate extinction at the hands of rum-crazed banana salesmen or man-eating pumas or Mexican bandits with unshaven chins and prune-like eyes.

After making several frenzied circuits of the States – occasionally calling in at a small hotel for a good night's sleep – I eventually reboarded my Aer Lingus flight along with my fellow-'students', including once again a large party of nuns, the red-faced farmers twisting their caps between their hands, and an identical team of labourers in navy-blue donkey jackets, with the mud of the Bronx firmly adhering to their boots. I changed planes in Dublin, and caught the train down to Seaford from Victoria in time for an evening bathe and a walk along the front. As I walked round from the station, sunburnt and begrimed, with a thousand lurid anecdotes waiting to be unleashed, I spotted my mother taking in the washing from the line which – to my sister's deep distress – stretched out in the waste land in front of the cottages, offering travellers on the Southdown bus to Brighton a unique insight into the underclothes of the English middle classes. From past experience, I knew that whenever my sister and I were out of the country she spent most of her waking hours poring over atlases and studying weather-charts and hearing terrible rumours of earthquakes or cyclones or communal massacres or outbreaks of the plague in the places through which we were passing and eagerly consulting her watch ('He must be arriving in El Paso just about now!') and gazing fiercely out to sea through a large Victorian telescope; but – as parents always do – she greeted my arrival with the calmest of nods, as though I had strolled back from a walk across the Downs, and seemed far keener on my getting a last swim in before it was too late than on listening agog to the adventures of a lifetime. In this she was, no doubt, both wise and right; either way, life was as it should be once again.

CHAPTER TEN

Dublin Daze

Back in Dublin for the beginning of our third year, we found ourselves sadly adrift with nowhere to live: we had had enough of landladies and doilies and the pursing of lips when we stumbled home long after the commercial traveller and the lady who stubbed cigarettes out in her hair had retired for the night, clutching cups of cocoa and hot water bottles in elaborately woven covers, and we decided that we would take a flat instead. Since none of us was terribly businesslike, we quite failed to do anything about it before the end of term, and arrived in Dublin with nowhere to lay our heads. I suggested that we might revisit the ancient public house with the sloping floors and the absence of locks on the lavatory doors, if only to find out whether the unpleasant byproduct of a well-aimed sneeze was still embedded in the butter, but this was felt to be going too far; instead we moved into what was - or so we soon learned - the most notorious address in Ireland at that particular moment.

That summer, while we had been trundling about America in Greyhound buses, a particularly gruesome murder had taken place of a kind I associate far more readily with the dingy streets of post-war London than with Dublin, which - perhaps wrongly - I assumed to specialize in sharp blows on the head with an empty stout bottle or raking bursts of fire from a Thompson sub-machine gun than with, as in this case, disagreeable scenes of dismemberment with kitchen knives, and the boiling of bones. The foul deed had been done in one of the elegant if decrepit Georgian terrace houses in Harcourt Street, off St Stephen's Green, and had, I seem to remember, involved some unhappy, lonely African student of the kind I associated with razor-sharp creases in cavalry twill trousers and natty blue blazers and silk scarves immaculately tied; none of us knew anything of the murder before returning to Dublin, and it was only after we had been in residence for a day or two that the grisly truth was revealed. For a few days we cheered ourselves up by drumming on the windows to attract the attention of passers-by and small crowds of ghoulish sightseers who had come to view the sight of the crime; but for all our bravado we found living in the murder flat an eerie and distasteful business – quite apart from anything else, it was extremely dirty and the oven was coated in what looked like orange axle grease but could, given the nature of the deed, have been something altogether worse – and after a week or so we gave in our notice and sought alternative accommodation.

We moved instead to a ground floor flat in one of the vast and even more elegant Georgian houses in Fitzwilliam Street – almost opposite a strip of houses which, shortly afterwards, were demolished by the philistine Gas Board, so ruining what must have been one of the finest and longest Georgian streets in the British Isles (the Board had taken the advice of an eminent English architectural historian, who pronounced the houses to be of little merit). We rented the flat from a prim lady with pursed lips in late middle age; she had never, she explained, let her flat to men before, let alone Trinity undergraduates, and was very chary about doing so, but when we assured her that we were the soul of reliability and in no way given to wild parties or late nights or – heaven forbid! – the consumption of alcoholic beverages or the stubbing out of cigarette ends on the furniture, she relented with a reluctant sniff and dabbing of the nose, and said that she would break her rules for once and give us a go.

That flat was decorated throughout in various shades of pink, abounded in doilies and flounces and antimacassars, and was crammed with dainty reproduction furniture: it was, in every way, far better suited to a trio of elderly spinsters – still more so since Shore and I spent so much of our evenings in the pubs, rolling home after midnight with foul-smelling bags of fish and chips in one hand and spare bottles in the other, while Ian was out till the early hours several nights a week, playing the piano and the ukelele and singing in pubs and clubs and dance-halls all over Dublin. To begin with, at least, we behaved with exemplary domesticity, removing our shoes and closing the front door with exaggerated care and tiptoeing stealthily up the stairs, taking especial care not to collide with the fern that stood at the bottom of the bannisters on a well wrought but flimsy wooden pillar;

well-trained at home, I proved a particularly anxious and nimble housewife, darting to and fro with the hoover, making sure the beds were made, emptying the ashtrays, plunging the lavatory brush up and down and round and round, and keeping an anxious eye out for the cigarette burns on the reproduction furniture. So houseproud did I become, and so worried about our querulous landlady, that I invariably did all the dusting and hoovering before the cleaning lady arrived, so enabling her to put her feet up and enjoy a quiet cup of coffee and a ruminative cigarette.

Ian and I shared a bedroom in the front of the house. Our beds were covered with plump pink eiderdowns, and their legs concealed with pleated pink valances; the lamp on the bedside table between us wore a pleated shade of pink; on the dressing-table in the corner, our landlady had daintily inserted items of lacework between the protective glass on top and the shining mahogany beneath. We felt decidedly out-of-place in these maidenly surroundings at first, but the beds were seductively soft and our voices grew steadily louder, and before long we began to feel quite at home in our ruched and rose-pink boudoir despite the curious and quizzical looks it excited among those who came to see us. Shore, in the meantime, had bedded down in a small corridor-like room that led through to the kitchen at the back of the house; his bed lay immediately behind the door, and since the bed was very large, and Shore was relatively small, late-night visitors – many of them over-excited with drink – would frequently fling open the door of Shore's room with a mighty crash and march noisily through to the kitchen talking as they went, quite overlooking the figure of their host as he lay in the middle of his outsize mattress, like a rowing boat adrift in an endless sea.

One of our most frequent and congenial visitors once the pubs had closed was a forceful figure in a greasy fawn gaberdine mac of the kind I associated with middle-aged men queuing up in an embarrassed, furtive way to see *Naked as Nature Intended* and *Nudes in the Snow* in a double billing at a cinema in Great Windmill Street. Although Weale was a couple of years younger than the rest of us, and had come up to Trinity when he was only seventeen, he had the gait, the demeanour and the battered, world-weary looks of a hard-living man in his early fifties. His face was the colour of porridge, and pitted like a pumice stone or the surface of the moon; everything about him seemed to slope down hill with a hangdog comicality, from his eyes and his mouth and his shoulders to the bottomless plunge of his hands into the pockets of his scrofulous, seldom-discarded mackintosh, giving him the look of an Anglo-Saxon Jean Gabin, or one of those sturdy, earthbound Frenchmen who seem to spend a good deal of time lounging about in marketplaces or on quaysides with cigarettes hanging from their mouths at angles impossible of achievement to the pedestrian English smoker.

He had a fine stentorian voice and was the outstanding student actor in Trinity at an unusually talented time, combining great delicacy and a strong sense of melancholy with a contagious relish for old-fashioned, thundering histrionics of the kind practised, I liked to think, by Sir Donald Wolfit and the stock company actors of Edwardian England. He was extremely bibulous, hopelessly in love with various unattainable women, and – though lunatically generous when money came his way, not least to the swarms of barefoot tinker children who flitted about the streets of Dublin like spectres from the London of Dickens or Mayhew – almost always broke: he slept, for the most part, on other people's floors, but had spent odd nights on park benches, in various Dublin prisons, and in a ditch by the side of the road in the Dublin hills; having fallen asleep on the bus following a heavy night in the pubs, he had woken to find himself adrift in the Irish countryside at one o'clock in the morning, and had set out to walk home before being overcome by the excitement of the evening.

Once or twice a week we would hear a mighty thundering on the outside door, accompanied by resonant, fruity cries and the clinking of bottles; and we would hurry downstairs as quickly as we could, reassuring the anxious, heavily curlered head of our landlady as it peered peevishly out from her bedroom door off the main hall, and usher our swaying, Micawber-like guest unsteadily upstairs, our forefingers pressed to our lips as he threatened to burst into song. Once upstairs he would, more often than not, produce from the pocket of his mackintosh some bottles of stout, or a half-drained bottle of Jameson's; after which he would stride about the house in his mac, declaiming like an old-fashioned orator, or Phiz's version of Mr Chadband, his right arm slicing the air while the other clutched his lapel; or he would wrestle with Ian among the reproduction furniture – the crash of their falling bodies bringing further puzzled protests from below – before bedding down on the sitting-room carpet so that the flat rang to his titanic snores.

His appetite was gargantuan, and admirably adapted – even more so than mine – to the grossness of the average Irish meal; a dreadful hunger used to come over him after closing time, causing him to stride through Shore's bedroom en route for the kitchen, loudly declaiming as he went, before making himself a cold porridge sandwich or a gigantic omelette containing a dozen eggs. Like Shore, he was given to passing out in the lavatories of public places, but whereas Shore specialized in theatres and places of entertainment, Weale had a penchant for restaurants: my wife, who has known and liked him even longer than I, remembers his taking her out for a Chinese meal after a night in the pub, disappearing to the lavatory after ordering his 'Universal Special' (a dish of rice and noodles and sweet and sour pork with a fried egg looking ill-at-ease on top) and never re-emerging; when he finally came round at about half-past three in the morning, and let himself out of the lavatory, he found his 'Universal Special' still awaiting his arrival.

So good an actor was Weale that, single-handed, he almost converted me from my ancient aversion to the theatre. When working in advertising I had felt – for the only time in my life – a terrible, anxious need to have seen every film and play then showing in London, and had spent more evenings than I care to remember sitting in the Curzon Cinema at 7/6 a time, or squatting alone in the gods at the Aldwych or Old Vic. Over-indulgence led to aversion: I have probably been to the cinema five times in the last twenty years, and no sooner had I arrived in Dublin than I conceived a peculiarly frivolous attitude to theatrical goings-on which, despite my recent conversion to opera, I find it quite impossible to shake off. Faced with some intolerably pretentious play at school, I had worked out – but failed to execute – a scheme whereby some friends and I would climb into boilersuits and greasy tweed caps and, cunningly disguised as workmen, with cigarettes drooping from our lower lips, saunter on stage at a moment of critical tedium and start removing the scenery from behind the actors' backs; and even now I find myself far more gripped than I should be by the mechanics of the theatre, craning eagerly forward with twitching nostrils as food and drink are brought on stage (are they real or are they false? This, far more than the complexities of plot or the fine flourishes on stage, seems to me the overriding issue of the moment) or holding my breath with terrible suspense as a jammed door causes the scenery to sway alarmingly to and fro before – in a perfect world – crashing forward onto the stage, revealing a team of startled stage hands picking their noses or draining enormous mugs of tea.

This aversion spilt over to important actors, in particular those of the resonant or sonorous school, with (or so it seemed to me) quite unmerited titles attached to their names; and from thence – and here the loss was all mine – to the unfortunate Shakespeare, the only tolerable productions of which appeared to be mounted by amateurs or schoolboys. (Thirty years ago at prep school I stage-managed a production of *Twelfth Night*, and a few years back I was almost won round to the old gentleman by a production of the same play in the gardens of Merton College, Oxford; in between, all seems to have been a dreadful waste of flatulence and affectation.)

Although I felt colourless and conventional beside Weale, I knew we were honoured by his patronage, and that to find so familiar a character of Trinity life snoozing loudly on one's sitting-room floor (his head beneath a 'nest' of tables, his feet in the fireplace, and the carpet rolled around his body) or making massive inroads into one's catering arrangements marked us out, if only by association, as characters in our own right, and ones who dwelt near the eye of the storm. He was, however, a good deal more than a waggish, comical buffoon: he was – and still is – an impeccable and inspired watercolourist and draughtsman, taking whole weeks out in the middle of the term to tramp about Kerry or Connemara with a sketchbook in his hand; and unlike most of those who, like him, were reading English, he had a natural and instinctive love of literature, and was ferociously well read. Certainly I had far more time for his views on the subject than for those of many of his colleagues, who read what they were told to read, never strayed from the straight and narrow, repeated the conventional wisdom that was handed down to them in pre-digested form, and seemed to regard literature as something to be 'got through' or as an academic exercise: we were at one in our liking for Dickens and Surtees, and enjoyed irritating those who knew best by comparing Fielding unfavourably with Smollett, knowing perfectly well that those who angrily repudiated our claims had never actually read that dyspeptic Scottish doctor, since he was not on the list of 'set books'.

By some miracle of brinkmanship, we managed to stay in our spinsterish flat for the whole of our third year, despite Weale's booming flights of oratory and the thundering on the door and the sound of frying at one o'clock in the morning and (for all my precautions) a burn on the arm of a G-plan chair and tell-tale rings on the reproduction furniture, and – worst of all – the destruction of a particularly virulent painting of a waterfall plunging over rocks, which Shore had taken an especial dislike to and eventually brought crashing over the head of a visitor, who wore it about his neck like an ungainly Elizabethan ruff. To our surprise, our landlady – who had mellowed greatly with the passing of time – never referred to this unfortunate incident, and we could only assume that she shared Shore's opinion of the painting, and had hung it in the first place purely from a sense of obligation.

The life we led that year continued to be idle, bibulous, convivial and consistently juvenile, and involved a good deal more travelling about the West of Ireland – on Shore's and my part, at least – in the company of Rivers and the Deaf Malvernian. To fill in the long hours I took to writing for two of the three university magazines – the monthly literary magazine, to which I contributed poems of childlike whimsicality and brightness, and a weekly affair, to which I initially submitted, greatly daring, pieces about Guatemala and the Aran Islands. The thrill and the feeling of self-importance that came from seeing one's name in print in those magazines was far greater than anything I have ever known since; my parents bought me a typewriter – which I once, in a fit of rage brought on by the sticking of one of the keys, hurled across my rooms with such force that, in my shame, I felt the only answer was to drop it into the foetid waters of the Liffey, and follow suit myself – and for the rest of my time at Trinity I spent more and more of my time banging out long and self-indulgent articles, laughing excessively at my own jokes as I crouched over my tiny machine and, as the eventual editor of both mags, taking particular care to publish pieces by my friends.

My editorship of the weekly magazine, *TCD*, was generally regarded as poor, and quite rightly. The practice was for those involved to choose the next editor at the end of the preceding term, so that he or she could brood on its contents over the vacation and come back with all kinds of bright ideas bobbing about; thanks to some active lobbying on my part, we chose Ian for the job, but no sooner had we reassembled than he announced his immediate resignation, and I was ordered to pick up the bits. Editing *Icarus* was a smoother affair, though I caused some irritation by employing outside contributors and by writing an over-jocular preface in which I announced my policy of printing no short stories on the grounds that no one read such things, and their absence would be regarded as a blessing all round. It was while I was editing this magazine that Derek Mahon brought into my rooms a red-haired Irish lady poet and told me - a terrible smile lighting up his features - that she would like to recite to me one of the poems I had (somewhat reluctantly) selected for the magazine: he then stood behind her, bouncing up and down with silent merriment, while the lady bard, clad in a black cloak and waving her arms with circular, prophetic movements, read in resonant, tremulous tones, modelled on those of the aged Yeats, a long and sombre poem about various birds cleaving the Irish air, and I gazed in dread at the floor, torn between a very English embarrassment and a dreadful urge to laugh out loud.

Every now and then I wandered down Fitzwilliam Street and stared up in a melancholic way at a back window in Merrion Square just as I had two summers before, when ffenella had lived at that address, and I had hoped (in vain, alas) that, gazing out of the window in an absent-minded way, she would spot me standing on the pavement, looking more like an old clothes salesman than the troubadour I imagined myself to be, and invite me in with a little cry of delight. Early in the summer term such ancient allegiances were eventually expelled, after Shore and I were invited to tea in Fitzwilliam Square with an assortment of Trinity girls. Shore's and my Central American adventures, suitably embellished, had provided us with the stuff of which club bores and dinner table anecdotalists are made, and the ladies were far too polite to interrupt as I boomed and rambled on about encounters with giant iguanas and Rivers's escapades in the hollowed-out tree-trunk and lavatories suspended over shark-infested waters; indeed, their kindly display of interest - stifling their yawns behind their hands - and an unending supply of bread and jam and pastries from Johnson, Mooney and

O'Brien excited us both to further flights of incoherent eloquence, in the course of which we both laughed heartily at our own jokes and thought ourselves wags of the very highest order.

Among this – as I liked to think – admiring circle of ladies (most of whom I noticed, with a patronizing smile, had spent their equivalent holidays in Donaghadee or Weston-super-Mare, or at most in Florence or the Haute Savoie) was a girl from Holywood in County Down, clad in a grey flannel pleated skirt and a black and grey striped jersey: framed by shoulder-length hair – which she often wore pinned up, in the fashion of those days – her face was a perfect oval, and seemed to combine great liveliness with an almost angelic resignation and sweetness in repose. She had, without doubt, the most beautiful eyes I had ever seen – normally I was fiercely averse to the very idea of large brown eyes, which I associated with spaniels and unreliable scoutmasters – and, unlike Maud Gonne, unusually lovely hands. I was in those days quite incapable of remembering anybody's name, particularly if I had to introduce them, at which I was overcome by a sense of panic so intense and so disruptive that the names of even my closest friends would quite escape me, and a year or so later, when I was temporarily engaged to the girl with the hazel eyes and needed to introduce her, I found myself quite incapable of remembering what she was called, and surprised both her and those poised to make the acquaintance of my fiancée by having to ask her who she was before proceeding with the introduction: in the meantime, however, I somehow managed to remember that her name was Suzanne, and although – for all my boastings about Honduran brothels and seedy hotels in the Yucutan – I was far too afraid to articulate my aspirations, let alone ask her out, so I went away crammed with cakes and hoping that we might meet again in the not-too-distant future.

It was about this time that I was introduced to a red-faced man with bright blue eyes and the look of a rubicund satyr, or a rather more robust, sporting version of those agreeably devilish characters that appear in the paintings of Cranach. Charles Sprawson was – and still is – invariably clad in corduroy trousers, well-scrubbed gym shoes and a sleeveless v-necked jersey worn over an open necked shirt. He was, I was told, a keen sportsman and a Knight of the Campanile; his favourite novel was *The Enormous Bed* by Henry Jones PhD; he was an unusual classicist and went on, after Trinity, to teach classics to the

Arabs in Saudi Arabia, where he was arrested by the desert police for dancing to 'La Bamba' on a portable gramophone among the sand dunes late at night, and blighted the reputation of a local stunt artist by strolling up in his bathing costume and diving off – as he often did – a hundred-foot cliff into a bottomless pool beneath just as the stunt man, heavily swathed in protective bandages and surrounded by admiring Saudi Arabians, was screwing himself up for the boldest feat of his career. Charles's conversational approach was peculiar and – to some at least – extremely disconcerting, consisting as it did of long silences during which he fixed his victims with his Cranach-like bright blue eyes before asking them about their sex lives or their views on some long-forgotten boxer or Oxford squash blue from the 1920s. Both he and Ian were gripped by schools and school life; but whereas Ian liked nothing better than to evoke his prep school days at Nutlands, peopling the corridors and classrooms with Will Hay-like masters swishing their canes and storming from room to room in ink-stained gowns, Charles was far more interested in unhappy classicists and in the doomed heroics of schoolboy sportsmen.

I immediately found Charles extremely sympathetic; and since his Germanic looks – and partial ancestry – were complemented by an interest in the seedy and the perverse, I immediately asked him to write about some aspect or other of life in Weimar Germany for my edition of *Icarus* (he later went on to establish himself as the authority on von Cramm, the great German tennis player of inter-war years). Charles in his turn asked me if I would join him in a game of tennis. I had, by now, got to know the hazel-eyed Suzanne, and she turned up with two of her friends to cheer me on. Although I had explained to Charles – who was one of the best tennis players in the university, and a squash partner of Jonah Barrington – that I was incapable of serving overarm and had only the dimmest idea of the rules, I was alarmed to see him turn up at the courts at the far end of College Park in full tennis gear and clutching several sets of rackets like a seeded Wimbledon player, whereas I was wearing my everyday clothes and a pair of sandals on my feet. Feeling a trifle unnerved, I took my place at the end of the court, and we started batting the ball to and fro.

I spun this out for as long as I could – since I was quite incapable of returning any of his shots, most of the time was spent retrieving balls from around the court, while Shore kindly recovered and threw back those that had struck my racket a glancing blow before rocketing skywards and out of the court altogether – but eventually Charles decreed that the game should begin. Holding my racket limply by my side and standing with my legs crossed (I hoped this parade of nonchalance would impress the spectators and prove off-putting to my opponent) I watched with a mesmerized dread as Charles bounced the ball several times on the ground before suddenly tossing it up and bending back his mighty serving arm to send it hurtling across the net towards me at something approaching the speed of light; but almost before any of this had registered I felt a terrible scalding, sickening pain amidships and crashed heavily to the ground, my hands clutched between my legs like a small boy cut short in a public place, and terrible moans and cries of anguish bursting from my foam-flecked lips. At the far end of the court, the demon stood laughing his wicked silent laugh, his shoulders pumping up and down and the tears coursing down his cheeks; while my three lady attendants rushed onto the court and carried me, rigid with pain and gasping for air, from this terrible arena and laid me out on the grass beyond, like some buffoonish French knight who had been knocked from his horse within seconds of his arrival on the field of battle, and was unable ever to rise again.

Some weeks later I was able to take unintended revenge on my tormentor. Ian and I had to come over to Dublin for the first part of our finals at the end of our third year (in expansive Irish fashion, finals were taken not in June but in September, so spinning out our university careers still further and making it even harder to adjust to the world beyond and the prospects of employment); we had nowhere to stay, and Charles suggested that we might like to stay the night with him in his flat in Mount Street, off Merrion Square. We took the last flight from London, rolled up at Mount Street at about half-past twelve, and pounded on Charles's front door. After about five minutes the door opened a good six inches, and the satyr looked out. He was clad, I noticed, in a silk dressing gown, and looked unusually hot and dishevelled, his hair shooting from his head in an unfamiliar way. We greeted him warmly and prepared to come in, dragging our luggage with us, but he resolutely barred the way. We couldn't possibly come in, he informed us; we remonstrated angrily; he looked puzzled and somewhat at a loss; and then, with a sudden surge of confidence, he confessed that his friend Agnew had unexpectedly arrived with thirteen friends, that they were spread out all over his floor, and that there was no way in which he could squeeze any more guests on board. After much protesting on our part the demon eventually drove us away, and we heard the rattle of the door chain behind us.

Ian and I felt surprised and rather put out. It was late; we hadn't eaten; it was beginning to rain; we could stay in a hotel, but it would cost us at least a guinea; we didn't have much money to hand, and – a promise being a promise – we didn't see why we should. We stamped round Merrion Square a couple of times, while the rain grew ever thicker, grumbling about Charles and his treacherous behaviour; and then we decided that, whether he liked it or not, we would climb in through his bedroom window and join Agnew and his thirteen friends on the floor. We headed back to Mount Street, climbed over the railings; pushed up the sash window of his basement room, and started to climb in. I had one leg over the sill when he loomed suddenly before me, his arms spreadeagled like a traffic policeman holding at bay a convoy of misdirected lorries, and his hair looking even wilder than it had half an hour before. He repelled us with some energy, heartlessly ignoring our pleas about the rain and the lateness of the hour, and continuing to evoke the mysterious Agnew and his thirteen friends, none of whom appeared to have been disturbed by the rumpus in the window. We managed, despite the hour, to book into a small hotel on the corner of Merrion Square, and after a leisurely breakfast we set out to find our faithless friend and subject him to the kind of withering reproach he so obviously deserved. When we banged on the front door in Mount Street he emerged at once, looking his familiar sporting self; his hair was as orderly as ever, and when we peered over his shoulder into his room there was no sign of Agnew or his thirteen friends. I asked him where they had gone, finding it odd that they should have decamped so rapidly, leaving no trace behind; Charles looked blank for a moment and then hastily explained that they had hurried off *en bloc* to catch a bus for Galway – and that of course we were free to stay with him for the next few days. This we did; our stay was made memorable by Charles's collection of unwashed socks, which steamed and bubbled in a giant wardrobe, and threatened to storm across the room at the slightest provocation; and by Charles's patiently piecing together while we slept a diary of mine which I had torn into tiny fragments, an activity that kept him fully occupied on the night before his finals. No further mention was made of Agnew and his thirteen friends, nor did they reappear from their Galway expedition. Years later I learned that we had, twice, disturbed our unfortunate friend in one of the most intimate moments of his career (it goes without saying that so obvious an explanation never occurred to me at the time); in the excitement of the hour he had quite forgotten about our coming to stay, and he had hastily invented Agnew and his thirteen friends in a desperate bid to prevent the ruination of a night of bliss.

Another new friend was a loud, kindly and ebullient figure called John Kelly; he was that rare occurrence, a scholar of Trinity – this entitled him to rooms in college throughout his four years, as well as a more elaborate gown than the plain affairs we wore for lectures or dining on commons – and has since become the fellow of an Oxford college, devoting his days to the letters of W. B. Yeats. Both Weale and Kelly were in the same English set as the girl with the hazel eyes who had so patiently listened to my ravings about Central America, and helped to carry me rigid from the tennis court at the far end of College Park; and it may well have been in his rooms that I had met her again earlier that summer term. She lived with her excellent flat-mate, Hilary, in a small, square house on the canal; I went to visit her there several times, and soon found that her eyes and the shape of her face had much the same effect on me as ffenella's auburn hair and exciting-looking bosom. We had hardly exchanged more than half a dozen words before the term ended, and once again the great wastes of the summer vacation stretched before us. On a luminous, rain-washed evening I rushed round to say goodbye before catching the Liverpool boat from the North Wall; and all the way across, as I tucked into that familiar cross-Channel combination of warm stout and cold pork pies and, defying the white-coated stewards, stretched out at length on a bench in a first-class lounge, I thought – as I was to think for the next two years at least – of nothing but her eyes and the melancholy beauty of her face.

* * *

That summer we travelled to the Middle East in a flexible foursome of which Shore and I were the constant factors, with Rivers and Sprawson coming and going as the mood or circumstances dictated. We took a train to Istanbul, where we stayed at the same agreeably seedy hotel in which, two years earlier, Shore and I had spent some time with ffenella and Jill. Istanbul seemed as grey and lugubrious as ever, rather like (or so I imagined, for I had never been to such places in my life) some sooty, rain-lashed industrial city in the North of England that had surprisingly sprouted domes and minarets: I was interested that the hotel lavatory – a porcelain hole in the ground of the kind more usually associated with the unhygienic French – was quite as clogged and repellant as it had been on last inspection, and that its customers were still advised to make their way into the firing position on a pair of gigantic wooden pattens that lifted them up, to some extent at least, above the horrid evidence of the inmates' inability to aim in the right direction. Our previous visit seemed to belong to a distant, long-forgotten age; and although, much later, our travels with ffenella were to assume, in my mind at least, an almost Arcadian aspect, revisiting the sights of this autumnal, wind-swept city stirred not the faintest tremor of regret.

Like most matters of this kind, our journey was vastly preferable in anticipation and in retrospect. I loved the idea of travelling in hot, exotic places, but as I lay sweating on my bunk in some Syrian boarding house or tramped across the interminable Anatolian plateau, my thumb moving excitedly up and down as an enormous lorry sped towards us in a cloud of dust, or fought in vain to make myself understood by gesticulating locals, I longed to trade these mighty vistas of rock and stunted shrubs and dessicated goats' messes for a nordic landscape of grass and trees and shade, and the delights of foreign travel for a storm-lashed seaside hotel and brisk walks through the August rain and the roar of the shingle at Seaford as great seas prepared to pound the promenade. Even so, the idea of not enduring such expeditions was quite out of the question, for grumbling about the weather or the food or the standard of accommodation was – and remains – an essential ingredient of the summer holiday; and this trip – which was punctuated, as ever, by a good deal of merriment and over-indulgence – was no exception to the rule. Apart from the booze and the beaches and the mild, benign adventures, I travelled – in much the same way as I read, or poked about ill-lit, frowsty-smelling churches, or pushed open attic doors into dark, neglected corners of decrepit country houses – in the vague, unfocused hope that somewhere, somehow, an elusive, impossible moment of revelation would occur, when everything would suddenly slot into place and God would step forward to claim his own, like a man jumping out from behind a bush to guide his children home.

In the middle of Anatolia we were pleasantly surprised to find Sprawson – who had left us several hundred miles earlier – asleep in the first-class compartment of a slow-moving Turkish train, the blinds drawn down and a handkerchief covering his face; we tried to persuade him to come with us to inspect the curious rock churches of Goreme, but his interests took him in other directions, and he leapt nimbly out as the train took a turn to the east. In Syria I won the approval of a busload of crones by cracking against my teeth and swallowing a raw egg which a ferocious, black-bearded Arab produced, after much scratching and hauling about of his robes, from some unwholesome nether garment; we slept in a prison near Petra, but since Shore and Rivers lay by my side I had no need to babble excitedly about Byzantine iconography or the problems of the early Church; shortly afterwards, Rivers vanished with a party of Bedouins and I found myself composing another regretful letter to Reigate, which I was able to tear up when he arrived, with a raging fever, just as Shore and I were about to go through the Mandelbaum Gate into West Jerusalem. I sat too long in the sun on the boat from Haifa; my legs blew up like enormous orange balloons, and I was left alone in a whitewashed hospital in Rhodes that was built around a flowering courtyard and run by nuns, a metal frame keeping even the lightest of sheets from touching my putrid blisters.

After tossing about the Aegean in a small steamer heavily laden with cardboard suitcases and chickens in wicker baskets and wizened crones clad entirely in black, who moaned terribly as the sea grew rougher and were violently sick over the rail on the windward side in such a way that their sick was immediately blown across the deck, like an airborne minestrone soup, and spattered about the heads of unheeding foreigners gazing keenly out to sea on the opposite side of the boat, I caught up with my companions in Crete – for Rivers had by now reappeared, while Sprawson was forever circling in the background, like a grinning, rubicund shark – and we made our way slowly north, through Athens and the great skybound monasteries of Meteora and Belgrade. It was raining in Vienna, and the leaves were beginning to turn. Over dinner in a youth hostel we fell into conversation with a party of English girls, one of whom had eyes of the kind I was pining for; it was time to be hurrying home.

CHAPTER ELEVEN

Closing Time

We spent our last year in a set of rooms in Trinity. To our disappointment, we were allotted what must have been the darkest and gloomiest rooms in the entire university, tucked away on the ground floor in a far corner of Botany Bay. The bedrooms looked out onto Botany Bay, so reminiscent of Dartmoor and the breaking of stones, and commanded an uninterrupted view of the bicycle sheds; apart from a patch of sky, we saw nothing from the sitting-room window except the grey granite wall with spikes on top which ran round large parts of the university, and the college dustbins, which were emptied from time to time to the accompaniment of much shouting and dropping of lids. We had dreamed of an elegant set of rooms in New Square such as had once belonged to the Deaf Malvernian and the world's leading authority on the caddis fly, with windows eight feet high and huge unfolding shutters and a vista of green and gold; instead we had to make do with these cramped and stygian quarters, more suitable for troglodytes or ill-featured goblins with beards and pointed ears than for such eminent members of the university.

It all seemed most unjust, still more so since all three of us had, in anticipation of a new and more elegant way of life, hurried round to Bryson's the tailors and ordered ourselves almost identical tweed suits with tubular trousers, twin slits at the back, and the waisted jackets I so admired. But normal service was resumed when, a few days after our arrival, a leg was thrown over the window-sill of Ian's and my bedroom in the early hours of the morning, to be followed by a grubby gaberdine mackintosh and a face with the features of ancient statuary, breathing a fiery mixture of stout and whiskey fumes. Such interruptions became an agreeable commonplace, as Weale pushed his way through our room en route for the sitting-room, where he bedded down in front of a sputtering gas fire and below a painting by William Scott, on the glass of which Rivers had – to Ian's annoyance – painted a moustache and a pair of spectacles. If particularly inflamed, he might pause to wrestle with Ian, hurling him out of bed and bringing him crashing to the floor in much the same way as he had wrestled among the reproduction furniture in our flat in Fitzwilliam Street. Shore, in the meantime, snoozed peacefully through such interruptions: neither Ian nor I ever set foot in his bedroom, which was full of canvasses; whether they were of naked women bursting out of eggs, or whether he had moved on to still stranger forms of subject matter, is something I shall never know.

Increasingly often, though, I was the only one to hear Weale puffing and gasping in the square outside as he struggled to force our window open, or to watch with weary amusement as his suede-clad foot swung into view, along with the elderly mackintosh and the leering lunar face and the sulphurous blast of breath; for Ian was spending more and more of his time playing in clubs and concerts in Dublin, and came creeping home with the dawn, finally climbing into bed long after Weale had drawn his mackintosh about him in front of the fire and abandoned himself to stertorous slumber; and before the year was out I too would be spending less and less of my days and nights in our crepuscular, cave-like rooms.

Every now and then Shore and I would go along to hear Ian play with a band called Bluesville, and listen agog as he described the propositions he had received from convent-educated scrubbers ('I would like to have intercoarse with you at your own convenience'). With what pride we watched him stride on stage wearing, on top of his jeans and t-shirt, the Provost's gown, rented for the occasion from the gown-maker to the university who, all unsuspecting, had offered him the full range of canonicals, from the robes of a Doctor of Divinity to those of the Vice-Chancellor himself! With what righteous anger we rose up when he stormed back to our rooms in the early hours of the morning with torn and bleeding knuckles after knocking out the two front teeth of some silly ass at a Trinity dance who had tried to amuse the ladies by banging down the piano lid on the hands of our star performer! And how important we all felt when one of his records rose to Number Seven in the American charts, poised to topple even the Beatles and the Rolling Stones, let alone the mighty Roy Orbison who, we were enraged to learn, had been refused entry to a party in New Square by – who could doubt it – the very same chinless wonder whose teeth had been so recently removed!

For several weeks our rooms were invaded by cigar-chewing agents and managers from New York and Wardour Street, talking percentages and royalties and splits in loud important voices while our old friend the bibulous hamster sat placidly in front of the fire in his cardigan reading the *Daily Telegraph* and Weale climbed in and out of the window and I squatted behind my typewriter pounding out articles on Dublin cinema audiences or 'My search for the perfect pork pie' for that week's *TCD*. Shore and I became, for a short while, eager readers of *Variety*, anxiously scanning the charts while Ian struggled to get through to Los Angeles on the ancient telephone outside the Hist, feeding in great columns of pennies and emitting loud cries of rage as he was cut off yet again, or found himself talking instead to the Swastika Laundry in St Stephen's Green, or fought to get some drunk off the line just as the president of the record company at last picked up his phone.

Those of us who lived in college were entitled – in fact, obliged – to dine on commons every evening. As in an Oxford or Cambridge college, the dons sat at the high table, while the riff-raff, clad for the most part in their commoners' gowns, occupied long benches in the main body of the hall. Above us hung enormous portraits of well-fed eighteenth-century Church of Ireland bishops and weatherbeaten members of the Anglo-Irish Ascendancy; and about us scurried even more purple-faced men in white jackets – including the old retainer who spent his days unblocking the college drains, lavatory brush in hand – handing out huge bowls of potatoes and brussels sprouts, and the great white jugs of stout with which we washed down the produce of the college kitchens. Although I could never match my friend John Kelly who, when invited out to dinner made a point of eating on commons before joining the party, somewhat belatedly, for his second dinner of the evening, he and I were as one in our anxiety to share a table with pallid serious-minded undergraduates and well-behaved Ulstermen in green blazers who, preferring not to cloud their brains with alcoholic fumes before a quiet evening in the Library, could be relied upon to wave away the pints of stout that were set before them; these we drained with eager cries and much smacking of the lips, while the bottle-nosed lavatory cleaner hovered solicitously behind us, jug in hand, waiting to replenish the barricade of glasses that hemmed us in. Those who sat at the head of the table were responsible for serving out the spotted dick or tapioca pudding that followed the main course; once again, Kelly and I made sure that one of us occupied this coveted position, and once again the modest or serious-minded did all that was required of them, either disdaining the suet altogether with a thin and watery smile, or insisting on so diminutive a portion that half the pudding at least remained for our private delectation.

Before we could tuck into whatever lay before us, a long and elaborate Latin grace was read out by a scholar; if, as was often the case, I found myself deep in conversation during this important ceremony, I invariably found myself brought up short by a peppery, censorious glance from an unusual-looking undergraduate with the bristling moustache, glaring protuberant eyes and short back and sides of the quintessential sergeant major. Although he can only have been in his early twenties, he had the look and the gait of a man in his fifties, including broken veins in his cheeks and sausage-like rolls of fat at the nape of the neck; he was dressed like an elderly prep school master - including leather patches on the elbows of his lovat tweed jacket, of the kind so coveted by Ian - and during the reading of grace he stood up very straight, his hands clutching his lapels and his watch chain glinting in the light from the chandelier overhead, and glared angrily about him like a splenetic martinet or a Latin master who had been pushed too far and was about to lash out with the cane that twitched, hidden, behind his back. Keen to forge ahead as a schoolmaster, this splendid figure went on to a teachers' training college at a time when liberal notions of education were in the ascendant: never a man to compromise, he unwisely insisted on introducing the subject of corporal punishment and the importance of the cane into the most unexpected places when writing his thesis for his Dip Ed, and was promptly failed by his shocked examiners, for whom he must have embodied all that they sought to sweep away.

*   *   *

I had come to love Trinity not only for its kindliness and its conviviality, but for its ambivalence, its lack of commitment, its tolerant cynicism, for its being, in so many ways, neither a part of England nor of Ireland; and I particularly relished the fact that, as far as England at least was concerned, we were very much out on a limb, and that Trinity – unlike its fiercer, more ambitious equivalents on the other side of the Irish Sea – could never be seen as part of the English Establishment, while sharing some of its graces and assumptions. This sense of detachment and the lack of self-importance or pomposity suited me down to the ground. Ever since I could remember I had tended to react against the ideas or the company in which I found myself – not boldly or heroically but in a furtive, derisive way – with the result that my own ideas and attitudes tended to be not only absurdly confused and fluid, but in a state of constant flight, of appalled repudiation of the here-and-now. A natural conservative, I approved – in theory at least – of ritual and tradition and formality and hierarchy, yet found their practical manifestations more often than not intolerably pompous, exclusive, selfish and self-congratulatory; egalitarian and liberal-minded (or so I liked to think) in my dealings with those about me, I found the pharasaical smugness and destructiveness of the left quite as unappealing as the world from which I had fled, and relapsed into a kind of quiescent, unobtrusive anarchism.

At school I had been a quiet and timid youth, and my failure to make any mark whatsoever was more the result of incompetence and general wetness than the spirit of revolt: I was neither brave nor enterprising enough to be bolshy, but from a very early age I regarded the goings-on of masters and boys alike with a kind of puzzled detachment. Not surprisingly, perhaps, I found it hard to understand, let alone take seriously, the solemn rites of institutional life, and remained impervious to their charms until I went to Trinity, where they formed an agreeable and unobtrusive part of the scenery, a kind of background hum – made up, perhaps, of a gaggle of Church of Ireland bishops in gaiters and frock coats bustling about the Fellows' Garden, a teacup balanced in one hand and an umbrella in the other, or the imposition by the Junior Dean of a fine of 7/6 for failing to wear a gown, or the unexpected appearance of the disgraced dentist from Mullingar in robes of vibrant purple – rather than an all-pervasive aspect of everyday life.

At school, on the other hand, I had found it quite impossible to take such matters with the necessary pinch of salt; I regarded boys and masters alike with the basilisk stare of one who considered almost every aspect of public school life as, in the last resort, a ludicrous waste of time. As a fag, I had bitterly resented having to make cocoa or clean shoes or polish gaiters for uncouth and lumpish seventeen-year-olds with spots and problems with shaving; when I was eventually made a house prefect in my turn I was felt to have let the team down badly by refusing to employ a fag of my own and insisting on doing such chores for myself. (Years later when, for some improbable reason, I was interviewed for a job as a spy – work I was patently ill-suited to, being quite incapable of keeping a secret and hopelessly addicted to gossip – I found, to my surprise, that my interlocutors were interested only in my attitude to fagging; my views on the subject excited disappointed glances, and my career as a master spy rapidly ground to a halt.)

Nor would I take part in the beatings which took place in the prefects' study after evening prayers and prep. The boy to be beaten would be summoned from his dormitory and brought down in his check dressing-gown and bedroom slippers to the study, where his seniors sat in a solemn, nodding ring, sipping mugs of cocoa brewed up by some unhappy fag, and looking insufferably middle-aged and smug. The odd cheeky boy or professional villain excepted, those about to be thwacked looked – to my eyes at least – wretchedly vulnerable and forlorn, and the prefects made the most of them, subjecting them to sonorous disquisitions on the iniquity of their crimes, or if in a skittish mood, hurling slippers at the victim before administering the regulation swipes with a shoe and sending him back to bed with a cold, dismissive nod. As the junior prefect, I was supposed to collect the miscreant as well as witness his punishment, but I refused to do either chore and sloped silently off to bed instead, or stamped angrily away to my study where I busied myself with my collection of ancient 78s. I had no particular objection to beating as such, but I felt very strongly that it should be left to the masters and not to the spotty seventeen-year-olds, for whom I retained my ancient disdain: what I found repellent was the rigidity and the smugness and the self-congratulatory gravitas of those who took these disagreeable ceremonies with such terrible seriousness.

Equally problematic was the school cadet corps, in which I found myself, at the age of seventeen, the oldest and by far the largest boy in the school holding no rank of any kind, not even that of the humblest lance-jack, and being marched up and down in a platoon full of fourteen-year-olds with high piping voices, none of whom came higher than the breast pockets of my ill-pressed battle jacket. I had, quite genuinely, been utterly baffled by the sight of a dismantled bren gun, proving quite incapable of putting the pieces together in any semblance of order, and I found it almost impossible to end up pointing in the right direction as the elderly NCOs – both veterans of the First World War – drilled us fiercely to and fro, their faces screwed up like angry babies' as they roared and strutted and puffed up their chests and crammed absurd little sticks under their armpits and shouted more hotly than ever as the senior geography master sauntered up to inspect us, saluting with such a trembling of the hand and so great a rush of blood to the face that I feared that either or both of them would shortly be carried from the parade grounds, struck down by a massive heart attack; but my own ineptitude, great as it was, was underwritten by the fatal suspicion that the spectacle of masters and boys stamping up and down pretending to be soldiers, however corrective to the character, was irremediably absurd.

And yet I knew that without discipline and hierarchies and rules, however fatuous or parochial, society at large and the school in particular would drift into a state of anarchy or terminal inertia; that my own somewhat lofty sense of the absurdity of institutional life was, in a very large part, a defensive measure, justifying or plastering over physical fear, timidity, a dislike of competition and a dread of making an ass of myself in public; and that the prefects and sportsmen and schoolboy sergeant majors whom I both feared and disdained, with their fresh pink faces and crinkly fair hair and stodgy, sensible expressions and silk cravats in house or school colours neatly tied about their necks, would duly and no doubt deservedly inherit the earth and set it spinning on its axis in a way that I never would.

Even in this apparently uncongenial wilderness, however, companionable fellow spirits could be found, like hardy grasses clinging to some arctic landscape. These included the Parsee with the peroxided hair, my two fellow-referees, and that civilized boy mentioned earlier who was even worse at games than I was, and was unkindly referred to as 'Grandma' on account of his cracked and quavering voice and somewhat fastidious ways. With them I founded, towards the end of my career, a body known – rather presumptuously – as the Intellectual Society. Anxious to avoid the sneers of the sporting set, we met after supper in a boiler room in the basement of our house. Festooned with gurgling Victorian pipes on which the jockstraps and footer shorts of the enemy were hung out to dry, our meeting place was uncomfortably hot and steamy: my spectacles invariably misted up within seconds of our assembly, and our solemn deliberations on Plato or T.S. Eliot were interrupted as members of the audience fought their way through the jockstraps for a draught of cooling air. From time to time I raised the tone of the meeting by letting fly a snarling, well-extended fart, which excited cries of indignation and much vigorous fanning of the scraps of paper on which we had typed out the evening's agenda.

Rather to our surprise, the Intellectual Society excited a certain envy and curiosity. Keen cross-country runners and muscular centre forwards asked if they could join; our meetings were transferred from the boiler room to the prefects' study; the headmaster came to address us, and singled us out for especial praise in his prize-giving speech at the end of term (an altogether admirable figure, he left the school a far more civilized place than he found it); the senior English master – a shambling, eloquent figure with an enormous head and yellowing spectacles that seemed somehow embedded in his skull – addressed us with fervour not, as we had expected, on Milton or on Wordsworth, but on the iniquities of towing sewage out to sea in barges instead of drying it on racks for subsequent use on the soil. Public schools nowadays are, for good or for bad, altogether more informal and relaxed than they were, and even the bleakest and most games-obsessed appear to have been touched by the optimistic, subversive notions initially propagated in places like Bedales and Dartington Hall; with our dislike of organized games, fagging, prefectorial beatings and the sonorous pomposities of Victorian public school life, we were, perhaps, feeble forebears of what was to follow in the 1960s, when masters would shed their gowns and address the boys by their Christian names; when black jackets and boaters and striped trousers, and the minute gradations of privilege in terms of buttons worn undone or hands in pockets or the wearing of coloured socks were jettisoned in favour of sports jackets, anoraks and jeans, and when art rooms and string quartets mysteriously flourished.

In the meantime, my academic career had advanced in a very average manner. I took my 'O' levels, failing maths four times; the time had come to specialize. I decided to take history at 'A' level; and, like most of my contemporaries who had opted for history, I hoped and expected to take English with it, since it was the only subject I was actually good at, and I had read far more widely and enthusiastically than most. Alas, this was not to be. Just as I was filing into a classroom to tell our form master what subjects I wanted to take at 'A' level, one of the geography masters rushed up to me and begged me, in tones both menacing and pathetic, to read geography instead. Although I have since come to suspect that, unjustly despised as it is, geography has rather more to offer as a subject of academic study than Eng lit, English had far more glamour to it, and I was already dreaming of reading English at Cambridge; geography was reserved for dullards and sportsmen with enormous skulls like those of Cro-Magnon Man and expressions of the kind more normally associated with those who have been recently struck severely on the head, and was taught by hearty games masters in tweed jackets who needed a simple subject to teach in between rushing about the games fields in blazers and knee-length shorts, blasting on whistles and shouting instructions from the touchline.

This particular geography-and-games master was, it seemed, desperate to include in his class one boy who might, with luck, rustle up an 'A' level and so save him from joshing humiliation in the common room, where masters stood about in their gowns between classes, knocking out their pipes and exchanging schoolmasterly badinage. Ever anxious to please, and touched by the geography master's unhappy plight, I agreed with a sinking heart; my dreams of a quiet life teaching Dickens and Smollett and Surtees to students at some obscure university evaporated at a word, and I abandoned forever the flatulent delights of literary criticism for terminal moraines and copper mining in Western Australia. (Much later – in my early forties, in fact – I came to regret not having done classics. Such an idea would never have occurred to me at the time. I had never learned a word of Greek; Latin seemed to be taken up almost entirely with Cotta and Labienus hurling darts at the Belgae or rushing about the country in their chariots like a team of over-eager travelling salesmen, though there was a moment of excitement when the senior Latin master – an elderly veteran of the First World War, with a damp, tobacco-stained moustache and yellowed spectacles held together with the inevitable adhesive tape – crept up on all fours on a snoozing boy at the back of the class, his gown trailing on the ground to either side of him, and woke him from his torpor by plunging the pointed leg of a compass into his thigh.)

Most of those whom I got to know towards the end of my time at Trinity were reading English, and towards them I felt a familiar, nagging mixture of envy and derision. Since any course of study seemed to involve sitting round in libraries reading books that one would almost certainly never get round to in civilian life, how much more sensible to be able to tick off *The Faerie Queene* or *Paradise Lost* – neither of which, I suspected, and rightly, I could see myself reading in the bath or on the beach in the years that lay ahead – than a history of liberalism or the life of Isaac Butt; yet how sheeplike and ill-read they seemed, loyally parrotting the views of tutors and critics, and seldom straying beyond the charmed (if often charmless) circle of set books. After I had got to know the girl with the hazel-coloured eyes I used, from time to time, to dip into the various works of lit crit which she and her friends were ploughing through with exemplary seriousness of purpose. They were, I uneasily felt, becoming experts in the subject, whereas I would remain forever an enthusiastic amateur; they understood the jargon, and knew about such matters as 'dissociation of sensibility' and 'negative capability', and I hoped that if I too mastered the important critics I would learn to speak the same elevated and difficult language, and be able to hold up my head in their company.

I found these ventures into the world of lit crit both baffling and oddly consoling: not only did the authors seem to me to be very much worse writers than the historians – and even the political theorists – with whom we were supposed to familiarize ourselves, but so much of what they had to say, if intelligible at all, seemed to me to be flatulent, unimportant and alarmingly vague. All this aggravated my growing suspicion that, as an academic discipline, Eng lit was something of a non-event, inclining as it did to long-winded and pretentious statements of the obvious or the meaningless. The only critics who seemed to write intelligible, straightforward English, or to have anything of interest to say, were themselves writers, like Eliot or MacNeice or Orwell or Edmund Wilson. A particular favourite of mine was Graves's *The Crowning Privilege*, in which he lashed out at Eliot, Auden, Pound and Dylan Thomas; like the criticism of most professional writers other than Eliot and Empson, this was, I noted, treated in a patronizing, dismissive way by the academic critics, as though an erratic child had been allowed into the company of the grown-ups, and had sadly misbehaved.

Not only – or so I rudely assumed – was English something of an easy option, albeit one that might not only have put me on easy terms with Shakespeare, but enabled me to struggle through to the end of Henry James's *The Ambassadors*, my Everyman copy of which – a birthday present from an old headmaster – I had, in a frenzy of frustration, followed by an awful sense of shame, snapped across my knee and hurled from a fifth-floor window with a cry of strangled rage; it was also, or so it seemed to me, yet another manifestation of the curious way in which the once brisk and commonsensical English middle classes, deprived of both God and a sense of national mission, had taken up the 'Arts' as a kind of substitute religion. Taught by schoolmasters and dons to despise the worlds of trade and industry, stolid young Englishmen of the type that might, in happier times, have become muscular curates or iron-jawed district officers in solar topees and knee-length shorts, ploughed their way through volumes of lit crit of theological obscurity; 'literature' – defined in terms of a restricted band of poets, playwrights and novelists – came to be seen as a baffling business, like astrophysics or Egyptology, that could only be understood, or 'decoded', by the professionals and their initiates; in the world of education, where 'creativity' and 'spontaneity' came to be prized above all, middle-class parents calmed their worries about the shortage of tables or the dates of kings and queens by reflecting on the excellence of the school orchestra, and the air was loud with the rasping of tiny violins and the streets aswarm with tuba-toting ten-year-olds, hurrying to their next appointments like gigantic, fast-moving snails. All this, we were told, formed the background to a great revival of the arts, and one that had made Britain the centre and the envy of the artistic world.

None of this quite rang true; in the meantime, as I read – with

increasing pleasure – Pieter Geyl and Hugh Trevor-Roper and Isaiah
Berlin, I began to see that reading history was not so bad a business
after all, and to realize that, after all, that intrusive geography master
may not have blighted my life to quite the same extent as I had
formerly suspected.

★   ★   ★

Shore and I spent far less time in our last year travelling round the
West of Ireland in his back district nurse's car (now equipped with a
spare steering wheel mounted on a broomstick; sitting beside Shore
in the front, I emulated his every motion, so giving puzzled passers-
by the impression of two drivers at the wheel), and far more in the
university library: the formal demands made upon us were as slight
– or even slighter – than ever, but conscience got the better of us
both; quite apart from which I discovered – very much to my
surprise, since I had no interest whatsoever in practical politics – a
curious fascination in the abstractions of political theory, and spent
more time than was necessary reading about Comte and Saint-Simon
and Feuerbach and the giant Bakunin pulling the communication
cord of a train in which he was travelling through Poland in order to
lend a helping hand to some peasants busily engaged in setting fire to
some unpopular country house.

In the evenings we often drove out beyond Phoenix Park – passing
en route the stables where, a winter or two earlier, my wife-to-be,
encouraged by her wooden-legged landlords, had fed the boiler with
the sawn-up remains of the dining-room table – to the Wren's Nest,
a small country pub overlooking the Liffey that seemed to me to
embody all that such places should, yet so seldom do. It was a plain,
whitewashed building of the kind preferred by eighteenth-century
builders and small children drawing houses – two floors, a door in the
middle, windows on either side, a slate roof, a puff of smoke hanging
over the suitably symmetrical chimney. In summer one could take
one's pint and stand or sit on the wall outside; but it was in the winter
that the Wren's Nest came into its own. To the left of the front door
was a diminutive bar behind which a very old man stood pouring
drinks extremely slowly and discussing the issues of the day with his
equally aged customers, many of whom wore cloth caps and flannel,

collarless shirts with studs in front of the kind I associated with my grandfather's farm; to the right was a bare, whitewashed room with a steel engraving of the Wicklow Mountains on one wall and a faded copy of the 1916 Declaration of the Republic pinned to another, bare stone flags on the floor, plain, backless benches and a couple of Windsor chairs drawn round a blazing fire, some silver Guinness barrels in a corner, and a hurricane lamp hissing overhead. Every now and then the elderly landlord would shuffle slowly in carrying an enormous white enamel jug full of stout, with which he replenished our glasses; after half-past eleven he still more slowly drew the shutters, and life would continue along very much the same lines as before.

The little world we had lived in for so long was slowly beginning to drift apart. The Deaf Malvernian was heaven knew where; Charles Sprawson was a swimming-pool attendant somewhere in Paddington; Ian was wrapped up in his music, and Shore in his mysterious works of art; and I found myself increasingly obsessed with Suzanne, reeling back to Trinity in the small hours of the morning and banging noisily on the Front Gate to attract the attention of one of the red-nosed college porters who, unlike their English equivalents, would cheerfully let us in at the most unsociable hours of the night.

Suzanne now lived with Hilary in the ground floor flat of an elegant early nineteenth-century terraced house in Pembroke Road. The flat next door was occupied by an unusual undergraduate in knee-length khaki shorts and a khaki bush skirt. For some inexplicable reason he seemed to exude a powerful animal magnetism, with the result that he lived with a harem of Trinity girls, all of whom bustled eagerly to and fro, cooking his meals, rubbing oils into his feet, keeping the flat spick and span and, presumably, competing decorously with one another for the honour of sharing his bed. The members of the harem were genteel, nicely brought up young ladies of the kind I associated with the Edinburgh middle classes, clad in green twinsets and kilts and thick green tights, and sporting a string of pearls and fair hair kept neatly in place with a black velvet band; to keep them in order (or so we surmised) he employed a large and hungry-looking Alsatian, which roamed about the garden licking its chops and gazing about through melancholy, bloodshot eyes; he also (or so we liked to imagine) kept a rhino whip at the ready, and the night air was, from time to time, punctuated by harsh cries of command and the crash of falling furniture. That summer he left for Afghanistan in a Land Rover, taking with him his entire harem; one of them (or so we were led to believe) died on the journey home, at which he unhooked a spade from the side of the Land Rover, dug a shallow grave in the desert, and motored steadily on in silence, his jaw set in a look of grim resolve.

Just up the road was a Mooney's bar, which had unwisely abandoned its black and white chequerboard marble floor and well-worn leather upholstery for great swathes of purple carpet and tiny, pert bar stools with buttons holding the stuffing in place, and we assembled there one evening after going to see the first of the Beatles' films. Although I secretely enjoyed their songs, which seemed to me to be above average in a pretty mediocre neck of the woods (though as nothing to the mighty Roy Orbison), I disliked the ludicrous and servile nonsense that was already being written about them and their contemporaries by those who should have known better; and as a long-standing champion of worried clerks and ground-down chief cashiers, I took particular exception to a scene in the film in which the 'zany' lads made mock of a tired if pompous commuter in a bowler hat making his way home to Penge or Potters Bar. Their behaviour, I learned from their admirers in the pub, was 'iconoclastic' and 'irreverent' and 'classless' and 'refreshing'; to me it seemed merely oafish and uncouth, but as I listened to the voices all about me raised in anger and derision at the stuffiness of my views, I knew with a weary sinking of the spirit that the new world of pop culture that was coming into being would not be one in which I would ever feel, or want to feel, in any way at home.

* * *

When it came to amorous matters I found that – despite my brief adventure with the Damsel in heavy tweeds on the streets of Dublin – I was quite as timid and as incompetent as I had been all those years before when the very thought of ffenella's bosom or auburn hair had sent me scurrying to my diary with pounding heart and racing pen, there to confide my innermost thoughts and burning passions for the future delectation of Charles Sprawson. I learned from the girl with the hazel eyes that there had been Other Men in her life: this came as a terrible blow, and I strode frenziedly up and down her sitting-room beating my brow with the palms of my hands and quoting – or, more probably, misquoting – lines from *King Lear* about the perfidy and general wickedness of women, and speculating loudly about the feasibility of hurling myself off the nearest cliff-top in the face of the appalling and unprecedented revelations.

And then, one night, I found that she had – not unreasonably, since it was well past one o'clock – climbed into bed, and that I was leaning over her, breathing rather heavily and, for some curious reason, bereft of shirt and shoes, and that she seemed to be suggesting – could this really be the case? – that I might like to join her in her bed, narrow as it was. All at once I realized that the terrible moment had arrived – the moment that would make me as one with the middle-aged Copt and the Bailey boys in their hacking jackets and tubular corduroy trousers and Mr Jawleyford in his canary-coloured waistcoat and the banana salesmen and rum-soaked sailors in the bars in Puerto C— and Agnew and his thirteen friends and the unspeakable cads who had only a day or two earlier caused me to tear my hair and stride about spouting Shakespeare in an unprecedented way.

Trembling all over, I hurried away to the bathroom to steady my nerves, like a soldier preparing to go over the top, and gazed at myself in the mirror – the features still as distressingly lard-like and bland as ever, just as they were when I left with ffenella for Greece – and wondered whether such things could possibly be happening to me; and then, when the trembling stopped, I plodded back to her bedroom to see what would happen next. I was wearing that evening a pair of very hairy grey and black herringbone tweed trousers: these I refused to discard, but clutched tightly to me as I climbed in beside her like a mobile bramble bush and prepared to seize her in my arms. After several minutes of fierce debate and expostulation, I was – very reluctantly – persuaded to remove the herringbone trousers and drop them overboard; and when it was over, and we lay beside each other in that narrow crumpled bed, I raised one arm in the air in exultation, like a runner coasting home, or one who has seen the light acclaiming the New Messiah.

*   *   *

My remaining term and a half at Trinity I spent mostly, and very happily, with Suzanne in her flat in Pembroke Road. So excited was I by my belated removal of the herringbone trousers that I announced to whoever happened to be listening that we were now engaged; beyond that, I did nothing about it apart from enjoying a brief, idyllic interval, much of it spent in bed – from which I occasionally sprang and locked myself in the bedroom cupboard when visitors unexpectedly called for tea. Towards the end of the summer term the real world rudely intervened in the form of the Trinity Ball, an ordeal even more daunting than the business with the herringbone trousers.

As far as I remember, dancing first cast its shadow over my life when I was about five, and had been sent to my otherwise admirable pre-prep school in Queen's Gate. About once a week we were expected to pull on a pair of shiny black elastic-sided pumps – not dissimilar to the shoes my mother later, and very sensibly, refused to send with me to my prep school – and attend a dancing lesson. A grey-haired matron was especially imported for the occasion, and spent an undemanding hour demonstrating steps and intoning 'One – two – three – HOP' while a second matron thumped the piano. On the command 'HOP' we were told to shoot one leg out sideways in a curiously uncomfortable way; since our shiny black pumps had even shinier leather soles, which our mothers had vainly scratched with pins in order to make them grip, and since the parquet floor was very highly polished, a good deal of time was spent colliding with one another and crashing to the ground. Although dancing lessons were enjoyed by those odd ruby-lipped boys with names like Nigel or Julian, most of us, I'm sure, regarded them as an imposition of the most tedious and disagreeable kind.

Nor did they prove of any use when, some years later, I started being asked to dances, for by then 'One – two – three – HOP' and 'Forward-side-together' had been elbowed out by the twist and the rock and roll. Quite apart from our technical ineptitude, both my sister and I were extremely gauche and anti-social, casting a blight on the merriest of proceedings, marching about the room with stern unsmiling faces and looking ostentatiously at our watches as the long hours ticked away. Even so, despite our worst endeavours, the odd invitation filtered through and, protesting feebly, we were shunted off to spend another interminable evening striding disdainfully round the garden or, if our luck was in, surreptitiously watching television with the father of the house while the revellers crashed and chortled all about.

Nemesis can't be dodged for ever, and very occasionally I was dragged from behind some protective pillar and forced, almost at gunpoint, onto the dance floor. Almost at once my glasses misted up with fear and embarrassment; my feet, large enough in civilian life, felt as though they had been encased in concrete, and that far from venturing out in the kind of footwear appropriate to the occasion I was sporting a pair of mud-encrusted brogues. Quite unable to see where I was going, I invariably steered my partner into a table covered with drinks and dainties, sending them spinning to the ground, or mowed down other couples as they spun about the floor, exciting frowns of disapproval and the kind of comment normally reserved for elderly motorists. Puce with shame, I spent those agonizing moments apologizing to my partner as I ground her tender toes beneath my iron-clad boots or drove her backwards down a flight of stairs; as soon as the band stopped playing we fled apart with gasps of mutual relief. And if I couldn't find a deserted room in which to read my book, or the night was too chilly to snooze beneath the stars, I spent as much time as I could talking to solicitous mothers or whisky-imbibing fathers, strenuously – and so unworthily – avoiding the gaze of the plainest girl in the room, who had been sitting out the last dozen dances and might even, if very pushed, have welcomed the pressure of my steel-tipped toes to relieve the tedium.

On this particular evening relief was at hand in the rubicund, satanic form of Charles Sprawson, who had abandoned his career as a swimming-pool attendant to come back for the Trinity Ball. In a very boorish, very English way, I left Charles – who was, to my amazement, an enthusiastic and rather dashing dancer – to dance the night away with Suzanne while I propped up the bar with my cronies. As the music throbbed and pulsed about me I wished – as I was often to wish again – that I could throw myself into the dance with the genial abandon of those I affected to despise, and that the same absurd self-consciousness that made me incapable of singing a note in public would suddenly drop away, like a mist in the morning sun; and I found it hard to suppress an uncomfortable suspicion that (as is so often the case) those awful Julians and Nigels probably had the answer all along.

★   ★   ★

A day or two later the term ended in a mire of drunkenness. We read in one of the Dublin evening papers an awe-inspiring article about a family of cockroaches who had made their home in the heavily lacquered beehive hairdo of a Dublin housewife and – here the story lost its charm – had burrowed into her brain and so proved the undoing of their landlady who seemed to have remained quite oblivious to all these goings-on right to the bitter end; overcome with drink and tiredness in a nightclub in a mews off Merrion Square – the manager was a cheerful Greek who held his trousers up with a knotted Trinity tie – I had a vision of my friends as skeletons, whirling and grinning in the blackness like characters in a mediaeval dance of death.

Ian went to America to make more records; Shore and Rivers hitchhiked to Nepal; my money was running out, and I wanted to work for my finals, so I travelled instead with my old friend Tom, poking absent-mindedly about the sites of Sicily and wishing I were in Holywood, County Down, instead. In September we gathered, for the last time, to take our finals. Whereas a year or two earlier – or so the story had it – Derek Mahon had concluded his scholarly career by staggering into the Exam Hall carrying a large block of concrete which he dropped with a mighty crash before the invigilator before striding purposefully out, lightly dusting his hands together, our finals proved a modest and decorous affair. After it was all over we stood on the steps and compared notes and exchanged addresses in a stiff, uneasy way and said goodbye, not to those – like Ian or Suzanne or Weale or John Kelly – whom one expected to go on seeing for ever, but to the figures from what already seemed another age: to ffenella and the bank manager and the man with the leather jacket who had asked for my views on existentialism and the middle-aged Copt (soon to be starting his fourteenth year) and the great army of Ulstermen in green blazers with filigree boars' heads emblazoned on the bosom, and the shades of Mr and Mrs Todd's ancestral roots in Teddington and their mauve-legged daughter and Holmes with his collection of cigarette stubs and the Deaf Malvernian and Mrs Brady and her hard-working husband and the constipated Wykhamist and Hector dancing in the dark and the Damsels striding purposefully by ... All about us, puzzled freshmen with spots and scarves and clean-looking duffel coats were anxiously opening doors and enrolling in Fabian or Gaelic-speaking societies and squash or cricket clubs and taking shelter with copies of *Punch* and *Country Life* among the snoozing trainee clubmen of the Hist and the Phil, where the windows were still uncleaned and the clocks ticked steadily on and the flies buzzed against the glass and everything stayed the same. Four years earlier it had seemed that this particular slice of life could never end, and would offer a refuge for ever; now the gates of the garden were open, and it was time to wander out.

EPILOGUE

Like most Trinity graduates, and especially those of English origin, I found adjusting to the outside world a hard and uncomfortable business, and could be spotted blinking and peering uneasily about like some unhappy mole who had been forcibly expelled on the end of a spade from its cosy, subterranean lair into the metallic brightness of midday. After four years of idling and drinking and travelling and quietly snoozing in the Irish countryside, one was both ruinously spoilt and wretchedly ill-equipped for the mundane mechanics of earning a living; and whereas Oxford and Cambridge students – by definition somewhat sharper and better equipped than their English equivalents from Trinity – prided themselves on haunting the ante-chambers of the Establishment, and remained firmly in touch with whatever made English society go about its business, we had haunted a curious, Edenic limbo, neither England nor Ireland and a refuge from both, in which the world of everyday – and certainly the world in which we would have to earn our keep – seemed blissfully abstract and remote. Not surprisingly, many Trinity men took to the bottle, or became chicken-farmers in the West of Ireland, or dabbled in double-glazing, or – like the middle-aged Copt – became lifelong undergraduates, flitting like melancholy ghosts about their adopted city, carousing with callow youths fifteen years their junior, ingratiating themselves with each year's intake of girls with exciting-looking bosoms, and watching generation after generation passing by through bloodshot, saurian eyes, as the waistline thickened and the hair thinned and the bones began to creak.

It took me at least two years to realize that, regrettable as it seemed, I would in the end have to earn myself a living; had I had private means, I would no doubt have spun things out still longer, and might still be on the brink of finding a job. Like the most tiresome type of don, I combined timidity with a quite unfounded arrogance: I expected to start at the top, but had no idea of how to set about getting there, and I had conventionally disdainful views about anything to do with industry or commerce. In my last year at Trinity an earnest, well-meaning girl from Hampstead, much given to thick bottle-green stockings and old-fashioned sandals with a flower pattern incised on their uppers, had – quite rightly – expressed concern about my refusal to take heed for the morrow, and insisted that I talk to her father, an important-sounding businessman who, she was sure, would be only too glad to find me a job. She arranged a picnic lunch in Merrion Square, and her father – a kindly, humourless man, quite oblivious to my graceless lack of interest, or the laughter of my fellow-guests at my evident discomfiture – spoke to me in measured, serious tones about a chain of supermarkets with which he was involved, assuring me (in reply to a flurry of self-deprecation on my part) that within a year I could well find myself in charge of the tinned foods counter in their Brighton branch. The very notion of my doing such work was too ridiculous to contemplate, but I was quite unable to come up with any alternatives: instead, I wasted time in a cheerless way, dimly hoping but never quite believing that if I waited long enough things would slot into place, or I might somehow find my way back to that Eden from which I had been so rudely expelled.

Nor was my reading matter exactly helpful: the first part of *Pickwick* and (a particular favourite) Gerald Durrell's *My Family and Other Animals* – that most magical of all evocations of escape – encouraged me to half-believe in, and certainly pine for, a world devoid of tedium, drudgery and responsibilities, in which money semed to present no problems, the old grew no older and the young remained forever young, and every day was lit with the luminous expectancy of a cloudless summer morning; I read and re-read Stephen Dedalus's intoxicating, subversive moment of revelation on the sands of Dublin Bay with the same sense of elation and revolt that I had felt when, some four years earlier, I had carefully copied it out in my diary, brooding all the while on my hopeless love for ffenella and the sharp white light of Greece; and, much as I enjoyed reading about harrassed, timid clerks or important-sounding businessmen in Dickens or Wells or the admirable Roy Fuller, I had no particular eagerness to meet their equivalents in the flesh.

The truth of the matter was that – like most university students, and especially those who dabble in the vague and often pretentious subjects loosely labelled 'the Arts' – I was hopelessly and irremediably spoilt. Egged on by my reading of the youthful Marx – whose writings on alienation have far more to do with Romantic angst and self-indulgence than with the iron laws of economics and the equally joyless notions associated with the sage in his later and more bad-tempered years – I saw even the most congenial and sympathetic forms of labour as a terrible intrusion on the self and a compromise with the forces of darkness. Those difficult French writers with whom I had wrestled from the depths of my deck chair before setting out for Byzantium with ffenella all those years before, with their message of lonely purity and defiance and contempt for the pale evasions and 'false' values of the 'bourgeois' world, infused with large doses of Stephen Dedalus pacing the strand in Dublin Bay in restless and titanic mood, seemed to be spot on to one who – like so many of his ilk – was strongly lacking in any sense of direction, had few firm convictions and (despite some notional nods to the left) felt that the only reasonable answer to life's problems, apart from the sudden but improbable bestowal of a private income, was the re-introduction of the feudal system, during the course of which, it went without saying, my friends and I would emerge as its principal beneficiaries.

Not surprisingly, I regarded even the most congenial form of labour – other than the academic life, which I imagined to be an enviable extension of the undergraduate world, involving little or no surrender of the self – with a prim and virginal shudder. In my post-Byzantium diary I had seen myself – quite unreasonably, since I could neither draw nor play a musical instrument, and was quite defeated by all known European languages other than my own – as leading the life of a kind of pilgrim-cum-wandering bard, strolling agreeably about the world with a notebook and a penny whistle: unlike the youthful Patrick Leigh Fermor, I no longer thought along quite such exuberant lines, but I regarded the prospect of any kind of office life with all the enthusiasm of a motheaten tiger confronted by a cage. It never occurred to me that the kind of work I was likely to do would, in all probability, be infinitely more entertaining and companionable and 'uncompromised' than that undertaken by the great majority of the population whom I so heartily despised, most of whom had left school at an alarmingly early age, and very few of whom had had the advantages, let alone the heady, indolent delights, of a university education.

Nor did I begin to appreciate – any more than I had in the self-important worlds of school and sport – that the suspension of disbelief and the playing of parts were an integral and piquant part of office life, or that the gulf between rhetoric and achievement, between the hen-pecked husband and the office tyrant, between professional greatness and neighbourly insignificance, provides institutional life as well as English social comedy with so much of its pathos and comicality; that even the dullest of jobs can be redeemed, in part at least, by the talking of shop or the endless fascination of office gossip and office politics, so compelling to those within and so meaningless to the world outside; or that those men in bowler hats I had so derided on the train from Victoria, dozing over their *Telegraph* crossword puzzles or struggling with the contents of their briefcases, may or may not have heard of Yeats or Auden or Robert Graves but were, in all probability, masters of an expertise or a knowledge quite beyond my power or ken and probably of far greater use to the rest of us than anything I would ever bring to bear.

Institutional life is only made possible, or even tolerable, by the shared pretence that everything we do is – as, in the long run, it must be – a matter of life and death, and in the years ahead I came to find the small hierarchies of office life and the ways in which, after a holiday, the office worker had to play himself back into his part, learning once more to feign rage or delight or indignation, both moving and extremely comic; but the life I had led to date – and my life at Trinity in particular – had been devoid of such devious intricacies, nor did I wish to become in any way involved. Like most undergraduates, I regarded 'hypocrisy' as the most terrible of sins: twenty years on I find myself increasingly uneasy with those brutal, forthright souls who insist on calling a spade a spade whatever the circumstances, and I regard a little mild hypocrisy and a kindly scattering of white lies as one of life's essential lubricants. Like most undergraduates, I bled for the world at large, but was fiercely intolerant of individual frailty and the sad, consoling myths that most of us survive by.

These arrogant assumptions were exacerbated – as they so often are – by a Micawber-life belief that somehow, sooner or later, something would turn up. If I waited long enough, an important-sounding job would materialize out of the brilliant Sussex air; I thought I would like to be a writer, but did nothing about it, on the assumption that one had to wait for inspiration to strike, and that one's hand would be mysteriously guided across the paper, like the glass on an ouija board, or Omar Sharif in the film of *Dr Zhivago*, when he rises in the middle of the night, climbs into a silken dressing-gown, writes out a short but perfect poem in an impeccable copperplate hand to the accompaniment of appropriate 'theme' music, gazes soulfully into the rising sun, and retires to bed rubbing his hands briskly together with the pleased demeanour of a man who has done a good night's job of work. I felt that one day I should grapple with the all-important question of the existence of God, but kept – and have continued to keep – the old gentleman waiting in the wings like some luckless tenant farmer wringing his hands in the expectation of a possible reduction in his rent. This terrible passivity afflicts me still. Only in the last year or two have I, very belatedly, come to realize the truth of those bracing aphorisms one finds printed on the back of matchboxes and in the pages of *Readers' Digest*, or – at somewhat greater length – in self-improving works by those earnest Americans with carefully combed hair and steel-rimmed spectacles who keep us informed about making sense of our lives or the need for positive thinking: that it is up to us to make things happen, and that, more often than not, we have only ourselves to blame for what we fail to achieve. Such notions were altogether unintelligible to me, as well as running counter to the prevailing dogmas of the age – in which I took a keen interest – which placed an overriding emphasis on the inescapable constraints of class, inheritance or general infirmities of character.

Nor was my dim desire to make my mark in the world or forge eagerly ahead, rudely elbowing my competitors aside, made any easier by my inability to take seriously the shibboleths of manliness, or to worry overmuch about which aspects of life were supposedly reserved for men, and which for women. Without in any way subscribing to the nuts-and-sandals school of thought – herbalists and vegetarians excited in them an Orwell-like derision – my parents had always expressed fairly advanced ideas about such matters as abortion or the desirability of couples living together rather than getting married right away; nor did they differentiate a great deal between who did what about the house. Both my sister and I grew up helping with the housework and the shopping; at home now I quite happily deal with the hoovering and the ironing, while my wife grapples with the car, discusses dry rot with builders' merchants and pays all the bills – areas strictly reserved for the menfolk in households in which the paterfamilias considers that to be driven around by the little woman, or to allow her access to an income-tax form, is somehow an affront to his virility, and insists on the insulting practice of giving her, from the generosity of his heart, a weekly 'housekeeping allowance' (plus a little bit extra for 'fripperies'), the over-expenditure of which excites in her heaving bosom terrible pangs of guilty dread.

Not surprisingly, I found many of the demands of the early feminists both sympathetic and oddly redundant, at least in the light of my own experience, having grown up in a family in which the women had, to say the least, an equal voice – an experience that has, perhaps, served me well in my professional life. Be that as it may, I had little interest in the 'virile' or 'manly' aspects of going to work: could things be so arranged, I thought, I would be quite happy to stay at home and do a little light dusting before retiring to bed for my afternoon rest with a large Victorian novel.

Towards the end of my time at Trinity a girl of whom I was particularly fond had told me in somewhat reproving tones that I was '*pas sérieux*'; and although I was, like most supposedly sensitive souls, extremely '*sérieux*' about my own feelings, I found it hard to be terribly '*sérieux*' about anything else. I was far more gripped by the surface of things than by their substance, more swayed by the cut of a pair of trousers or a see-through nylon shirt than by what their occupant had to say for himself, more likely to remember from the back of an old-fashioned Penguin where the author went to school than what his book was all about, and, when asking for instructions in the street, far too intrigued by the motion of my informant's adam's apple or his curious tone of voice to take in what he had to say. I found (and still find) it quite impossible to make up my mind on any of the great issues of the day, agreeing eagerly with whoever spoke last and whizzing across the political spectrum in sharp reaction against the company I had to keep, moving sharply to the right when confronted by a gaggle of smug, omniscient *Guardian* readers and bouncing leftwards once again at the very notion of a property developer or the kind of 'blue-rinsed' matron so dear to the heart of political journalists. I was, in short, in something of a dither; and the future looked baffling indeed.

★   ★   ★

For want of anything better to do I went to stay with a Trinity friend in Paris, sleeping on his floor in the Ecole Normale Supérieur. I was – in my mind at least – still engaged to the girl with the hazel-coloured eyes, though I had done nothing whatsoever to advance my cause, least of all buying a ring; I felt obscurely aggrieved that she was very sensibly pressing ahead with her own career, still more so since she had decided to take up journalism – which, equally obscurely, I felt to be somehow my patch, not hers, while once again doing absolutely nothing about it. From time to time we exchanged letters: mine were replete with whimsicality and lachrymose self-pity, while hers were brisk and to the point, and the enclosed cuttings from a Ballymena newspaper and, later, the *Belfast Telegraph* only served to point up the contrast between her purposeful professionalism and my inadequate escapism, and made it all too brutally plain that broken-hearted pining in Paris was likely to prove a futile, self-defeating business.

In the meantime, I found myself a job teaching English to foreigners in a Berlitz school near the Opéra. I found – very much to my surprise – that I greatly enjoyed baffling foreigners with the inconsistencies of English, drawing wildly on the blackboard and enticing strange and strangled cries from a roomful of eager clerks and jolly-looking housewives. From time to time I gave individual tuition. Among my prize pupils was a very plain, middle-aged lady in a fox fur with a tight, pursed little mouth that reminded me, rather unflatteringly, of that part of pug's anatomy that should, in a half-way decent world, be concealed beneath a pair of trousers. She was, I gathered, very anxious to master the language, and took her studies extremely seriously; unfortunately she was quite incapable of imitating even the simplest English word, however slowly and clearly I enunciated it, producing instead an identical, costive mooing noise as her version of whatever I happened to toss in her direction. I found it increasingly hard to control my laughter as this poor lady sat before me like an unhappy, pop-eyed fish, gasping and struggling to master the precise pronunciation of 'desk' or 'chalk' or 'pen' or even 'blackboard', yet always producing the same lugubrious lowing sound. After several hours of this I found my head beginning to spin: I felt an irresistible urge to lean forward in the middle of a moo and, seizing hold of those pursed, protruding lips between my thumb and forefinger, cut off the terrible sound at source; and so strong did this unworthy urge become that I had to clamp my hands together beneath the desk lest one of them got the better of me, while my pupil sat before me smiling with gratitude and a sense of progress being made and hooting at my every word like a foghorn running riot.

Unkind as I was – or felt – towards the lady with the lips, my own progress in a foreign language was wretchedly inadequate. I spent long hours reading – or trying to read – Sartre and Merleau Ponty and Raymond Aron and the memoirs of General de Gaulle, but when it came to speaking the stuff, let alone grasping what the man in the street was trying to say, I found myself utterly at sea. Instead I devoted much time to playing clock golf and consorting with English-speakers: among the most convivial of these was John Montague, the Ulster poet, who lived in a large studio flat in Montparnasse, round the corner from which I found a flat of my own after my friend at the Ecole Normale had decided to reclaim his floor.

Having wasted a year in this way, I now wasted another by enrolling for an MA at the University of Sussex, obtaining a handsome grant in the process. In those heady, expansive days the new universities in particular were adept at offering vague, interdisciplinary postgraduate degrees, the curricula of which had a colour-magazine-like quality of modish, predigested knowledge of a kind that was all too tantalizing to pampered perpetual students with no strong sense of where they wanted to go, or why. I rashly enrolled for a course advertised in the brochure as 'European Studies': this sounded admirably diffuse and undemanding and would, I fondly imagined, give me an opportunity to read those 'difficult' Continental novelists with whom I had hoped to impress ffenella all those years before, as well as the likes of Foucault and Marcuse and Lacan, all of whom were magic names to Englishmen with pretensions of a certain kind. To my dismay I learned – too late – that I had instead embarked upon a course specially designed for budding Eurocrats, and that far from idling about on the grass reading about the Human Condition I was writing essays on the founding of the Coal and Steel Community and the operation of pressure groups in the European Parliament, and reading enormous, utterly yawn-inducing volumes about Professor Hallstein and Jean Monnet and the Dutch electoral system (whether they were, in fact, any more unreadable than Foucault is another matter altogether). There were four of us on the course, and I felt very much the odd man out, and sadly unable to conceal my boredom or abysmal lack of interest: our tutor was a passionate Eurocrat, and my fellow-students shared his cold-eyed enthusiasm for standardizing poultry regulations and hurling down inoffensive tariff barriers and doing away with all those tiresome national idiosyncracies – like bowler hats or pounds, shillings and pence – that seemed to me to add a certain spice to life as well as being a source of irrational national pride. We went to a couple of 'European' conferences in Amsterdam and Grenoble, attended by well-scrubbed, brisk-looking trainee bureaucrats in button-down shirts and grey herringbone jackets, all of whom smiled a great deal and discussed the brotherhood of man in flat, inflexionless voices in a cosmopolitan version of English more akin to semaphore than speech. Nothing, it seemed to me, could be more deadly than to spend one's days making polite, anodyne conversation with interminably smiling foreigners, however amiable or well-intentioned. In Grenoble I found, to my surprise, a kindred spirit who looked as unhappy and ill-at-ease as I did, and seconds before the opening of a spirited debate on 'Whither the Nation State?' we climbed out of a window at the back of the hall, jumped ten feet to the ground, and made for the nearest bar. Back in England, I packed my bags and made for London where, many months later, my wife very sensibly persuaded me to finish my thesis on 'The Labour Party and the EEC', earlier rejected on the grounds of being altogether too journalistic, and to claim my unwanted degree; after which I put the whole unhappy business behind me, and thought no more of the European Court of Justice or the great work of the Fathers of the EEC.

Once in London, I had no alternative but to try to find a job. My efforts to take such matters seriously were gravely impeded by my mother's admirably frivolous attitude towards office life – she liked to tell us how she had had forty-seven jobs before she got married, including the supervision of a troupe of midgets – and by my belated discovery of P. G. Wodehouse. I had tried the old boy when I was about twelve – at about the same time as I was feverishly working my way through the Saint and Bulldog Drummond, and dreamt only of puffing insolent clouds of smoke into the faces of master-criminals – and had found him a good deal less entertaining than my contemporaries, all of whom emitted loud and annoying barks of laughter when confronted with the doings of Gussie Fink-Nottle and Catsmeat Potter-Pirbright. One day, having typed out my twenty-fifth application letter of the morning and posted off a great wodge of envelopes to various publishers, each of them containing a pitiful plea for admission, I called in at the Army and Navy Stores, bought myself a Wodehouse and, unable to face any more *curricula vitae*, spent the rest of the day learning about the Drones Club and Bertie's domineering aunts. So much did I enjoy this novel experience that, on my way back to my parents' flat in Ashley Gardens, I called in once again at the Army and Navy Stores, and bought another book about Bertie Wooster; and, far from advancing my career, I spent the next three weeks sitting in a deck chair in St James's Park, every now and then hurrying back to the Army and Navy to replenish my stocks.

Such masterly inactivity could not go on for ever, and as the days grew chillier and the evenings began to close in I stirred myself from my deck chair and went for the occasional interview. Like the girl with the hazel-coloured eyes – who was shortly to land a job on the old *Daily Sketch* before moving on to the *Mail*, and a good many points beyond – I really wanted, I think, to be a journalist, but I knew it would involve me overmuch with my old enemy, the telephone. I very much disliked the idea of open plan offices, and had a strong suspicion that, when it came to putting a foot in the door, I would prove a broken reed, and that my terrible sense of the futility and the transience of things might well prove stronger than my sense of commitment or ambition; so I concentrated my efforts on publishing instead.

Like most self-important applicants with university degrees, I imagined publishing to be a matter of standing about in hairy tweeds or a corduroy jacket drinking sherry with celebrated authors and, in the afternoon, turning the pages of a masterpiece in a languid, desultory fashion: this seemed a way of life to which I was eminently suited, and I had no doubt that, before long, some purple-nosed publisher in a bow tie and loud striped shirt would offer me the kind of important editorial job for which I was so obviously equipped. In the meantime I made it quite clear that there were certain kinds of work that I was, quite simply, not prepared to contemplate: when, after a long and apparently cordial interview, an eminent publisher – who had himself started, as the best publishers always do, at the bottom of the heap – told me that I seemed a reasonable sort of chap and that I could start work in the warehouse within the month, my face fell with so evident a display of outrage and distress that the conversation was brought swiftly to an end; and as for the suggestion, some weeks later, that I might be interested in a job in the Glasgow office ...

To fortify myself against such outrageous suggestions I spent as much time as I reasonably could in a pub under Piccadilly Circus called Ward's Irish House; and I became so attached to this unusual spot that on particularly happy nights I used to dream that I had been appointed its manager and was allowed into those mysterious vaults in which were stored enormous silver barrels of stout and outsize bottles of Jameson's with the labels pasted on upside-down. Visiting Ward's filled me with a terrible nostalgia for Ireland, and my heart went out to those select few who shared my enthusiasm for its green and white lavatory tiles, stone floor, dripping barrel-vaulted ceilings, faded red leather benches and ancient, badly stained sepia photographs of the Wicklow Mountains or the main street of Mullingar. Except for on Saturday nights in winter, when crowds of drunken football fans picked their way unsteadily down the steep steps and sang those hideous dirges that are, I suppose, the nearest thing modern England has to genuine folk song, Wards was a surprisingly mild and peaceful place in which to enjoy a ruminative pint. It was mercifully free of those twin banes of the modern pub, pounding music and clattering fruit machines, and its conversational clientèle consisted of bus crews, red-faced Irish labourers in donkey jackets and mud-encrusted boots (no doubt some of them would soon be boarding the Holyhead train) and the occasional publisher or literary man tucking into the regular lunch of boiled bacon and cabbage.

Perhaps its most colourful customer was a bibulous Irishman who had worked in the royalties department of Faber and Faber. The author of 'Tshombe's Lament' and a fine poem about his place of employment which began 'I don't give a jot/For Eliot/For Auden/ I don't give a damn', he achieved a brief celebrity when he was photographed in The *Sunday Times* clutching a pair of false teeth which, he claimed, had belonged to T. S. Eliot, and had been discovered by him among some yellowing papers in the basement in Russell Square. Derek Mahon and I spent a good deal of time talking to this comical, melancholy figure; some years later we learned that he had been discovered, dead, in a frozen attic in Camden Town.

Among the barmen, our particular friend was a large, pale-faced man from County Tipperary; he was a keen reader, and always asked me about the books I was tackling at the time. One day I happened to be clutching an excellent if rather gloomy novel called *The Sinner's Bell* by Kevin Casey. At the sight of its somewhat austere jacket the Man from Tipp became unusually animated. Of course he knew Kevin Casey, he cried: one of the most famous wrestlers in Ireland; this must be his autobiography, a book he had been waiting for years to read. In vain I tried to persuade him that this particular Kevin Casey was very far from being a champion wrestler; he begged me to lend him the book – a sad story of marital frustration in the Irish Midlands, the opening chapter of which was set in some seedy honeymoon hotel in Paddington – and put it carefully away on a shelf behind him for safe removal to Kilburn or Camden Town. I never saw *The Sinner's Bell* again, and from then on the Man from Tipp seemed less anxious to meet my gaze than in the innocent days of yore.

One evening I met my old friend John Kelly for a drink in Wards, and after we'd had a pint or two he asked me if I'd like to come with him and his wife to visit an old Trinity friend who was living in a flat in Cadogan Square. This turned out to be the best of many good turns Mr Kelly had done me: the friend – whose name was Petra – was a cheerful, very dear person with black eyes (like those of an Outer Mongolian) and hair like a badger, and within a month or two we were married; but that is another story.

*   *   *

After much writing of letters and a certain lowering of expectations,

I eventually found myself a job with a large and distinguished firm of publishers. Their offices were off St James's Street, in a rickety Georgian house which seemed to swallow up and absorb an unreasonably large number of people. In the panelled reception area was a full-length portrait of an earlier member of the ruling dynasty, raffishly smoking a cigarette and looking like a shrewder, fiercer version of Catsmeat Potter-Pirbright or even Bertie Wooster himself; the illusion of country house life – swiftly dissipated once one set foot in the offices themselves – was sustained by comfortable, battered-looking sofas and creaking boards more appropriate, I felt, to a decrepit rectory than a hard-headed and highly successful firm of publishers. As the junior member of the publicity department, my job was to book advertising space in various newspapers and magazines – had *nothing* changed in the years between? – prepare and design advertisements for provincial papers and, with the help of a ruler, work out exactly how much of the cost of the advertisement should be assigned to each of the books listed therein; I was also charged with making a note of exactly who reviewed what kinds of books for which particular paper, and was occasionally allowed to fill in a 'tick list' of those newspapers that should receive review copies of the books we were publishing that week. This gave me access to a large and tempting room in which these brand new books were stored, and over the next few months many of my friends and relations – to their grateful surprise – found themselves joining the lists of literary editors and VIPs to whom free copies should be sent.

Utterly unaware – as most newcomers are – of the depth of my own ignorance, and of the unflattering fact that a couple of degrees, however good in themselves (and neither of mine was in any way remarkable), were of absolutely no practical use or even interest to my employers, I felt this to be tedious and decidedly anti-climactic work; when I said as much to one of my colleagues – a jolly, fair-haired girl with a gap in her teeth, who later left to become a successful journalist and the writer of equally jolly novels – she kindly and patiently explained the facts of life and told me, quite correctly, that the first six months were always the worst; after which I felt altogether more cheerful and resigned to my lot.

The head of the publicity department was a woman in her thirties with shoes like small grey mice who looked very much as William Pitt the Younger might have done had he been kitted out with Mary Whitehouse spectacles. She was a kind but worried soul, and slightly daunting to work for, in the manner of the old-fashioned school matron: we minions were careful to keep on the right side of her, and I quickly learned the tell-tale signs of a storm in the making, including a blackened brow and angry, pursed-out lips. Every now and then the old gentleman who ran the firm would submit this unfortunate lady to the most terrible basting, after which she would limp back to the office looking bedraggled and woebegone; a terrible silence would fall over the publicity department, broken only by the sound of sobbing from within, while we exchanged part-fearful, part-gleeful glances with one another and waited for the next stage in the drama to unfold. My friend with the gap in her teeth was greatly given to jolly, bibulous lunches, and in the dog hours of the afternoon could often be spotted snoozing behind her typewriter, her arms across the carriage and her long fair hair entangled in the keys. At the sound of these terrible sobs she would slowly uncoil herself from her typewriter, and pad in bare feet into the dragon's lair; after a few minutes of reassuring noises the sobbing died away, to be replaced by the sound of noses being blown and Kleenex scrumpled and thrown away; the girl with the gap in her teeth would come padding out again, closing the door behind her, and give us the nod in much the same way as, years earlier, an air raid warden might have signalled the All Clear; and life returned to normal once again.

Within a day or two of my arrival I was informed that, as the most junior member of the department, it would be my job to work the office projector, and that I was to show a group of distinguished journalists and émigrés a film that had recently been smuggled out of Russia showing the funeral of an important dissident writer published by the firm. I had no idea how a projector worked, and felt baffled by the very idea of a Box Brownie, but I carefully watched as one of my colleagues explained how to take the film from its can and thread it onto the various hooks and spools that protruded from an ancient projector of the kind I remembered so well from prep school showings of *The Ghost Train* when we weren't being addressed by vicars emulating the cry of the heron or fraudulent clerks disguised as deep sea divers. After twenty minutes or so I had, I felt, mastered the machine – after all, if the games master had understood its workings, surely I could too? – and I set off to the laboratory off the Tottenham Court Road where the precious film was being developed for its first ever showing west of the Iron Curtain.

That afternoon a bevy of journalists, academics and excitable grey-haired Russian ladies, all of them clad in black and speaking in impenetrable accents, gathered in one of the conference rooms downstairs, and seated themselves in eager, anticipatory rows on gold court chairs of the kind associated with marquees and catering firms and dubious-looking men in morning dress. I put up the screen, drew the curtains, clipped the full spool I had collected from the laboratory onto the back of the projector, and carefully threaded the loose end over the various wheels and knobs as instructed before hooking it into the empty spool at the front. I asked the émigré ladies, whose voices were now rising to fever pitch, if they were ready to start; they assured me they were with an eager, impatient cry; I turned out the lights and pressed the starting button, and a reverential, awesome silence fell on the little gathering as the distinguished guests craned eagerly forward for their first glimpse of this moving and historic scene. I knew that the film would show a sombre group of black-clad pall-bearers in fur hats and enormous overcoats carrying a coffin across a waste of snow, followed by a cortège of mourners, shuffling sadly forward with wreaths in their hands; yet here – as the film sputtered suddenly into life – were white luminous figures on a background of overwhelming black, moving rapidly backwards, retrieving the coffin from a hole in the ground like black-faced versions of Burke and Hare, hoisting it onto their shoulders, and carrying it off in quite the wrong direction, stepping sharply backwards like overdressed ballet dancers across the interminable wastes of coal-black snow! As the cortège disappeared into the distance a terrible cry went up from the émigré ladies and the distinguished Slavonic scholars, after which they started jabbering to one another in angry, disappointed voices, and gathered hotly about the projector, wagging their fingers and thrusting their faces forward like a flock of well-appointed crows.

Nor was I through with the world of Russian dissidents. I had been at work for about a week when, to my horror, the telephone on my desk – which had been mercifully silent hitherto – began to ring in a loud, insistent way. I had lost none of my old dread of the telephone in the intervening years: I jolted back in my seat, like a man who has touched an electric fence; my heart began to pound; I stared at the loathsome instrument as though it were a serpent coiled upon my desk before eventually picking it up. 'A Mr Solzhenitsyn wishes to speak to you,' the lady on the switchboard informed me in a disapproving voice: 'He sounds like a foreign gentleman.' In those days the bearded sage was not yet the household name he has since become, but he did ring bells of a kind. 'Put him through,' I commanded in my most impressive tones, after which a guttural-sounding voice began to tell me at great length about his next book, and to ask if we might be interested in publishing it. Dimly aware that I had been plunged straight into the heart of the publishing business, and that I might, in my first week, be about to pull off the coup of a lifetime, I asked the great man to hold on and, clamping my hand over the receiver, turned to my room-mate for advice, my eyes revolving in their sockets with excitement. 'I've got that chap Soljey-something on the line,' I said. 'Isn't he one of those Russians who write about prison camps and people standing around with snow on their boots? What should I tell him?' 'Never heard of him,' my colleague replied, busily buffing his nails, one leg crooked over the arm of his chair: 'I should get rid of him if you can. He's almost certainly a maniac. Put him through to editorial.' Anxiously I turned back to work - only to find Solzhenitsyn inexplicably convulsed with mirth. The brute turned out to be my old friend Tom, who was now working in the City, and for whom impersonation of distinguished Russian writers was an agreeable way of filling in the long hours of office life. Was this the shape of things to come?

Afterword

Many books come into being by accident rather than by design, and when, one evening in the early Eighties, I began — for no apparent reason — to write an account of how some twenty years earlier I had clambered aboard the boat-train at Euston Station, *en route* for Holyhead, the Irish ferry and a new life as an undergraduate at Trinity College, Dublin, I had no idea that I was laying the foundation stone of what would eventually become two volumes of autobiography. Not long before we had moved back to London after six years of exile in Oxford, and were living in a rubble of possessions, as yet unsorted and unpacked; I typed at a table in our bedroom, hemmed in by a teetering mound of books and clothes and children's toys, but as I inched my way slowly down the page, the years and my surroundings dropped away and, as though in a trance, I found myself reliving, in the minutest and most vivid detail, that heady moment when I first spotted ffenella striding about the deck of the Dun Laoghaire ferry, the wind lashing her auburn hair and her magnificent bosom jutting out like the prow of a Viking ship, or the anticlimactic misery in which, the following morning, I dragged myself round the grey, granitic squares of Trinity, bleary-eyed from lack of sleep and ruinously indigested from a diet of draught Guinness and stale pork pies.

So immersed was I in the minutiae of my vanished youth, and so over-whelmed by the long-forgotten details bubbling to the surface, that I quite felt as if I had written a full-length book by the end of that first evening, and was surprised and disappointed to discover that I had notched up 400 words at most. Over the next week or so I produced some 4000 words in all, and since they seemed to make a satisfyingly self-contained item, I posted them off to Alan Ross at the *London Magazine*. I knew he had a soft spot for memoirs, and was prepared to publish pieces which, for reasons of length or obscurity, were unlikely to find homes in more conventional outlets. Prompt as always, he sent me one of his familiar postcards by return. To my relief, he liked ffenella very much, and would be printing her in the next issue of the magazine: he longed to know what happened next, and hoped I would keep his readers informed. Dutiful as ever, I produced a second instalment, and then a third in which I revealed how, to my everlasting regret, I had failed to take advantage of the situation while sharing a prison cell with ffenella on the Greco-Turkish border. That might have been the end of the story, had not a publisher from Collins written to say that she had greatly enjoyed my pieces, and hoped they might form the germ of a book. Nothing had been further from my thoughts, but the opportunity was too good, and too flattering, to pass by, and before long I had signed up to write a slice of autobiography based on my time at Trinity. I have always enjoyed notions of circularity, of ending up pretty much where one started out, and since I had worked, unhappily, for an advertising agency before going up to university, and went to work in publishing once it was all over, I decided that I would begin and end the book in the office, with my gazing gloomily out of the window, wondering quite what I was doing and how soon I could make my escape. Between these two poles of office life I would suspend my Irish adventures, like a literary washing-line with various autobiographical escapades pegged along its length. The fact that Collins was publishing my book was entirely apposite, since theirs were the unnamed offices in which my story ends: in those days it was still a patrician family firm, ruled by a hyperactive and heavily tweeded old gentleman with eyebrows like bolts of carbonated lightning, and both Rupert Murdoch and the Harper-prefix lay in the unfathomable future.

Most writers are avid recyclers of their own work, and the writing of *Playing for Time* was made a good deal easier by the fact that, a year or two earlier, Derek Mahon — an old friend from Trinity, and easily the best (and most underrated) Irish poet of his generation — had offered me a monthly column on the *New Statesman*, where he was then spending long and dissolute afternoons. Many of the pieces I had written for him were essentially autobiographical, and I eagerly pressed them into service. In due course the book was finished, and sent on its way. I had enjoyed writing it a very great deal, and — to my shame — had found myself rocking with laughter over my own jokes while typing them out. Apart from a couple of stinkers, the reviews couldn't have been kinder or more appreciative. A particular fan was the wine-loving Oxford historian Richard Cobb, who liked it so much that he somehow managed to review it twice; and I was bowled over by a fan letter from my hero James Lees-Milne, whose *Another Self* is almost certainly the funniest autobiography of them all. Since publishers always enjoy the mixture as before, Collins commissioned a second volume, *Kindred Spirits*, which dealt with my alarmingly unsuccessful career in publishing, and was eventually published in 1995.

Writing one's autobiography is a presumptuous undertaking at the best of times, and after *Playing for Time* was published I found myself being asked — politely for the most part, but sometimes carrying an accusatory twist in the tail — the same three questions over and over again: how could I remember my past in such detail, how much of it had I in fact made up, and why on earth should anyone want to read (let alone publish) the memoirs of someone who had not only led a very humdrum life, but had failed to distinguish himself in any way whatsoever, and was completely unknown to the world at large?

As far as memory is concerned, I suspect — on the basis of no scientific evidence whatsoever — that everything that ever happens to one is somehow recorded on a giant videotape, and that although the replaying of the tape in full would be, quite literally, a lifetime's work, much more of it is recoverable than one might suspect. I have never kept a diary, but — as I have said — I was amazed by the amount of stuff that came bobbing to the surface once I had thought myself back into the past and bent my mind to the job.

Woefully lacking in imagination, I am quite incapable of inventing or making up stories, and (as far as I know) everything I recorded in my autobiographies actually occurred: but, like most writers, I tend to burnish and embellish. Autobiographers, like all the travel writers I know, concentrate their fire on unusual or memorable occurrences, prompting their readers to believe that they lead wilder or funnier or more adventurous or more colourful lives than is, in fact, the case, and I am no exception to the rule. Shortly after the first of my pieces had appeared in the *London Magazine*, my old Trinity friend Charles Sprawson — whose book *The Haunt of the Black Masseur* also started life in the *London Magazine*, and is one of the few works of literature given over to the subject of swimming — pointed out that although I had ffenella clutching a copy of Günter Grass's *The Tin Drum* in the face of a Force Eight gale, its English translation had yet to be published, and my memory must have been at fault. I deliberated long and hard about correcting this in the book itself, but finally decided against: I liked the idea that if a perceptive reader gave this loose end a tweak, the entire garment might begin to unravel. Besides which, none of us is infallible.

I was in my early forties when I began writing *Playing for Time*, and was looking back at a period of my life for which I felt intense nostalgia — heightened a year or two earlier by the sudden and unexpected reappearance of ffenella, looking disturbingly like the ffenella I had worshipped twenty years before, yet somehow not the same. On the cusp of middle age, I wanted to both celebrate a lost youth and at the same time exorcise it, to get it out of my system and move on to other things, at work and with my family. My feelings were, I suspect, all too prosaic and all too familiar: which is why — to answer the third and most needling of the questions that were shot in my direction — I believed that (provided they could write well enough) nonentities were often far better placed than famous names to write in ways that made sense to the reading world at large. Publishers ache to commission the memoirs of celebrities, yet they are, for the most part, doomed and hopeless undertakings by their very nature: public figures are miserably prone to pomposity, self-importance, name-dropping, discretion in all the wrong places, and a benign but fatal urge to cram on board all their well-known friends and colleagues irrespective of whether they have anything interesting to say for themselves. Some years after the publication of *Playing for Time* I was commissioned to write the authorised biography of the writer and critic Cyril Connolly, and although I wanted, at times, to give him a sharp retrospective kick, I found his prose and his cast of mind more sympathetic than those of any other writer I know. Everything he wrote, including the most humdrum book reviews, was essentially autobiographical, and I share to the full his autobiographical bias; for all his snobbery and greed and cowardice and indolence — or, more probably, because of them — he wrote better than anyone else about feelings (and failings) common to us all. One's reading of Connolly is punctuated by starts of recognition, by disconcerting glimpses of oneself: and it is this ability to empathise with and articulate the familiar as well as the unexpected that marks out the autobiographies I admire and reread, and not the quantity of well-known names or important events that litter the page.

Modern English poetry is a pretty dismal business, and few post-war English novels are worth the bother of reading, but autobiography is one area in which the English have excelled in the last half-century. Writers of memoirs — like historians and travel writers — tend to be overlooked by Eng Lit academics and their pupils in literary journalism, most of whom have been taught that Literature equals Novels, Poetry and Plays, and bestow on dim and badly-written novels and sub-fusc verse a reverence withheld from what are thought to be less 'creative' and 'imaginative' forms of writing: but I like to think that our time will come round at last. The best English autobiographies — Lees-Milne's *Another Self,* Julian Maclaren-Ross's *Memoirs of the Forties,* John Gale's *Clean Young Englishman,* T. C. Worsley's *Flannelled Fool,* Gerald Durrell's *My Family and Other Animals,* Patrick Leigh Fermor's pre-war hike across Mitteleuropa, the multi-volume memoirs by Alan Ross and by Michael Wharton — combine comicality with a sense of the sad absurdity of life, a delight in the oddities of human behaviour with a deceptive authorial modesty. *Playing for Time* was written in conscious emulation of a tradition I admire and long to be a part of, and if it gives a tenth of the pleasure these works have bestowed I shall feel I have not typed in vain.

Jeremy Lewis
March 2000